Selected Poems of Thomas Hood

Selected Poems of Thomas Hood

Edited, with an Introduction and Notes, by
John Clubbe

Harvard University Press
Cambridge, Massachusetts, 1970

For Robert E. Cameron

Preface

Thomas Hood is the chief poet of his generation for whom no adequate "selected poems" is available. Only a selection chosen for range and quality can provide the basis for a reevaluation of his poetry. The most complete edition, that edited by Walter Jerrold and published by Oxford in 1906, remains a too formidable volume. The sheer bulk of its nearly eight hundred pages, in part double-columned, deters all but the most determined readers. Furthermore, the arrangement of the Oxford Edition is awkward, its text somewhat "modernized." Notwithstanding, a new complete edition is not needed today. A "selected poems" very much is. Much of Hood's poetry, no one denies, borders on the second-rate and hardly merits republication; yet buried within the mass of hackwriting lie many poems of interest and quality. These I have tried to sift out for the present edition.

Hood's poetry poses difficult problems of selection and arrangement. Though many editions appeared in the nineteenth century, most left out important poems; none arranges them in a way that makes sense today. Jerrold sums up the difficulties in the preface to the Oxford Edition:

It has for sixty years been the custom to divide Hood's poetical writings into "comic" and "serious," or into "serious poems" and "poems of wit and humour." This was done in Moxon's editions shortly after Hood's death, it was done by Samuel Lucas twenty years later, and the arbitrary differentiation was maintained by Canon Ainger in the two volumes of selections which he issued in the Eversley Series in 1897. That it is an arbitrary form of classification may be seen by comparing some of those earlier editions, in which we find that one editor includes poems in the "serious" section which another allots to the "comic," and vice versa. Lucas, to cite but one example, puts "Miss Kilmansegg" in the latter, while Ainger puts it in the former. Certain of Hood's poems are definitely comic and others are definitely serious in both thought and treatment, but many of them while deeply serious in intent are presented with all the machinery of wit and humour at his command.

Despairing of finding suitable categories, Jerrold decided "to break away from this traditional and unsatisfactory method of classification, and to give the poems in a certain chronological order." Chronological arrangement, for a complete edition, is

as satisfactory a solution as any other, but "a certain chrono-
logical order," in effect neither "chronological" nor an "order,"
falls between two stools. A "selected poems" requires a more
satisfying method of classification. The five headings under
which I present Hood's poems, though perhaps as arbitrary as
any other division, offer a compromise between the awkward
(and false) dichotomy of "serious" and "comic" and the refusal
to impose some semblance of order that chronological arrange-
ment implies.

No selection of poems will satisfy everyone. In this edition I
have made every effort to choose poems that reveal Hood's
many-sided genius. An uneven poet, he benefits especially from
strict selection. For this reason the reader will find excluded, in
the section "Romantic Poems," all the longer poems from *The
Plea of the Midsummer Fairies* (1827). Though contempo-
raries criticized Hood for not writing more in this vein, his
romantic poetry has not stood the test of time. Critics today
concur that—a few exceptions aside—the romantic poems are
too heavily imitative to rise to genuine creativity, that it is in
his comic vein that he truly excels. The selection of "Comic
Poems" concentrates on his ballads, many with grotesque and
supernatural overtones, and on his poems of domestic humor.
The choice of "Verse Narratives" reveals Hood's story-telling
skill in many styles over a period spanning nearly twenty-five
years.

In the 1830's Hood's understanding of life deepened, his
vision darkened. English life—specifically social injustice and
the miserable state of the poor—increasingly occupied his
mind's best energies. His poems of social protest, in technique
largely a development from his comic verse, culminate in the
well-known "Song of the Shirt" and "Bridge of Sighs." But the
publication date—1825—of the first poem in this section shows
that Hood's social consciousness was no sudden development.
Standing between the "Verse Narratives" (also extensions of
his comic vein) and the "Poems of Social Protest" is "Miss
Kilmansegg and Her Precious Leg," the longest of the verse
narratives and the severest of the poems condemning society.
In this, Hood's most important poem, "comic" and "serious"
intimately blend.

Hood's poems pose only minor textual problems. Few holograph manuscripts survive; I mention in the notes the location of those I have found. Unless otherwise indicated, the text of each poem is that of the last published version which Hood revised during his lifetime. This text has been collated with earlier editions and with previous versions published in journals. The texts for the *Comic Annuals* were, however, more carefully prepared than those for *Hood's Own* (1839) and have thus been accorded greater respect in the choice of punctuation, accidentals, and other printing variants. Hood did not revise his poems extensively once published; he almost never rearranged stanzas, omitted or added lines, or made other major changes. For only a few poems do two radically different versions exist. Thus, except for correcting obvious printers' errors and making about two dozen changes in spelling, punctuation, and capitalization, I have followed the last revised edition, keeping its inconsistencies and occasional archaisms. Emendations have been kept to a minimum. Important textual variants —diction always, spelling and punctuation occasionally—I give in the notes.

Hood's poems abound in allusions to now-forgotten personages and events, in localisms of the day and puns, in mode words, slang, and colloquial expressions. Some of his poems of social protest, it is no exaggeration to say, require as many notes as a Roman satire. Because Hood's vocabulary was so large and because he often punned on multiple senses of words, I gloss, with the aid of dictionaries, some of the more unusual meanings. A few words he used seem to have passed from the language without other written trace. Hitherto, except for the collected *Works* (London, 1869–1873) and Jerrold's Oxford Edition, no other edition of Hood has provided annotation. The notes in both, however, are grossly inadequate. Those prepared for the present edition develop the lines that connect Hood with a literary past and present and attempt to show him working within linguistic and literary tradition. For this reason I include the more relevant of the notes his son, Tom, prepared for the collected *Works,* indicate as many of Hood's literary allusions as I (or others) have found, and make selective use of the criticism on Hood. The notes, which for some poems approach a commentary, are profuse by design; in defense let me cite Dr. Johnson's comment in the Preface to his edition of Shakespeare: "It is impossible for an expositor not to write too little for some, and too much for others." Though I have not succeeded in solving all mysteries, I do think that in some poems my annotation now makes it possible to understand more clearly what Hood was trying to do.

Hood was artist as well as poet, and this edition attempts to bring out his duality of vision. He illustrated many of his poems himself and upon first publication the comic woodcuts accompanied the written text. Some poems achieve a complementary effect: neither poem nor illustration stands alone. Others ("The Haunted House," "A Drop of Gin!" "The Lady's Dream") Hood wrote around another artist's illustration. Later reprintings of the poems usually omit the illustrations; in the standard *Works* the woodcuts are scattered helter-skelter over the first four volumes and often bear no relation to the text they supposedly elucidate. The Oxford Edition has no illustrations. The present edition contains most of the woodcuts Hood designed —and many of those he commissioned—to accompany the poems included. Even when not by Hood, these illustrations are not merely pretty or amusing pictures: most have an integral relation to the poems. The interaction of illustration and poem has never been adequately studied because of the difficulty of finding the original volumes even in large university libraries. Some of the woodcuts may seem, at first glance, to have no more than tangential relevance. Yet, as Goethe was the first to point out, even when they seem to have no literal bearing upon the text, careful perusal will usually discover thematic counterpoint. The inclusion of so many illustrations in this edition makes it possible to read Hood's poems as he intended them to be read, text and illustration printed in appropriate conjunction and mutually complementing.

Acknowledgments

In preparing an edition of this kind one incurs many debts to libraries and to individuals. Libraries, through the magic carpet of Inter-library Loan, have generously yielded their distant treasures or permitted Xerox copies to be made. I wish to thank here a few of the many individuals who have helped me in bringing this edition to completion: Florence Blakely, Mary Canada, Jane McKean, and Cheryl L. Swan, among the helpful reference librarians of the Duke University Library, for aid often beyond the call of duty; J. Emerson Ford, director of the Inter-library Loan Service at Duke, for perseverance in obtaining the many rare volumes necessary; Robert Krueger, for a year's loan of his *Oxford English Dictionary;* Ian M. Campbell, for sterling help in tracing Scottish allusions; C. Hilburn Womble and Wesley Kort, for similar aid in identifying, respectively, Latin quotations and biblical references; Eric Gaskell, librarian of the Wellcome Institute of the History of Medicine, London, for ingenious solutions to two matters within his special competence; Peter F. Morgan, for use of his doctoral dissertation, "Thomas Hood's Literary Reading, as Shown in His Works," a rereading of which complemented my researches at a late stage; George W. Williams, for expert counsel on matters of editing; Carl Woodring and the late William H. Marshall, for invaluable guidance; and Dorothy Roberts, for her generous enthusiasm and unflagging concern. I also acknowledge with gratitude the generosity of the Duke University Council on Research in awarding me a Faculty Research Fellowship for the summer of 1969 and this edition a publication subvention. Most of all, I wish to thank Robert E. Cameron of Portland, Oregon, for his epistolary discussions of Hood over the years and his loan of rare volumes from his unequaled Hood collection. Without his aid, freely and unfailingly given, this edition would not have reached completion.

I have abstained from extensive documentation of fact in the Introduction, passages of which have previously appeared in my *Victorian Forerunner: The Later Career of Thomas Hood.* For permission to reprint them thanks are due to Duke University Press, Durham, North Carolina.

J. C.

Durham, North Carolina
July 1969

Contents

Contents

Introduction

Many think of Thomas Hood either as a romantic poet manqué or as a comic punster. He would have disliked either categorization. Today, looking back over the Victorian era, we begin to see its literary figures in clearer perspective. The versatility of Hood's talent has become increasingly recognized, and he has, in recent years, been getting something more like his just due. His poetry, often misunderstood since his own time, once again finds discerning admirers. In 1930 William Empson had lauded its amazing technical virtuosity. More recently, W. H. Auden, reevaluating the comic poems, proclaimed Hood "a major poet." [1]

Hood's life span (1799–1845) embraced three periods of English literary culture. Although Neoclassic ideals still prevailed at his birth and were to continue in favor with the general public and the leading critical journals for three decades to come, Wordsworth and Coleridge had ushered in the romantic era in 1798 with their *Lyrical Ballads* and the second decade of the nineteenth century saw the emergence of Byron, Shelley, and Keats. But, although his poetry reveals indebtedness to the younger romantics, Hood never met them. Nor did he ever meet two of the more gifted of his contemporaries, George Darley and Thomas Lovell Beddoes. His one close literary friend, John Hamilton Reynolds, had exhausted his romantic vein by the time Hood came to know him well and soon abandoned literature for the law. Romanticism, as Hood knew it from his own experience, had already receded into the past. His romantic poetry was, from first effusions to the poems of the 1840's, imitative, chiefly because he saw no need to formulate his own artistic credo. When he died in 1845, a new generation of writers—Thackeray and Dickens in fiction, Tennyson and Browning in poetry—had begun to gain recognition. Thomas Hood, wandering between two worlds, two different conceptions of literature, did not feel quite at home in either.

"The early Victorian poet," writes Jerome Hamilton Buckley, "sometimes no more certain than his contemporaries, was expected to furnish instruction as well as amusement." [2] Hood would have agreed. The "highest office" of literary men was, he wrote in 1838, "to make the world wiser and better"; "their lowest, to entertain and amuse it without making it worse." [3] Through his poems of moral humor Hood attempted both to reform the world and to amuse it. His poetry's enormous appeal throughout the nineteenth century lay in this humor tinged with a morality that closely reflected contemporary standards. The Victorian middle class, where, like Dickens, he found the great majority of his readers, relished the domestic sentiment and the puns that pointed a moral.

Hood groped for an understanding of the problems that beset his rapidly changing society. He took up—indirectly at least —many of the social and political questions that aroused men's interest at that time. More easily comprehensible to the Victorians than to us, Hood's poems of social protest are necessarily topical in nature; but this topicality often becomes difficult to fathom as the political, social, and religious controversies of his day fade into obscurity.

Hood was scrupulous in keeping every word, every image, within the narrowing bounds of the feminine sensibility of the age. He abhorred indelicacy. "I have at least been a decent writer," he wrote in his "Literary Reminiscences" of 1838; "I feel some honest pride in remembering that the reproach of impurity has never been cast upon me by my judges." [4] Hardly a typical "romantic" trait, this desire to keep his poetry fit reading for the entire family reflects the dominant Evangelical influence upon the Victorian *Weltansicht*.

In most ways, then, Hood was a Victorian poet. Yet it has, until recently, been the custom to regard him as a late romantic, a poet whom a sterner age did not permit to develop his lyrical talent. In his lifetime, members of the *London Magazine* circle —"Barry Cornwall," Allan Cunningham, Charles Lamb, Hartley Coleridge—almost without exception urged him not to forsake his romantic, "serious" work, where they considered his true talent lay, for the frivolity of comic verse. Subsequent writers, such as S. C. Hall in *The Book of Gems*, have enshrined for later generations the image of Hood as a pauper who pined to compose "serious" poetry for the ages, but whom necessity forced to write comic poetry to keep the bill collector from the door. When told that Hall thought him a romantic poet gone awry, Hood was amused and attributed the characterization to Hall's knowing him but slightly: "You will judge how well the author knows me when he says 'we believe his mind to be more serious than comic, we have never known him laugh heartily either in company or in rhyme.' But my methodist face took him in, for he says, 'the countenance of Mr. Hood is more solemn than merry.'" Even Thackeray, throwing a retrospective glance back over his own career, deplored Hood's forced labor.[5] Insofar as we know his opinions about his métier, Hood never did.

The view that Hood was a dedicated romantic poet led astray by his misguided inclination to comic punning has few adherents today—and, I believe, rightly. After all, of the thirty years, from 1815 to 1845, during which Hood was active as a poet, he devoted not more than two or three of them—and then not exclusively—to "romantic" poetry.[6] Once he had tired of his Keatsian vein, he felt in later years but slight inclination to revive it. Only his *Plea of the Midsummer Fairies* can properly be called romantic; but the poems there, a few of the lyrics excepted, are no more than pale copies of themes and techniques no longer vital.

Hood retains our attention today not as a late romantic, nor even, in William Michael Rossetti's description, as "the finest English poet between the generation of Shelley and the generation of Tennyson,"[7] but as the first Victorian poet—a poet who anticipated many trends in modern poetry. His comic grotesquerie combined with technical virtuosity, his moral humor, his social and humanitarian concern, these—rather than the romantic echoes of an outworn poetic fashion—represent the deeper currents in Hood's literary career.

Thomas Hood was born on 23 May 1799 in the Poultry, a district in the heart of the City of London. Except for five years of exile on the Continent, the mature man always evinced a decided preference for living in or near the capital. He was the second son and third child of Thomas Hood, a leading bookseller and partner in the firm of Vernor and Hood, and of Elizabeth Hood, née Sands. Thomas had a brother several years older, James, reputedly gifted beyond the rest of the family in genius, who, the *Memorials of Thomas Hood* records, "died at an early age, a victim to consumption, which ultimately carried off his mother and two sisters."[8] Two other sisters survived to maturity. In 1811, the year of James's death, Thomas's father died "of a malignant fever, originating from the effects of the night air in travelling."[9] After his death the family fell into relative poverty; two years later, when about fourteen, Thomas, to help support his mother and sisters, left school and began work as a clerk in a counting house.

Despite the witty, caustic remarks in his "Literary Reminiscences" about school being time wasted, he did develop there a fondness for reading and he won a Latin prize. He also mastered French well enough, he said, to help edit a translation of *Paul et Virginie*, but no one has succeeded in finding it. Throughout his youth he read voraciously. Though in later life he read a good deal less, his writings give evidence of wide reading and of an apt memory that could recall an appropriate quotation when wanted.

Instead of concentrating on the figures before him, Thomas found his thoughts in the counting house unaccountably straying to his favorite authors. Worse, bent over a table all day, he impaired his health. Happily, uncles on his mother's side took an interest in him. First under the patronage of James Sands, later of Robert Sands, he served an apprenticeship as engraver; afterward he worked for one of the well-known Le Keux brothers, probably John Le Keux. His health still did not improve, and, in the language of the day, he bade fair to "submit to a decline."

Doctors recommended fresh air and exercise, so off he went in 1815 to Scotland, where at Dundee and neighboring villages lived aunts and uncles on his father's side. Installed first in a boarding house, later in his Dundee aunt's home, he soon made the acquaintance of several young men whose interests complemented his own. Early endowed with an enthusiasm for literature and art, Thomas continued to read voraciously and to draw, began to write poetry, even sent several prose contributions to local newspapers, none of which can be identified with certainty. Nor did the carefree invalid forget the purpose of his Scottish sojourn: to get well. He swam, rambled through the countryside, and took up fishing, a favorite pastime throughout life. Moderate health recovered, he returned in the fall of 1817 to London.

During the three to four years following, Thomas continued, first as apprentice, then on his own, his work as engraver. His commissions being such that he could do them at home, he began work on the plate in hand at about nine, labored through the morning, lunched, and with a break for tea continued to work through the afternoon. In the evenings he relaxed with his mother and sisters in their suburban Islington home. In the later hours he read or sketched. He always loved to draw and the hundreds of comic woodcuts scattered through his many volumes testify to genuine artistic talent. Often his mind did not cease its restless activity until the morning's early hours. Though strengthened by his stay in Scotland, at no period in his life did Hood achieve good health. Eventually he even had to give up playing the flute because the effort placed too great a strain on his lungs.

Around 1820 he joined a literary society, composed mainly of prim young ladies who encouraged him to read his original verse. He had already begun to write poetry in Dundee: his earliest poem, "The Dundee Guide," a Hudibrastic satire, mocked the grave limitations of Dundee and its inhabitants much in the manner that its model, Christopher Anstey's *New Bath Guide,* had ridiculed those of Bath. Only a few passages, printed in the *Memorials* from letters, survive of this poem: they show Hood already a highly perceptive critic of society, indignant at the "strict bigoted tenets" of Scottish Calvinism. In his next effort, "The Bandit," he molded his irresolute "Chieftain" on various romantic heroes, finally showing preference for the robust, hugely popular Conrad of Lord Byron. Before the literary society he read several poems, including two showing newfound range, one in the style of Keats, another which later became the comic narrative "Bianca's Dream."

Although the society's gatherings had quickened his interest in literature, it was not until John Taylor offered Hood a position on the *London Magazine* that he conceived a change in occupation possible. He accepted the offer with evident joy, and, as a "sort of sub-editor," came to know the magazine's famed contributors: John Clare, "Barry Cornwall," De Quincey, Lamb, Hazlitt, Reynolds, Allan Cunningham. It was the one close association he was to form in his lifetime with literary men of genius. At first his tasks hardly consisted of more than proof-reading articles, but Taylor soon recognized his talent and entrusted to him the answers-to-correspondents column, "The Lion's Head." From punning retorts to readers young Hood rapidly passed to poetry. Contributing to the magazine over a two-year period (July 1821 to June 1823), he came during this time to maturity as a "serious" poet in the style of Keats. In the pages of the *London Magazine* he first published the poems that appeared, with minor revisions, in 1827 under the title of *The Plea of the Midsummer Fairies;* and on *The Plea,* his only collection of "serious" poems, rests Hood's claim to recognition as a romantic poet. For these romantic poems he took as models first Byron, then Shelley, before he finally submerged himself in Keats. This imitative verse—though patterned after the younger romantics it has echoes of many English poets since the Elizabethans—marks him as a predecessor of Tennyson and Browning, whose poetry passed through similar if not exactly parallel stages of influence. With him submersion in the romantics did not preclude—as it also did not with Tennyson and Browning—the later development of a distinct personal idiom.

Critical journals accorded *The Plea* a mixed reception. Though Hood's friends on the *London Magazine* responded to it warmly, the general public did not buy. Perhaps fortunately so. Had financial success crowned this venture, Hood might never have developed his more genuine talent for poetry of other kinds, but squandered it on more of the same—for him surely an esthetic cul-de-sac. One weakness in the longer poems, George Gilfillan noted in 1850, stands out as paramount: "We find in [them] . . . no effective story, none that can bear the weight of his subtle and beautiful imagery." In the title poem especially, "Hood has not been able to infuse human interest into his fairy or mythological creations." [10]

Despite oppressive echoes of Keats, apparent even in the titles, several of the shorter poems—the three "Autumn" lyrics, "Ruth," the "Ode to Melancholy"—succeed as imitations. If one's memories of Keats's poem have dimmed, a first reading of Hood's "Ode: Autumn" may impress; if Keats's ode is kept in mind, however, Hood's seems little more than a thematic variation, too imbued with the poetic vocabulary of his older contemporary to rise to genuine originality. Keats constructs his ode "To Autumn" upon a series of images of "mellow fruitfulness"; in all three of Hood's poems it is the sadness and decay of this season that prevail. "Ruth" and the "Ode to Melancholy," written even later in the romantic afternoon, reveal only wistful discontent, not the deep understanding of life that Keats expressed when he wrote, "Ay, in the very temple of delight, / Veil'd melancholy has her sovran shrine." Hood, brooding over each image of decay with morbid sweetness of tone, never rises further than the recognition that "There's not a string attun'd to mirth, / But has a chord in Melancholy." Among the sonnets, "Silence," more genuinely Hood's, resists the Keatsian overtones, though Keats too knew well how to evoke the desolation of solitude. Many literary critics have considered, with William Sharp, that among sonnets "Silence" takes a "place in the very front rank." [11]

Hood's poems modeled on Keats founder, I believe, because Hood did not regard Keats's kind of poetry with instinctive sympathy. In the 1820's he did not have a temperament that took seriously either life or art; moreover, he never found, as had Keats, deep meaning in the world of myth. His letters do not illuminate, as Keats's do, the nature and kinds of poetry. Nor does Hood speak of the poet's role as creator; "unlike Keats," writes Elizabeth Jennings, "he never felt the need to work out a personal aesthetic for the writing of verse." [12] Gilfillan saw the failure in plot construction and in creating living beings. Hood's unease in his imitative Keatsian style appears also in other weaknesses: uncertain and never fully mastered technique; flaccid vocabulary and "Cockneyisms"; above all, too heavy a dependence on the phraseology of the Elizabethans refined through the sensuous ears of their romantic disciple John Keats. Hood's genius for language, overflowing in his comic poems, remains cramped and unfulfilled in his romantic poems. Alvin Whitley's perceptive analysis of Hood's reaction to Keats's influence can hardly be bettered:

The tenor of his reaction is of some importance, for it was that of most of the nineteenth-century imitators of Keats. Hood retained, with considerable dilution, the mood, the music, the imagery, the diction, the atmosphere, the settings of Keats's poems; he ignored their principal themes, the intellectual content which we now loosely consider the philosophy of Keats. In two titles, Hood and the Victorians seized on "La Belle Dame sans Merci" and abandoned, to their cost, the "Ode on a Grecian Urn." More particularly, Hood not only exploited the trappings of the Keatsian style; he grafted them on themes conventionally sentimental and moral.

And further: "When Hood attempted, in the mode of Keats, the allegorical narrative or the narrative for its own sake, he tended to flatten symbolic meaning by rendering it merely moral or to introduce a moral to provide a wholesome application." [13]

Whitley here adumbrates the genesis of what became a chief characteristic of Hood's later poetry: its moral concern. Many of his poems have an implicit ethical content, some close with an explicit "moral." Much of his writing, Hood once said, had as its purpose "to hint that a writer may often mean in earnest what he says in jest." [14] This desire to instruct unites in purpose writers as diverse in technique as Dickens, Thackeray, Carlyle, Ruskin, R. H. Barham—and Thomas Hood. It gives their work, even when humorous in tone, its underlying moral earnestness. If Hood, in his poetry, could not respond fully to the symbolism, the philosophy, the mythmaking power of Keats, he knew he could still render his imitations of Keats wholesome—and clearly useful—reading. By tacking an explicit *moralitas,* similar to the admonitory closing paragraph of medieval writers, onto dozens of his poems and tales written in later years, Hood reveals his persistent desire to instruct.

Hood criticism today does not rank high the poems in *The Plea of the Midsummer Fairies.* J. C. Reid dismisses them as "faint carbons." Laurence Brander is equally positive: "It is impossible to disagree with the judgement of the time that the 1827 volume of serious verse was very minor. Hood was going to write genuine poetry later in his life, but everything here is Romantic imitation." [15] By 1824 Hood had abandoned any thoughts of a career as a romantic poet. Neither impulse nor dedication had ever been strong and during the remainder of his life he produced few romantic poems of importance. He learned to write comic verse with facility, recognized that it earned him a living, and never voiced regrets.

More successful than *The Plea* from a commercial point of view was his first volume of comic poems, coauthored with John Hamilton Reynolds, the *Odes and Addresses to Great People* (1825). Styled after James and Horace Smith's *Rejected Addresses,* the volume enjoyed sufficient popularity to run through three editions within a year. Hood's concern for the betterment of English society stamps several of these early poems, especially the "Ode to H. Bodkin, Esq." In this poem, addressed to the "Secretary to the Society for the Suppression of Mendicity," the poet clothes his serious message—banning beggars from the streets in effect condemned them to death—with brilliant and humorous wordplay: "What ills can mortals have, they can't / With a bare *Bodkin* end?" In 1825 few of his poems carry a moral; ten years later, many do. This same year Hood also published his Hogarthian engraving *The Progress of Cant,* depicting the hypocrisies of the age. Though he focused on no single abuse, the engraving does show his concern early in life with the world elsewhere. It would seem that over the next two decades cant, especially religious cant, progressed by leaps and bounds. Hood's awareness of it, at least, did so progress.

The year 1825 also marks his marriage to Jane Reynolds, eldest of the Reynolds sisters. He had been engaged to her since the fall of 1822. Seven and a half years older than her husband, Jane Hood proved an ideal wife: her maturity lent her the patience to deal with his whimsical nature and her own background of ill health gave her the sympathy necessary to nurse him through his frequent illnesses. Mutual dependence and love formed the cornerstone of twenty years of married happiness. Upon the rare occasions of separation Hood wrote her letters of remarkable tenderness. Of firm yet pliable character, Jane Hood was a good wife to her husband, a good mother to her children. Hood's happy domestic life, first at his mother's home, later as husband and father, contrasts sharply with the failure of the romantic poets—Coleridge, Keats, Shelley, Byron —ever to still their longing for an idealized relationship and find happiness in married love. Family ties always meant much to Hood, and they are reflected in many domestic poems, comic in form yet sincere in their celebration of family life. In one of the best of them, "A Parental Ode to My Son, Aged 3 Years and 5 Months," the antics of the all-too-real boy ironically undercut the father's sentimental evocation of childhood. His background of domestic harmony and his deep sense of the domestic virtues, reflected in his work, were to make Hood a favorite family author of Victorian England.

The Hoods' first child, a girl, died soon after her birth in 1827. Her death moved Charles Lamb to write his touching poem, "On an Infant Dying as soon as Born." The saddened father wrapped a wisp of golden hair in the following lines:

Little eyes that scarce did see,
   Little lips that never smiled;
   Alas! my little dear dead child,
Death is thy father, and not me,
I but embraced thee, soon as he! [16]

Another child was born in 1830, and she lived. Christened Frances Freeling in honor of Hood's friend the Postmaster-General Sir Francis Freeling, she soon became known to all as Fanny.

In formal society Hood always remained reserved, naturally shy; but in his family and among close friends he relaxed and became a delightful host. Partial deafness, from which he suffered all of his adult life, no doubt explains his quietness at social gatherings. Mary Balmanno describes him at one such gathering in 1828 at the home of Charles and Mary Lamb:

In outward appearance Hood conveyed the idea of a clergyman. His figure slight, and invariably dressed in black; his face pallid; the complexion delicate, and features regular: his countenance bespeaking sympathy by its sweet expression of melancholy and suffering.

And Jane:

Mrs. Hood was a most amiable woman—of excellent manners, and full of sincerity and goodness. She perfectly adored her husband, tending him like a child, whilst he with unbounded affection seemed to delight to yield up himself to her guidance. Nevertheless, true to his humorous nature, he loved to tease her with jokes and whimsical accusations and assertions which were only responded to by, "Hood, Hood, how can you run on so?" [17]

Hood was an inveterate punster. Both in speaking and in writing he punned continually and, it would seem, compulsively. His punning indicates that his mind possessed a fundamental, unresolved dichotomy: he perceived the comic in the tragic and the tragic in the comic—but this discovery of life's incongruity caused him distinct unease. Equivocation came easily to his nature, and his puns provided a means by which he could shy away from the full implications of his vision. He used puns, William Empson observes, "to back away from the echoes and implications of words, to distract your attention by insisting on his ingenuity so that you can escape from sinking into the meaning." [18] His marked reluctance in his social poems to affirm directly his beliefs on controversial subjects reveals a basic insecurity; through punning, the outlet his gifts permitted him, he was able to reconcile his embarrassment before unease. Rarely did he boldly face a political or social problem: hence the puns and anticlimactic endings of so many works. Tomfoolery by itself would not do; neither would a wholly serious implication. Consequently, a compromise—presenting the moral in comic verse—became, for the greater part of his career, the most adequate solution.

Hood stands as the unquestioned master of the pun in English. How recognition for this verbal wizardry should be qualified has long caused critical debate. Upon reading the *Odes and Addresses* Coleridge wrote Lamb that the "puns are nine in ten good, many excellent, the *Newgatory* transcendant!" [19] and insisted that Lamb must have written the volume. Lamb, however, had a truer perception of the strengths and weaknesses of Hood's style. He reviewed the *Odes and Addresses* in words that could apply, with equal aptitude, to many of Hood's succeeding volumes:

A too great aim at brilliancy is their excess. We do not think that in any work there can be too much brilliancy *of the same kind* . . . What we allude to is a mixture of *incompatible* kinds; the perpetual recurrence of *puns* in these little effusions of humour; puns uncalled for, and perfectly gratuitous, a sort of make-weight; puns, which, if *missed,* leave the sense and the drollery full and perfect without

11

them. You may read any one of the addresses, and not catch a quibble in it, and it shall be just as good, nay better; for the addition of said quibble only serves to puzzle with an unnecessary double meaning. A pun is good when it can rely on its single self; but, called in as an accessory, it weakens—unless it *makes* the humour, it *enfeebles* it.[20]

The author, probably Leigh Hunt, of the article on Hood published in the *Edinburgh Review* after his death, presented the case even more unfavorably:

His brain teems with humorous fancies, but he cannot afford to part with one. Every quip or crotchet which the train of associations suggests, he insists on imparting to the public; and, as might be expected from this indiscriminate effusion, for every stroke really successful we have ten which are forced or unnatural . . . Once caught by a play on words, his course defies calculation: one conceit brings on another, till we lose sight entirely of the point from which we started.

Hunt, who would have known, blamed these "unfortunate effects" upon Hood's "constant connexion with, and dependence on periodical literature." [21] To my mind, however, Hunt misjudges the case: the bent of Hood's mind led him naturally to play on words. Having to churn out his many volumes of "fun" could only aggravate—not cause—this irrepressible tendency within his mental makeup. Modern critics have showed more charity than Lamb and Hunt: both Empson and Auden esteem Hood's acute, if not always discriminating, sense of the possibilities of language.

In the early nineteenth century the pun was still, in part because of the revived interest in Shakespeare, very much a topic of criticism; with the romantic critics it had not fallen into the neglect—and disfavor—from which it now suffers. Even Lamb, though he occasionally found Hood's puns "gratuitous," wrote in defense of punning elsewhere and punned incessantly himself; Coleridge, who could find a pun by Hood "transcendant," offers several brilliant analyses of the pun in his Shakespearean criticism. With other popular writers of the 1820's and 1830's— Pierce Egan in *Life in London* and its sequels, Barham in *The Ingoldsby Legends*, Dickens in *Sketches by Boz* and *The Pickwick Papers*—Hood responded to the exuberant language of the London streets, its cant terms, its racy expressions, its turf, gambling, and theater jargon, in short the words which made his comic and satiric poems much more alive to his own generation than they can possibly be to a later one. He usually justified his puns on the ground that they helped him thrust his point home—"A double meaning shews double sense"[22]— or reenforced his moral. No one denies that many of his puns and morals are badly, sometimes irrevocably, dated, and often have now no more than historical interest, but to Hood their didactic value justified their use. The ease and brilliance with which he manipulated words may still command respect. His mastery of language is one of his chief claims to our attention today—perhaps why, for Auden, he is "a major poet."

In the late 1820's Hood began to attract attention as a popular playwright. For three months in 1826 he wrote a weekly column on the theater for a new periodical, the *Atlas;* this journalistic experience probably helped bring his long-standing interest in the stage to creative endeavor. He wrote in all perhaps half a dozen plays of all kinds—farce, pantomime, musical comedy—for the comedians Charles Mathews and Frederick Henry Yates. Of those extant none is read or readable today.[23] Indeed, the literary merit of the surviving fragments and songs leaves no reason to bemoan Hood's turning away from the drama after several years of varying success. But his writing for the stage did lead him to experiment with vocabulary and meter: onto the traditional meters of English poetry he learned to graft the rhythms of popular songs. "Thomas Hood's apprenticeship to the music hall," observes J. M. Cohen, "his writing of sketches and songs by the popular comedian Charles Matthews [*sic*], vastly extended the vocabulary, the metres, and the allusiveness of nineteenth-century poetry."[24] Hood also knew intimately the dramatic works and musical comedies of the writers of his generation and that previous—men such as the two Charles Dibdins, father and son, T. J. Dibdin, John Poole, George Colman the Younger. He followed closely the careers of leading comic actors, including the favorite of Dickens's childhood, the beloved clown Joseph Grimaldi, for whom he wrote the farewell at his final Drury Lane benefit. It becomes obvious that through his work as a drama critic in 1826, his writing for the stage which extended through 1829, and his lively interest in the melodramas, musicals, farces, comic operas, vaudevilles, pantomimes, and reviews of his contemporaries, Hood succeeded in enriching considerably his literary experience. His saturation in current colloquialisms, derived in part from his knowledge of the stage in all its aspects, enabled him to extend his range of expression more widely than any poet of his generation.

Whims and Oddities, his first volume of comic verse of the kind that became synonymous with his name, appeared in 1826. It enjoyed immediate popularity and the public soon called for new editions. To meet the demand Hood published the next year *Whims and Oddities, Second Series.* These two volumes established him as the leading comic poet of his day and represent the high point of his career as a humorist. In his comic ballads Hood used the traditional ballad stanza to parody serious themes. Many of the ballads dramatize the conflict between love and death: the lover returning to find his sweetheart untrue—"Faithless Sally Brown" and "Faithless Nelly Gray"; the ghost of the beloved paying a midnight visit to her lover—"Mary's Ghost"; the disillusioned husband murdering his new wife—"Tim Turpin." After Hood, the serious literary ballad in English poetry lacks vitality; in effect, his burlesquing its themes helped destroy their credibility within the form. On the other hand, his comic ballads had an important influence on those of Edward Lear, Lewis Carroll, and W. S. Gilbert. Besides the comic ballads, several verse narratives, notably "The Last Man" and "Jack Hall," and sea tales, particularly "The Demon-Ship" and "The Sea-Spell," show Hood's temperamental fondness for writing about death in grotesque forms, often with an infusion of the supernatural. "The Last Man," the most dramatic of the narratives, more than holds its own with treatments of the same theme by Byron, Thomas Campbell, Beddoes, and Mrs. Shelley. The charnel house, gravediggers and body snatchers, human decay and decay in nature, demons and ghosts: all fascinated Hood. Early developed, this *Galgenhumor*—the depicting of the horrible as the natural—stayed with him throughout his career.[25]

Hood was, in many ways, an imitative writer. Confronted with the romantic achievement, he adopted one of two courses, occasionally, even in the same poem, both: he consciously imitated another poet's style, or he consciously parodied a romantic theme. Though Keats dominates *The Plea of the Midsummer Fairies,* some poems in this volume echo Lamb and Wordsworth ("I remember, I remember," "A Retrospective Review") and Shelley ("The Sea of Death"). *Odes and Addresses* does not disguise its borrowings from the Smiths' *Rejected Addresses.* "The Demon-Ship," "The Sea-Spell," and "The Last Man" of the two *Whims and Oddities,* as well as "The Dream of Eugene Aram" of a few years later, reveal the pervasive, if more subtle, influence of Coleridge's "The Rime of the Ancient Mariner." The novellas in *National Tales,* a volume published in 1827, recall Boccaccio. Indebtedness in poems and prose extends to eighteenth-century models: Swift, Sterne, Smollett, Gray, Dr. Johnson. The *Arabian Nights' Entertainments* influenced passages of fantasy in several poems, including the realistic "Miss Kilmansegg and Her Precious Leg." Other poems reflect Hood's extensive knowledge of folklore, his desultory browsing in books on many different subjects, his absorption in the daily press, his fascination with all kinds of miscellaneous out-of-the-way information. His mind displays amazing retentivity of facts culled from his reading, and his poetry displays that reading filtered, the bits of information startlingly and often strikingly juxtaposed.

When Hood assumed the editorship of an annual, *The Gem,* in 1828, he succeeded in attracting distinguished contributors: Charles Lamb, Bernard Barton, Hartley Coleridge, and even the star attraction of the "Annual" trade, Sir Walter Scott. He inserted several of his own poems in its pages, including his fine Coleridgean tale of a man's sin and remorse "The Dream of Eugene Aram," which he later published separately, with illustrations by William Harvey, in 1831. The year 1829 saw the publication of *The Epping Hunt,* a long, punning poem that ran into a second edition the next year. In 1830 he also published *Comic Melodies,* songs from his plays set to music by Jonathan Blewitt.

Success with *The Gem* encouraged Hood to edit his own annual. At the end of 1829, when his readers saw the first *Comic Annual,* they learned in the preface that they might consider it a "Third Series of 'Whims & Oddities.' " For ten consecutive years (1830–1839) the poet turned out an annual volume of fun. Viewing the series when nearly complete, Henry Fothergill Chorley in the *London and Westminster Review* for April 1838 found that "the contents . . . make them, independent of their own intrinsic worth . . . valuable as a Pantagruelian commentary upon the follies, fancies, and manners of the world we live in." Although others contributed articles, poems, and woodcuts to the first *Comic Annual*, Hood did more and more of the writing in succeeding volumes, as he also did more and more of the comic woodcuts.

Critics of the poetry have persistently neglected the accompanying illustrations. Hood spent as much time designing the woodcuts as he did writing the poems, judged them of equal importance, and meant each to complement the other. Popular demand led his publisher to issue the woodcuts separately as well. Not the least attraction of the *Comic Annuals* and often misplaced or omitted in later editions of the poems, Hood's woodcuts are vital to a full understanding of the written text; some of them, moreover, evince a fine eye for externals and a genuine skill in grotesque art. Others embody a pun. Still others of Hood's woodcuts may be considered the artistic counterpart to Henry Mayhew's *London Labour and the London Poor.* "It will be seen from the illustrations of the present work," Hood wrote modestly in the preface to the first *Whims and Oddities*, "that the inventor is no artist;—in fact, he was never 'meant to draw.' " But he never pretended to correctness. On the contrary, except for their vigor and pointed effect, his drawings purposely resemble those of a child. They are intriguingly similar to the work of Thomas Rowlandson, even, here and there, to Daumier's cartoons. Contemporaries praised Hood's artistic skill,[26] as they did Thackeray's, and his chief collaborators, William Harvey for "The Dream of Eugene Aram" and John Leech for "Miss Kilmansegg and Her Precious Leg," enjoyed considerable renown in their day. Even when Hood did not design the illustrations himself, he worked closely with the illustrators, all personal friends, and the resultant interaction of text and illustration compares to that achieved, for example, by Dickens and "Phiz" in *The Pickwick Papers.*

During the 1830's, aside from occasional reviews and poems

contributed to periodicals, Hood depended for the greater part of his income on the success of his yearly volume. A survey of the ten *Comics,* however, leads irresistibly to the conclusion that they represent a decline in creativity within his humorous vein. Several of the comic ballads—"John Day," "Sally Simpkin's Lament," "A Waterloo Ballad"—show imaginative power, but do not quite equal the best of the two *Whims.* Among the verse tales "The Desert-Born" stands out: its narration of a nightmarish ride across the desert recaptures the unearthly magic of "The Last Man" and "Eugene Aram." Using romantic irony, Hood takes wry pleasure in undercutting suspenseful moments with last-minute comic twists. But his handling of romantic irony, though influenced by German romantic writers and the Byron of *Don Juan,* remains invariably his own: after presenting an apparently serious poem (often one with humanitarian, social, or supernatural overtones), he undercuts its reality in a quick pirouette, either with a pun or with a revelation that all has been a dream—or, as in "The Desert-Born," with both. He had a pathological fear of being taken at face value.

After five years of often-interrupted labor, Hood completed his first novel in mid-1833. Published in three volumes at the end of 1834, *Tylney Hall* is somewhat better than the complete oblivion into which it has fallen would suggest. In its day it obtained, with the exception of the vituperative *Fraser's,* generally favorable critiques and mild popularity. Lamb's judgment is perceptive: "a medley, without confusion, of farce, melodrama, pantomime, comedy, tragedy, punchery, what not." [27] Though minor characters entertain and some scenes sparkle with subdued humor, the novel as a whole does not cohere.

The winter of 1834–35 marks a crisis and a turning point in the career of Thomas Hood, for at this time he formed the decisions that would guide him during the remaining years of his life. The crisis was both financial and personal. Though his finances collapsed completely only in late 1834, at no time in his life were they stable. As early as 1829 creditors had pressed him to discharge his debts. His annual income, dependent upon the uncertain success of his comic volumes, fluctuated widely in the years that followed, and he never did get out of debt. In 1834 he severed dealings with his publisher of several years, Charles Tilt. His break with Tilt constitutes, however, only the prelude to a series of events whose sequence still remains, in part, conjectural. The apparent causes for Hood's financial collapse seem to be two: the failure about 1834 of an engraving firm with which he was associated, and his living at Lake House, Wanstead, his home since 1832, in a style well beyond his income.

Proceeding concurrently with the financial crisis was a series of personal calamities that included rupture of ties with his wife's family, the Reynoldses. On 19 January 1835, Jane gave birth to a son, Tom; Charles Wentworth Dilke, editor of the *Athenaeum* and Hood's good friend, was the child's godfather. Jane had been ill after the birth of each of her other children, and this time she came close to death. For ten days—Hood recalled them as "The Most Terrible Ten Days of my Life" —he despaired for her life. Night after night he watched by the bedside; twice he pitched headlong from his chair in extreme exhaustion. Without the devoted care given Jane by Dr. William Elliot, who was to become a lifelong friend of the family, Hood believed she would not have survived her ordeal.

The tension and the day-to-day pressure of an increasingly untenable position weakened his health, always as sensitive to mental as to physical strain. Creditors pressed him; local merchants refused him necessities of life; furthermore, his humiliation before impending destitution augmented his sense of frustration. Laboring under the triple burden of his weak health, his wife's grave illness, and his uncertain future, Hood truly went through the most soul-searching moments of his life. Later he was to be in weaker health, in even more embarrassing financial straits, but never did despair assume such awesome proportions as it did in the early months of 1835.

Despair prompted him early in February to write a long letter to Dilke, his strength and prop during the crisis, in which he voices his personal agony. Extremely painful to read, this letter is a key document for an understanding of Hood's later career—and writings. Nowhere else does he bare with such frankness his innermost feelings about life. He writes as a man deeply, suddenly upset, yet as a man who still could smile amidst infinite pain. "My dear Dilke," he begins,

Here I sit, solus, in that large drawing-room, with a sick wife upstairs, —a sick child in the next room to this . . . and a fly-load of company has just departed . . . What was done to oppress me in my sore time of trouble I cannot forgive or forget . . . I believe I shall be an altered man—more of a philosopher—scorning the hollow & enjoying the real in joy or grief . . . Think me not mad, my dear Dilke, but I am writing of things words cannot reach. Horrors, horrible, most horrible, must have been her portion . . . And now you know more of T. Hood than you could gather from a Comic Annual, or the whole series, or the Whims, or anything I have ever written, saving this letter . . . My views in life are changed—& would have been whether Jane lived or died, as you know . . . In some things my eyes are opened & my heart is shut. I disdain hypocrisy. Toward Jane I must feel more devoutly loving than on that dear day that made me her husband . . . My eyes have been widely opened—to the present, the past, & the future.[28]

The crisis determined Hood to leave England. Owing his creditors between £200 and £300 and without hope of immediate repayment, he thought to economize by living on the Continent. Certainly the English scene did not hold pleasant prospects for him; life abroad, under almost any circumstances, might well have seemed more promising. Although his decision to go to Germany may appear, in the light of subsequent events, unfortunate, it also seems unavoidable.

In March 1835 Hood left for Germany; his wife and children soon followed. In many respects Germany appeared an ideal place for Hood to settle and work. He took up residence at Coblenz, on the Rhine. For about a year after his arrival his letters back to English friends expressed general contentment. Then came, as so often in his career after a change of residence or scene, the inevitable disillusionment: he turned bitterly against the Rhinelanders and things German. For reasons of health and economy, above all to escape his environment and be within striking distance of London, he moved to Ostend in June 1837. He had never adapted himself fully to life in Germany; he was, again after an initial period of elation, to have a similar experience of disillusionment and depression in Belgium. After nearly three years of living in Ostend, he realized that if he were ever to regain his health he must return to England and return he did in April 1840.

Hood's five-year sojourn on the Continent, though physically debilitating, broadened his base of experience and resulted in literary work of significance. After 1835, his verse tales and fiction show him turning, as one might expect, more frequently to German themes and to the techniques of romantic irony. In Germany he made a new friend, the Anglo-Prussian Lieutenant Philip von Franck, and in his company he observed at close hand a foreign culture he could respect, if never like. He revenged himself for all the petty hardships he had to endure when he incorporated his impressions of Germany in a largely autobiographical novel, *Up the Rhine* (1840), modeled closely upon Smollett's *Humphry Clinker*. In Hood's novel a heterogeneous party of tourists decide to voyage up the Rhine. That they decide to make an extended stopover at Coblenz should not surprise: they have stumbled there upon "our old friend Markham," an English expatriate and obviously a persona for an irate Hood. With force and conviction "Markham" expresses Hood's frustration as he holds forth on the dozens of irritations he has suffered living in a foreign land. The novel, though marred by its increasingly bitter tone, is notable for its skillful rendering of German life and manners.

In 1839, the year before *Up the Rhine* was published, had appeared in volume form *Hood's Own: or, Laughter from Year to Year,* a collection of his best work from the *Comic Annuals,* and including "an infusion of new blood"—chiefly his "Literary Reminiscences." Modesty preventing Hood from writing an extensive autobiography, he gave only those "circumstances that prepared, educated, and made me a literary man." The chief interest of the "Literary Reminiscences" lies in its vivid pen portraits of the giants of the *London Magazine* in the twilight of English romanticism. Hood's punning style captures well the gay atmosphere of the monthly *London* dinners, presided over by editors John Taylor and James Hessey, when Hazlitt, De Quincey, Clare, and Lamb sat around the table. Later, after Lamb and his sister moved to Colebrooke Cottage, Hood often came over for an evening's chat and there met Wordsworth and Coleridge. The last pages of the "Literary Reminiscences" evoke a moving recollection of Sir Walter Scott.

During his years abroad, Hood also wrote three "letters" in support of bills favoring more equitable copyright laws and published them in the *Athenaeum* in April 1837 (he published two further "letters" in the same journal in June 1842). In "Copyright and Copywrong" he reaffirmed his vibrant belief in the integrity of the literary profession and in the men who comprised it; his third letter concluded with eloquent testimony to his own "debt" to books, those "silent instructors" from whom he had "learned something of the divine, and more of the human religion." [29]

The most important and lasting benefit Hood derived from his foreign experience was that, in the strength of his reaction against it, he came to full awareness of himself as an Englishman and of the social and political malaise that haunted English society. He began to reexamine his own conscience. He had never been blind to the inhumanity of England's laws against the poor—witness the "Ode to H. Bodkin, Esq." of 1825 and the "Ode to Mr. Malthus" and "Answer to Pauper" of 1832. But these and a few other poems aside, his poetry before 1835 does not possess strong humanitarian feeling. With the *Comic Annual* of 1835, written at the time of his shattering financial and personal crisis, a more thoughtful attitude toward life emerges. A poem like "A Lay of Real Life" reveals a man deeply shaken, acutely aware of the misery of others. After 1835 Hood's illnesses frequently kept him bedridden for long stretches of time. Between his decline in health and his awakening consciousness of society's injustices there exists a close parallel. Social and humanitarian themes, though still in humorous guise, gain prominence in his work. Poems pointing a moral become even more numerous. Hood's writings after 1835 often reveal him in a role other than funnyman. Misread since his own day as pleasant trifling, this supposedly comic verse deserves recognition for its serious ethical tenor. Though many of Hood's readers enjoyed his moral bent, most of them enjoyed his poetry without realizing it was there. But at least one contemporary penetrated to the "solid truth" behind the "light laugh":

We readily admit that the character of Mr. Hood's writings was fun and laughter, and that, as a writer, he was a most facetious one; but we deny that laughter was his only object. He amused the multitude in order to attract their attention; his aim was to make mankind

21

wiser, better, happier; and he made use of his wit and his humour as vehicles wherewith to convey his wholesome and more lasting lessons of morality. The light laugh passed away, but the solid truth remained. Thus many imbibed lessons of kindness and charity, who would have turned away from the inculcator of principles presented with a serious aspect. In truth, Hood was most serious in his purpose when he was most comic in his manner . . . Thus, in an age of reform, Hood was one of the most effectual of reformers.[30]

The preface to the *Comic Annual* for 1837 records Hood's heightened interest in English politics and society. Though he always took care in his published writings to demonstrate strict neutrality in politics, comments in his letters place him in the forefront of liberal, even on occasion of radical, opinion. Several poems of this time, among them "A Plain Direction," stand out as spirited if punning critiques of the age's ills. Seemingly invented with the most joyous insouciance, the puns that caused thousands to laugh Hood brought forth only at the cost of immense physical anguish and mental exhaustion. "No gentleman alive," he remarked bitterly in 1840, "has written so much Comic and spitten so much blood within six consecutive years."[31]

The "Ode to Rae Wilson, Esquire," published in the *Athenaeum* of 12 August 1837, is Hood's best-known poem denouncing the religious hypocrisy of the period. Rae Wilson, a wealthy and very pious Scot, spent much time traveling in foreign lands solely for the purpose, it seems, of drawing pointed comparisons between the moral purity of English Protestantism and the immoral decadence of foreign Catholicism. Hood had drawn Wilson's ire because of his relaxed attitude toward church attendance and alcohol—in Victorian England intemperance generally connoted irreligion—and had more than once come under attack in Wilson's travel books. The poet finally decided to retaliate. His "Ode to Rae Wilson, Esquire," despite the topicality of many allusions, makes excellent reading today for the acerbity of its attack against the Evangelical "piety" Wilson embodied and for its statement of Hood's own humane tolerance amidst Victorian intolerance:

I pray for grace—repent each sinful act—
Peruse, but underneath the rose, my Bible;

And love my neighbour, far too well, in fact,
To call and twit him with a godly tract
That's turn'd by application to a libel.
My heart ferments not with the bigot's leaven,
All creeds I view with toleration thorough,
And have a horror of regarding heaven
   As anybody's rotten borough.

In July 1840, once again settled in England, Hood signed an agreement to contribute to Henry Colburn's *New Monthly Magazine*. For this journal he wrote his most ambitious poem, "Miss Kilmansegg and Her Precious Leg." When it was later republished in the *Comic Annual* for 1842, Colburn commissioned John Leech, probably the most talented humorous artist between Cruikshank and Du Maurier and then at the outset of his career, to provide a series of illustrations. Though overlong —Hood was paid by the sheet and had no qualms about filling the poem out with digressions and moralistic reflections—"Miss Kilmansegg" remains his most significant achievement in the domain of moral humor. Its savage protest against the crass commercialism corroding British society makes it an earlier poetic pendant to Dickens's *Hard Times*. Through his heroine's pretensions Hood satirizes the vulgar aspirations to gentility characteristic of the new class of philistine plutocrats. Throughout, he contrasts the corrupted Miss Kilmansegg and the idle luxury surrounding her with the virtuous poor humbly enduring life's vicissitudes. He shows no compassion for his egotistic heroine and she dies at the end unredeemed by self-knowledge. With "Her Moral" the poem ends; the word "gold," a leitmotif throughout, has by now become more a dirge than a refrain:

Gold! Gold! Gold! Gold:
Good or bad a thousand-fold!
   How widely its agencies vary—
To save—to ruin—to curse—to bless—
As even its minted coins express,
Now stamp'd with the image of Good Queen Bess,
   And now of a Bloody Mary!

Upon the death in August 1841 of the *New Monthly*'s editor, Theodore Hook, Hood was asked to assume the editorship on what seemed to him, at the time, generous terms: £300 a year—with additional remuneration for his contributions. He accepted and for two years he and his family knew prosperity as they had not known it before. But the heavy demands of editing limited his time for creative endeavor and from these years few poems of distinction emerged. Financial security, moreover, acted as a balm upon his social conscience. Hood prosperous wrote on different subjects than Hood destitute; and he wrote less well. Adversity was needed to ignite his social conscience: relative affluence brought relative indifference. Many of his *New Monthly* contributions he collected in two volumes of *Whimsicalities,* published in late 1843 (the volumes carry an 1844 imprint).

Two new friendships of these years came to mean much to him. That with Charles Dickens, whom he first met sometime in 1841, brought him into contact with a man whose humanitarian sympathies well accorded with—and spurred on—his own. That with the Reverend Joseph Hewlett, author of numerous forgotten novels, gave him a companion with whom he could relax in fishing and hunting jaunts at Hewlett's parsonage in Wantage, Berkshire.

When Hood decided to terminate his contract with Colburn in August 1843, he took a fateful step. His income as editor had been stable; from then until his death, less than two years later, he faced a series of deepening financial crises. Ill health continued to plague him incessantly. But if these last years brought personal misery, they also brought widespread recognition by the general public. On 16 December 1843, for its Christmas number, *Punch* published his humanitarian poem "The Song of the Shirt." Such was the poem's immediate success that it changed both the course of that magazine's history and of Hood's life.

Hood had contributed occasionally to *Punch* almost from its inception in 1841, but mainly caustic or humorous epigrams. The publication of "A Drop of Gin!" (November 1843), his first "serious" contribution, marks a turning point in his career: from this time until his death his commitment to expose contemporary injustice and to help remedy it by his verse never faltered. The poem begins a series of eight (all included

in this edition) in which Hood's seriousness of purpose is un-
questionable. These eight poems are, in order of publication,
"A Drop of Gin!" "The Pauper's Christmas Carol," "The Song
of the Shirt," "The Lady's Dream," "The Workhouse Clock,"
"The Bridge of Sighs," "The Lay of the Labourer," and "Sug-
gestions by Steam." "A Drop of Gin!" in essence a sincere plea,
though written in a humorous style, serves as transition from
the often boisterous "Miss Kilmansegg" to the deeply serious
"Bridge of Sighs" and "Lay of the Labourer."

"The Song of the Shirt" established both *Punch*'s and Hood's
contemporary reputation: *Punch*'s circulation trebled, Hood's
popularity soared. Though he had always had a large audience
for his comic verse, he now found his name known all over the
land. The "Song" caught the conscience of the age as did no
other poem. Its opening stanzas depict the plight of a starving
seamstress forced to sew shirts together all day, every day, in
her shabby, bare room, in order to earn a miserable pittance.
To while away the interminable hours she sings the "Song of
the Shirt":

"Work—work—work
Till the brain begins to swim;
  Work—work—work
Till the eyes are heavy and dim!
Seam, and gusset, and band,
  Band, and gusset, and seam,
    Till over the buttons I fall asleep,
  And sew them on in a dream!

"O! Men, with Sisters dear!
  O! Men! with Mothers and Wives!
It is not linen you're wearing out,
  But human creatures' lives!
    Stitch—stitch—stitch,
  In poverty, hunger, and dirt,
Sewing at once, with a double thread,
  A Shroud as well as a Shirt."

As he did in almost all of his poems of social protest, Hood
based "The Song of the Shirt" on real-life incidents he read
about in the newspapers. Taking details from several reports

in the *Times* about the abject circumstances under which London seamstresses struggled for existence, he wove them into a poem of moving simplicity and pathos. With his poetry of social protest he stood side by side with Ebenezer Elliott, the "Corn-Law Rhymer," who fought for decades in verse against the "bread-tax," and Elizabeth Barrett, whose "Cry of the Children," published the same year as Hood's "Song," led to the passing of measures limiting abuses of child labor. Hood's powerful poem ends on the hope—one of its morals—that "the Rich" will hear the "Song of the Shirt."

While the "Song" "ran through the land like wild-fire," the poet engaged in negotiations to found his own magazine. January 1844 saw the appearance of the first number of a new periodical: *Hood's Monthly Magazine and Comic Miscellany*. The magazine's "Prospectus" promised "harmless 'Mirth for the Million' " to "a public sorely oppressed . . . by hard times, heavy taxes, and . . . 'eating cares' "; it took care to affirm, as well, Hood's ever-present desire never to raise a "maiden blush." [32] Half the first number he wrote himself, and it included, among the poems, "The Haunted House." In atmosphere and theme the poem recalls the eerie Gothic horrors of the 1790's, now more parodied than taken seriously; in imagery it recalls the "waste lands" of Browning's "Childe Roland" and of Tennyson's later *Idylls*. But stylistically the poem recalls Keats—and Hood's romantic poetry of the early 1820's. It reminds us that at all stages in his career he wrote poetry remarkably diverse and assimilative, that, though the example of Keats faded over the years, he never forget it entirely.

The narrator in "The Haunted House" explores first the garden, then the house itself. Climbing the stairs, he sees a "BLOODY HAND" on banner, curtain, and casement. But the heavy suspense and the carefully wrought images of interior decay lead to no climax; the poem ends with its mystery unresolved. As Hood had several times implied that the poem was a "dream," he could not, as he so often did, undercut the dramatic illusion by having the reader wake up at the close. Nor could he make that illusion credible. It is a characteristic of romanticism in its decline not to believe in the reality of the world created; Hood could establish and sustain an atmosphere quite skillfully, but he could not make that world meaningful.

Why Keats's influence remained a persistent, if not a powerful, factor in Hood's later career remains a question difficult to answer. Although it seems that Hood came to disbelieve—or distrust—the philosophy of Keats, he never quite rid himself of the stylistic influence, once so overwhelming. "Miss Kilmansegg" as well as "The Haunted House" contain clear verbal echoes of Keats. Nor was this all. In later years Hood found he could still respond genuinely, if differently, to Keats. By 1840 he had become more than a compliant imitator of Keats's technical proficiency or a pallid admirer of his sense of life's evanescence. His understanding of the pain of existence and the release of death, to which Keats's sensitivity was early so acute, came only after a personal crisis in mid-career. So too did his awareness of injustice within the social system, present in stanzas 14 and 15 of the earlier poet's *Isabella*. Though as Hood matured he developed his own distinctive style, he still echoed Keats on occasion, though no longer did he imitate him slavishly. Alvin Whitley is correct when he writes that after *The Plea of the Midsummer Fairies* Hood "never again published a wholly serious volume" but misjudges some later poems when he states that Hood never after "attempted the Keatsian manner or level." [33]

Unlike Keats, Hood never had the patience to revise and rewrite, to pose in his mind the half-dozen possible words before choosing the right one. Either his temperament resisted such self-discipline or publishers' deadlines forbade his practicing it. Probably both. In any event, seldom did he retain a manuscript until he could rework and improve it. Even in "The Haunted House," which contains superb descriptive passages and much sure handling of detail, inexcusable stylistic lapses obtrude. An examination of Hood's few surviving working drafts of poems reveals that the first draft was often the last. He had a compulsive need to keep active, to write or sketch, and he did both things well and quickly. The more demanding tasks of revision, requiring reflection and patience, held less appeal. "His brain teems with humorous fancies, but he cannot afford to part with one," wrote Leigh Hunt, in a passage already cited. And for this reason Hood could not develop a disciplined style such as that Keats evolved. Although Hood never met Keats,[34] why he made no reference in letters to the poet who molded his romantic poetry of the early 1820's and who held interest for him intermittently thereafter must continue a puzzle. Perhaps Hood grew reticent about admitting a debt that he, the first of Keats's imitators, came to find embarrassingly great.

Hood's Magazine, after achieving instantaneous success with its first number, soon ran into financial difficulties and nearly foundered. Its backers turned out to be insolvent. Hood, forced to disengage himself from them, sought new support. Largely through the energy of F. O. Ward, who worked in the capacity of an unpaid subeditor, no issue of the "Mag" failed to appear. But mental strain and a severe attack of influenza in March 1844 shattered Hood's delicate constitution. In May he hovered near death. Recovery came—but it was only partial: rarely in the year left him did he rise from his sickbed.

He continued to write indefatigably. Several poems of social protest—"The Lady's Dream" (February 1844) and "The Workhouse Clock" (April)—came out in *Hood's Magazine.* The May issue contained "The Bridge of Sighs," probably his best poem in this genre; it was based on the case of a seamstress named Mary Furley, which the *Times* had covered extensively in its daily "Police Report." Unable to support herself and her two children by making shirts at 1¾d. per piece, Mary Furley threw herself and her youngest child into the Regent's Canal. Although she was rescued, the child drowned. During her trial, at which she was undefended, she said "that death would have been a happy release to her."[35] The *Times,* protesting that the "New Poor Law [had] brought this creature to the verge of madness," maintained that neither legally nor morally was Mary Furley guilty.

Hood shared this view. In his poem he romanticized the sordid details of Mary Furley's case, made her young instead of middle-aged, childless instead of many times a mother. The squalid Regent's Canal metamorphosed into the grander Thames and Waterloo Bridge, the traditional jumping-off place of suicides. But for his poor seamstress there was no rescue:

One more Unfortunate,
Weary of breath,
Rashly importunate,
Gone to her death!

Take her up tenderly,
Lift her with care;
Fashion'd so slenderly,
Young, and so fair!

This last stanza, five times repeated with variations, unifies the poem and prepares the reader for the moral. In Hood's eyes, society compelled her to choose death, thus had no right to judge her act. The crime, he thought, lay rather in society itself for permitting such misery to exist in its midst: its inhumanity forced her to do what she did.

Another poem of the *annus mirabilis* that was 1844, "The Lay of the Labourer," depicts the plight of starving farm laborers denied the right to work. Not being able to find work, Hood believed, could drive sane men to insane acts: they would do anything to avoid the workhouse. Individuals, as always, aroused in him greater compassion than abstract causes, and "The Lay of the Labourer," like "The Song of the Shirt" and "The Bridge of Sighs," had its origin in an actual case—that of Gifford White. White, an unemployed farm youth, had sent a letter to the farmers in Bluntisham, Huntingdonshire, threatening that if he and his fellow laborers were not given an opportunity to work, they would "set fire to the whole of this place." [36] For his threat alone he was sentenced to transportation for life. In his prose essay, of which the poem forms a part, Hood, pleading the defendant's extreme youth, argued the penalty too severe. "The Lay of the Labourer" enjoyed much enthusiastic comment in the newspapers, but it did not, apparently, change White's sentence.

Though Hood had strained his creative powers to their uttermost, he was not satisfied that he had produced sufficient work of social value. A writer for the *Eclectic Review* who knew him remembered that he "lamented greatly" his inability to do more, "for he seemed to view himself as having a work— a great work to do, and earnestly did he desire to accomplish it. This was to have made a complete series of poems, illustrating every form of social misery, and earnestly advocating its removal."[37] To Sir Robert Peel, then prime minister and long an advocate of humanitarian reform, Hood wrote a death-bed letter expressing his anguish over his uncompleted achievement:

I would have written one more paper—a forewarning one—against an evil, or the danger of it, arising from a literary movement in which I have had some share, a one-sided humanity, opposite to that Catholic Shaksperian sympathy, which felt with King as well as Peasant, and duly estimated the mortal temptations of both stations. Certain classes at the poles of Society are already too far asunder; it should be the duty of our writers to draw them nearer by kindly attraction, not to aggravate the existing repulsion, and place a wider moral gulf between Rich and Poor, with Hate on the one side and Fear on the other.[38]

But in the end, though his sense of duty gave him qualms that he had not spoken out forcefully until too late, Hood had achieved not only understanding but full emotional empathy with the plight of the English poor. Rarely has anyone less deserved an uneasy conscience.

The last year of Hood's life was a period of increasing domestic strain, of near separation from his wife, of quarrels with Ward, of continuing crises with the magazine edited now "by proxy," of collapsing health, of accumulating debts. Throughout, he held up remarkably well. His spirits seldom failed him, and he did his pathetic best to continue—at a mere half sheet a month—the novel, *Our Family,* he had begun in May for his beloved "Mag." Friends and acquaintances responded generously to pleas from the indefatigable Ward for contributions. Robert Browning, Edward Bulwer, Richard Monckton Milnes, and Walter Savage Landor were among those who offered—gratis—poems and stories to help keep the magazine afloat. That so many people, known and unknown, rallied around him cheered the dying poet, and in his last months, though he was tortured physically, his mental anxiety was alleviated. In July 1844, some of Hood's friends began negotiations for a pension for him, and in November Sir Robert Peel announced a Civil List pension of £100 to be conferred, at the poet's request, upon his wife. Hood's exchange of letters with Peel provided him with the opportunity to express his admiration for the prime minister—an admiration reciprocated, Peel claiming that he had read almost every one of Hood's volumes.

His last poem, "Farewell, Life! My senses swim," shows him unafraid of death, now even welcoming it. Through March and April 1845, he lingered on, tended by his wife and adoring children, cheered by friends and even strangers, but when on 1 May he lapsed into a deep coma, all hope was finally abandoned. He died on 3 May. A week later, with his widow, children, and a few close friends as mourners, he was buried in Kensal Green Cemetery.

His death left Jane Hood and the children in reduced circumstances. Jane applied to the Royal Literary Fund for aid and was awarded a grant of £75. Moreover, plans were soon afoot for a subscription, organized by Ward and Thomas Reseigh; by August 1845, nearly £1400 had been collected, but even with this impressive sum, and despite the continuance of Hood's pension, Jane's situation remained precarious. Worn out and frequently ill, she died on 4 December 1846, having outlived her husband by only a year and a half.

Upon the instigation of Eliza Cook, the poetess, a committee was formed in 1852 to raise funds for a funeral monument in Hood's memory. The project, sponsored by the Whittington Club, advanced rapidly. Although many of Hood's friends from the literary world gave generously, his children recorded with especial pride the contributions from the nameless poor: "trifling sums from Manchester, Preston, Bideford, and Bristol —from a few poor needlewomen—from seven dressmakers— from twelve poor men." [39] By 1853 the committee had raised sufficient funds to commission the sculptor Matthew Noble for a monument. The unveiling took place on 18 July 1854, at which time Monckton Milnes, before many of Hood's friends and admirers, gave an oration commemorating his services to literature. Coupling Hood with Dickens, he praised both as "great benefactors of our species, not only on account of the amusement which they give us, but because they are great moral teachers." [40] Underneath the bust of Hood crowning the monument are engraved, at the poet's wish, the words he thought best fit to characterize his life: "He sang the Song of the Shirt."

Selected Poems of Thomas Hood

Dedication,
To the Reviewers

What is a modern Poet's fate?
To write his thoughts upon a slate:—
The Critic spits on what is done,—
Gives it a wipe,—and all is gone.

—*Whims and Oddities* (1826)

I Romantic Poems

I remember, I remember

I

I remember, I remember,
The house where I was born,
The little window where the sun
Came peeping in at morn;
He never came a wink too soon,
Nor brought too long a day,
But now, I often wish the night
Had borne my breath away!

II

I remember, I remember,
The roses, red and white,
The vi'lets, and the lily-cups,
Those flowers made of light!
The lilacs where the robin built,
And where my brother set
The laburnam on his birth-day,—
The tree is living yet!

III

I remember, I remember
Where I was used to swing,
And thought the air must rush as fresh
To swallows on the wing;
My spirit flew in feathers then,
That is so heavy now,
And summer pools could hardly cool
The fever on my brow!

IV

I remember, I remember
The fir trees dark and high;
I used to think their slender tops
Were close against the sky:

It was a childish ignorance,
But now 'tis little joy   30
To know I'm farther off from heav'n
Than when I was a boy.

A Retrospective Review

Oh, when I was a tiny boy
My days and nights were full of joy,
   My mates were blithe and kind!—
No wonder that I sometimes sigh,
And dash the tear-drop from my eye,
   To cast a look behind!

A hoop was an eternal round
Of pleasure. In those days I found
   A top a joyous thing;—
But now those past delights I drop,   10
My head, alas! is all my top,
   And careful thoughts the string!

My marbles—once my bag was stor'd,—
Now I must play with Elgin's lord,
   With Theseus for a taw!
My playful horse has slipt his string,
Forgotten all his capering,
   And harness'd to the law!

My kite—how fast and far it flew!
Whilst I, a sort of Franklin, drew   20
   My pleasure from the sky!
'Twas paper'd o'er with studious themes,
The tasks I wrote—my present dreams
   Will never soar so high!

My joys are wingless all and dead;
My dumps are made of more than lead;
   My flights soon find a fall;
My fears prevail, my fancies droop,
Joy never cometh with a hoop,
   And seldom with a call!   30

My football's laid upon the shelf;
I am a shuttlecock myself
   The world knocks to and fro;—
My archery is all unlearn'd,
And grief against myself has turn'd
   My arrows and my bow!

No more in noontide sun I bask;
My authorship's an endless task,
   My head's ne'er out of school:
My heart is pain'd with scorn and slight,   40
I have too many foes to fight,
   And friends grown strangely cool!

The very chum that shared my cake
Holds out so cold a hand to shake,
   It makes me shirk and sigh:—
On this I will not dwell and hang,
The changeling would not feel a pang
   Though these should meet his eye!

No skies so blue or so serene
As then;—no leaves look half so green   50
   As cloth'd the play-ground tree!
All things I lov'd are alter'd so,
Nor does it ease my heart to know
   That change resides in me!

O, for the garb that mark'd the boy,
The trowsers made of corduroy,
   Well ink'd with black and red;
The crownless hat, ne'er deem'd an ill—
It only let the sunshine still
   Repose upon my head!   60

O, for the riband round the neck!
The careless dog's-ears apt to deck
   My book and collar both!
How can this formal man be styled
Merely an Alexandrine child,
   A boy of larger growth?

O for that small, small beer anew!
And (heaven's own type) that mild sky-blue
   That wash'd my sweet meals down;
The master even!—and that small Turk   70
That fagg'd me!—worse is now my work—
   A fag for all the town!

O for the lessons learn'd by heart!
Ay, though the very birch's smart
　　Should mark those hours again;
I'd "kiss the rod," and be resign'd
Beneath the stroke, and even find
　　Some sugar in the cane!

The Arabian Nights rehears'd in bed!
The Fairy Tales in school-time read,　　　　　　　　80
　　By stealth, 'twixt verb and noun!
The angel form that always walk'd
In all my dreams, and look'd and talk'd
　　Exactly like Miss Brown!

The *omne bene*—Christmas come!
The prize of merit, won for home—
　　Merit had prizes then!
But now I write for days and days,
For fame—a deal of empty praise,
　　Without the silver pen!　　　　　　　　　　　90

Then home, sweet home! the crowded coach—
The joyous shout—the loud approach—
　　The winding horns like rams'!
The meeting sweet that made me thrill,
The sweetmeats almost sweeter still,
　　No 'satis' to the 'jams!'—

When that I was a tiny boy
My days and nights were full of joy,
　　My mates were blithe and kind!
No wonder that I sometimes sigh,　　　　　　　　100
And dash the tear-drop from my eye,
　　To cast a look behind!

Fair Ines

I

O saw ye not fair Ines?
She's gone into the West,
To dazzle when the sun is down,
And rob the world of rest:
She took our daylight with her,
The smiles that we love best,
With morning blushes on her cheek,
And pearls upon her breast.

II

O turn again, fair Ines,
Before the fall of night,   10
For fear the Moon should shine alone,
And stars unrivall'd bright;
And blessed will the lover be
That walks beneath their light,
And breathes the love against thy cheek
I dare not even write!

III

Would I had been, fair Ines,
That gallant cavalier,
Who rode so gaily by thy side,
And whisper'd thee so near!—   20
Were there no bonny dames at home,
Or no true lovers here,
That he should cross the seas to win
The dearest of the dear?

IV

I saw thee, lovely Ines,
Descend along the shore,
With bands of noble gentlemen,
And banners wav'd before;
And gentle youth and maidens gay,
And snowy plumes they wore;—   30
It would have been a beauteous dream,
—If it had been no more!

V

Alas, alas, fair Ines,
She went away with song,
With Music waiting on her steps,
And shoutings of the throng;
But some were sad, and felt no mirth,
But only Music's wrong,
In sounds that sang Farewell, Farewell,
To her you've lov'd so long.   40

VI

Farewell, farewell, fair Ines,
That vessel never bore
So fair a lady on its deck,
Nor danc'd so light before,—
Alas for pleasure on the sea,
And sorrow on the shore!
The smile that blest one lover's heart
Has broken many more!

Ruth

She stood breast high amid the corn,
Clasp'd by the golden light of morn,
Like the sweetheart of the sun,
Who many a glowing kiss had won.

On her cheek an autumn flush,
Deeply ripened;—such a blush
In the midst of brown was born,
Like red poppies grown with corn.

Round her eyes her tresses fell,
Which were blackest none could tell,   10
But long lashes veil'd a light,
That had else been all too bright.

And her hat, with shady brim,
Made her tressy forehead dim;—
Thus she stood amid the stooks,
Praising God with sweetest looks:—

Sure, I said, heav'n did not mean,
Where I reap thou should'st but glean,
Lay thy sheaf adown and come,
Share my harvest and my home.   20

The Sea of Death

A Fragment

—————Methought I saw
Life swiftly treading over endless space;
And, at her foot-print, but a bygone pace,
The ocean-past, which, with increasing wave,
Swallow'd her steps like a pursuing grave.

Sad were my thoughts that anchor'd silently
On the dead waters of that passionless sea,
Unstirr'd by any touch of living breath:
Silence hung over it, and drowsy Death,
Like a gorged sea-bird, slept with folded wings   10
On crowded carcases—sad passive things
That wore the thin grey surface, like a veil
Over the calmness of their features pale.

And there were spring-faced cherubs that did sleep
Like water-lilies on that motionless deep,
How beautiful! with bright unruffled hair
On sleek unfretted brows, and eyes that were
Buried in marble tombs, a pale eclipse!
And smile-bedimpled cheeks, and pleasant lips,
Meekly apart, as if the soul intense   20
Spake out in dreams of its own innocence:
And so they lay in loveliness, and kept
The birth-night of their peace, that Life e'en wept
With very envy of their happy fronts;
For there were neighbour brows scarr'd by the brunts
Of strife and sorrowing—where Care had set
His crooked autograph, and marr'd the jet
Of glossy locks, with hollow eyes forlorn,
And lips that curl'd in bitterness and scorn—
Wretched,—as they had breathed of this world's pain,   30
And so bequeath'd it to the world again
Through the beholder's heart in heavy sighs.

So lay they garmented in torpid light,
Under the pall of a transparent night,

Like solemn apparitions lull'd sublime
To everlasting rest,—and with them Time
Slept, as he sleeps upon the silent face
Of a dark dial in a sunless place.

Ode: Autumn

I

I saw old Autumn in the misty morn
Stand shadowless like Silence, listening
To silence, for no lonely bird would sing
Into his hollow ear from woods forlorn,
Nor lowly hedge nor solitary thorn;—
Shaking his languid locks all dewy bright
With tangled gossamer that fell by night,
    Pearling his coronet of golden corn.

II

Where are the songs of Summer?—With the sun,
Oping the dusky eyelids of the south,   10
Till shade and silence waken up as one,
And Morning sings with a warm odorous mouth.
Where are the merry birds?—Away, away,
On panting wings through the inclement skies,
    Lest owls should prey
    Undazzled at noon-day,
And tear with horny beak their lustrous eyes.

III

Where are the blooms of Summer?—In the west,
Blushing their last to the last sunny hours,
When the mild Eve by sudden Night is prest   20
Like tearful Proserpine, snatch'd from her flow'rs
    To a most gloomy breast.
Where is the pride of Summer,—the green prime,—
The many, many leaves all twinkling?—Three
On the moss'd elm; three on the naked lime
Trembling,—and one upon the old oak tree!
   Where is the Dryad's immortality?—
Gone into mournful cypress and dark yew,
Or wearing the long gloomy Winter through
  In the smooth holly's green eternity.   30

IV

The squirrel gloats on his accomplish'd hoard,
The ants have brimm'd their garners with ripe grain,
    And honey bees have stor'd

The sweets of Summer in their luscious cells;
The swallows all have wing'd across the main;
But here the Autumn melancholy dwells,
  And sighs her tearful spells
Amongst the sunless shadows of the plain.
    Alone, alone,
      Upon a mossy stone,   40
She sits and reckons up the dead and gone
With the last leaves for a love-rosary,
Whilst all the wither'd world looks drearily,
Like a dim picture of the drowned past
In the hush'd mind's mysterious far away,
Doubtful what ghostly thing will steal the last
Into that distance, grey upon the grey.

V

O go and sit with her, and be o'ershaded
Under the languid downfal of her hair:
She wears a coronal of flowers faded   50
Upon her forehead, and a face of care;—
There is enough of wither'd every where
To make her bower,—and enough of gloom;
There is enough of sadness to invite,
If only for the rose that died,—whose doom
Is Beauty's,—she that with the living bloom
Of conscious cheeks most beautifies the light;—
There is enough of sorrowing, and quite
Enough of bitter fruits the earth doth bear,—
Enough of chilly droppings for her bowl;   60
Enough of fear and shadowy despair,
To frame her cloudy prison for the soul!

Autumn

I

The Autumn skies are flush'd with gold,
And fair and bright the rivers run;
These are but streams of winter cold,
And painted mists that quench the sun.

II

In secret boughs no sweet birds sing,
In secret boughs no bird can shroud;
These are but leaves that take to wing,
And wintry winds that pipe so loud.

III

'Tis not trees' shade, but cloudy glooms
That on the cheerless vallies fall,   10
The flowers are in their grassy tombs,
And tears of dew are on them all.

Autumn

The Autumn is old,
The sere leaves are flying;—
He hath gather'd up gold,
And now he is dying;—
Old age, begin sighing!

The vintage is ripe,
The harvest is heaping;—
But some that have sow'd
Have no riches for reaping;—
Poor wretch, fall a weeping!   10

The year's in the wane,
There is nothing adorning,
The night has no eve,
And the day has no morning;—
Cold winter gives warning.

The rivers run chill,
The red sun is sinking,
And I am grown old,
And life is fast shrinking;—
Here's enow for sad thinking!   20

Ode to Melancholy

Come, let us set our careful breasts,
Like Philomel, against the thorn,
To aggravate the inward grief,
That makes her accents so forlorn;
The world has many cruel points,
Whereby our bosoms have been torn,
And there are dainty themes of grief,
In sadness to outlast the morn,—
True honour's dearth, affection's death,
Neglectful pride, and cankering scorn,   10
With all the piteous tales that tears
Have water'd since the world was born.

The world!—it is a wilderness,
Where tears are hung on every tree;
For thus my gloomy phantasy
Makes all things weep with me!
Come let us sit and watch the sky,
And fancy clouds, where no clouds be;
Grief is enough to blot the eye,
And make heav'n black with misery.   20
Why should birds sing such merry notes,
Unless they were more blest than we?
No sorrow ever chokes their throats,
Except sweet nightingale; for she
Was born to pain our hearts the more
With her sad melody.
Why shines the sun, except that he
Makes gloomy nooks for Grief to hide,
And pensive shades for Melancholy,
When all the earth is bright beside?   30
Let clay wear smiles, and green grass wave,
Mirth shall not win us back again,
Whilst man is made of his own grave,
And fairest clouds but gilded rain!

I saw my mother in her shroud,
Her cheek was cold and very pale;
And ever since I've look'd on all
As creatures doom'd to fail!

Why do buds ope, except to die?
Ay, let us watch the roses wither,   40
And think of our loves' cheeks;
And oh, how quickly time doth fly
To bring death's winter hither!
Minutes, hours, days, and weeks,
Months, years, and ages, shrink to nought;
An age past is but a thought!

Ay, let us think of Him a while,
That, with a coffin for a boat,
Rows daily o'er the Stygian moat,
And for our table choose a tomb: 50
There's dark enough in any skull
To charge with black a raven plume;
And for the saddest funeral thoughts
A winding sheet hath ample room,
Where Death, with his keen-pointed style,
Hath writ the common doom.
How wide the yew tree spreads its gloom,
And o'er the dead lets fall its dew,
As if in tears it wept for them,
The many human families   60
That sleep around its stem!

How cold the dead have made these stones,
With natural drops kept ever wet!
Lo! here the best, the worst, the world
Doth now remember or forget,
Are in one common ruin hurl'd,
And love and hate are calmly met;
The loveliest eyes that ever shone,
The fairest hands, and locks of jet.
Is't not enough to vex our souls,   70
And fill our eyes, that we have set
Our love upon a rose's leaf,
Our hearts upon a violet?
Blue eyes, red cheeks, are frailer yet;
And, sometimes, at their swift decay

Beforehand we must fret:
The roses bud and bloom again;
But love may haunt the grave of love,
And watch the mould in vain.

O clasp me, sweet, whilst thou art mine,   80
And do not take my tears amiss;
For tears must flow to wash away
A thought that shows so stern as this:
Forgive, if somewhile I forget,
In woe to come, the present bliss.
As frighted Proserpine let fall
Her flowers at the sight of Dis,
Ev'n so the dark and bright will kiss.
The sunniest things throw sternest shade,
And there is ev'n a happiness   90
That makes the heart afraid!

Now let us with a spell invoke
The full-orb'd moon to grieve our eyes;
Not bright, not bright, but, with a cloud
Lapp'd all about her, let her rise
All pale and dim, as if from rest
The ghost of the late buried sun
Had crept into the skies.
The Moon! she is the source of sighs,
The very face to make us sad;   100
If but to think in other times
The same calm quiet look she had,
As if the world held nothing base,
Of vile and mean, of fierce and bad;
The same fair light that shone in streams,
The fairy lamp that charm'd the lad;
For so it is, with spent delights
She taunts men's brains, and makes them mad.

All things are touch'd with Melancholy,
Born of the secret soul's mistrust,   110
To feel her fair ethereal wings

Weigh'd down with vile degraded dust;
Even the bright extremes of joy
Bring on conclusions of disgust,
Like the sweet blossoms of the May,
Whose fragrance ends in must.
O give her, then, her tribute just,
Her sighs and tears, and musings holy!
There is no music in the life
That sounds with idiot laughter solely;   120
There's not a string attun'd to mirth,
But has its chord in Melancholy.

Song

There is dew for the flow'ret,
   And honey for the bee,
And bowers for the wild bird,
   And love for you and me.

There are tears for the many,
   And pleasure for the few;
But let the world pass on, dear,
   There's love for me and you.

Ballad

It was not in the winter
   Our loving lot was cast!
It was the time of roses,
   We plucked them as we passed!

That churlish season never frowned
   On early lovers yet!—
Oh no—the world was newly crowned
   With flowers, when first we met.

'Twas twilight, and I bade you go,
   But still you held me fast;—   10
It was the time of roses,—
   We plucked them as we passed!

What else could peer thy glowing cheek
   That tears began to stud?—
And when I asked the like of Love
   You snatched a damask bud,—

And oped it to the dainty core
   Still glowing to the last:—
It was the time of roses,
   We plucked them as we passed!   20

Still glides the gentle streamlet on

Still glides the gentle streamlet on,
    With shifting current new and strange;
The water that was here is gone,
    But those green shadows do not change.

Serene, or ruffled by the storm,
    On present waves, as on the past,
The mirror'd grove retains its form,
    The self-same trees their semblance cast.

The hue each fleeting globule wears,
    That drop bequeaths it to the next,
One picture still the surface bears,
    To illustrate the murmur'd text.

10

So, love, however time may flow,
    Fresh hours pursuing those that flee,
One constant image still shall show
    My tide of life is true to thee!

The Forsaken

The dead are in their silent graves,
And the dew is cold above,
And the living weep and sigh,
Over dust that once was love.

Once I only wept the dead,
But now the living cause my pain:
How couldst thou steal me from my tears,
To leave me to my tears again?

My Mother rests beneath the sod,—
Her rest is calm and very deep: 10
I wish'd that she could see our loves,—
But now I gladden in her sleep.

Last night unbound my raven locks,
The morning saw them turn'd to gray,
Once they were black and well belov'd,
But thou art chang'd,—and so are they!

The useless lock I gave thee once,
To gaze upon and think of me,
Was ta'en with smiles,—but this was torn
In sorrow that I send to thee!   20

Queen Mab

A little fairy comes at night,
  Her eyes are blue, her hair is brown,
With silver spots upon her wings,
  And from the moon she flutters down.

She has a little silver wand,
  And when a good child goes to bed
She waves her wand from right to left,
  And makes a circle round its head.

And then it dreams of pleasant things,
  Of fountains filled with fairy fish,   10
And trees that bear delicious fruit
  And bow their branches at a wish:

Of arbours filled with dainty scents
  From lovely flowers that never fade;
Bright flies that glitter in the sun,
  And glow-worms shining in the shade:

And talking birds with gifted tongues,
  For singing songs and telling tales,
And pretty dwarfs to show the way
  Through fairy hills and fairy dales.   20

But when a bad child goes to bed
  From left to right she weaves her rings,
And then it dreams all through the night
  Of only ugly, horrid things!

Then lions come with glaring eyes,
  And tigers growl, a dreadful noise,
And ogres draw their cruel knives,
  To shed the blood of girls and boys.

Then stormy waves rush on to drown,
  Or raging flames come scorching round,   30
Fierce dragons hover in the air,
  And serpents crawl along the ground.

Then wicked children wake and weep,
  And wish the long black gloom away;
But good ones love the dark, and find
  The night as pleasant as the day.

Lear

A poor old king, with sorrow for my crown,
Thron'd upon straw, and mantled with the wind—
For pity, my own tears have made me blind
That I might never see my children's frown;
And may be madness, like a friend, has thrown
A folded fillet over my dark mind,
So that unkindly speech may sound for kind,—
Albeit I know not.—I am childish grown—
And have not gold to purchase wit withal—
I that have once maintain'd most royal state—   10
A very bankrupt now that may not call
My child, my child—all-beggar'd save in tears,
Wherewith I daily weep an old man's fate,
Foolish—and blind—and overcome with years!

False Poets and True

Look how the lark soars upward and is gone,
Turning a spirit as he nears the sky!
His voice is heard, but body there is none
To fix the vague excursions of the eye.
So, poets' songs are with us, tho' they die
Obscur'd, and hid by death's oblivious shroud,
And Earth inherits the rich melody,
Like raining music from the morning cloud.
Yet, few there be who pipe so sweet and loud,
Their voices reach us through the lapse of space: 10
The noisy day is deafen'd by a crowd
Of undistinguish'd birds, a twittering race;
But only lark and nightingale forlorn
Fill up the silences of night and morn.

Sonnet Written in Keats's Endymion

I saw pale Dian, sitting by the brink
   Of silver falls, the overflow of fountains
From cloudy steeps; and I grew sad to think
   Endymion's foot was silent on those mountains,
And he but a hush'd name, that Silence keeps
   In dear remembrance,—lonely, and forlorn,
Singing it to herself until she weeps
   Tears that perchance still glisten in the morn;—
And as I mused, in dull imaginings,
   There came a flash of garments, and I knew   10
The awful Muse by her harmonious wings
   Charming the air to music as she flew—
Anon there rose an echo through the vale
Gave back Endymion in a dream-like tale.

Sonnet

It is not death, that sometime in a sigh
This eloquent breath shall take its speechless flight;
That sometime these bright stars, that now reply
In sunlight to the sun, shall set in night;
That this warm conscious flesh shall perish quite,
And all life's ruddy springs forget to flow;
That thoughts shall cease, and the immortal spright
Be lapp'd in alien clay and laid below;
It is not death to know this,—but to know
That pious thoughts, which visit at new graves   10
In tender pilgrimage, will cease to go
So duly and so oft,—and when grass waves
Over the past-away, there may be then
No resurrection in the minds of men.

Sonnet: Silence

There is a silence where hath been no sound,
  There is a silence where no sound may be,
  In the cold grave—under the deep deep sea,
Or in wide desert where no life is found,
Which hath been mute, and still must sleep profound;
  No voice is hush'd—no life treads silently,
  But clouds and cloudy shadows wander free,
That never spoke, over the idle ground:
But in green ruins, in the desolate walls
  Of antique palaces, where Man hath been,   10
Though the dun fox, or wild hyena, calls,
  And owls, that flit continually between,
Shriek to the echo, and the low winds moan,
There the true Silence is, self-conscious and alone.

The Death-Bed

We watch'd her breathing thro' the night,
Her breathing soft and low,
As in her breast the wave of life
Kept heaving to and fro!

So silently we seemed to speak—
So slowly moved about!
As we had lent her half our powers
To eke her living out!

Our very hopes belied our fears
Our fears our hopes belied—
We thought her dying when she slept,
And sleeping when she died!

For when the morn came dim and sad—
And chill with early showers,
Her quiet eyelids closed—she had
Another morn than ours!

The Ballad

O, when I was a little boy—
  This print the time recalls—
What strips of song there hung along
  Old palings and old walls!

The ballad

O, how they flaunted in the air,
 And flutter'd on their strings!
I'd heard of Muses, and they seemed
 Like feathers from their wings—

Dim flimsy papers, little fit
 With Newland's bills to rank;
But O! there seem'd whole millions there
 In notes of Boyhood's Bank!

With what a charm of black and white
 They witch'd the urchin sense!
How blest if I could stop and buy!
 How pensive—without pence!

How hard, alas! if forced to pass
 By that enchanted place,
In dismal sort—a farthing short—
 To long for "Chevy Chase."

One comfort liv'd—if pence were scant,
 There still was Mary Dunn—
So stored with song, she seem'd the whole
 Nine Muses rolled in one.

Her pocket-money never went
 For cheesecake or for tart;
She purchased all new songs, and had
 The old ones each by heart.

When Mary sat to sing or read,
 All sport and play stood still—
Her words could lock a waggon-wheel,
 And stop the march to drill.

Meanwhile, the tragic tale she told
 Of Babies in the Wood
And gentle Redbreast,—or that bold
 Cock Robin, Robin Hood,

Will Scarlet, and his merry mates
　　Who Lincoln green had on—
I listen'd till I thought myself
　　A little Little John.　　　　　　　　　　　　　　40

O, happy times! O, happy rhymes!
　　For ever ye're gone by!
Few now—if any—are the lays
　　Can make me smile or sigh.

Perchance myself am changed—perchance
　　I do their authors wrong—
But scarce a modern ballad now
　　Seems worthy "an old song."

II Comic Poems

To a Critick

O cruel One how littel dost thou knowe
How manye Poetes with Unhappyenesse
Thou may'st have slaine; ere they began to blowe
Like to yonge Buddes in theyr firste Sappyenesse!
Even as Pinkes from littel Pipinges growe,
Great Poetes yet maye come of Singinges small;
Which if an hungrede Worme doth gnawe belowe
Fold up their stryped leaves and die withal.
Alake, that pleasant Flowre must fayde and fall
Because a Grubbe hath eat into its Head,—   10
That els had growne so fayre and eke so tall
Towards the Heaven and opende forthe and spreade
Its Blossoms to the Sunne for Men to read
In soe bright hues of Lovelinesse indeede.

The Fall of the Deer

[From an old MS.]

Now the loud Crye is up, and harke!
The barkye Trees give back the Bark;
The House Wife heares the merrie rout,
And runnes,—and lets the beere run out,
Leaving her Babes to weepe,—for why?
She likes to heare the Deer Dogges crye,
And see the wild Stag how he stretches
The naturall Buck-skin of his Breeches,
Running like one of Human kind
Dogged by fleet Bailiffes close behind—   10
As if he had not payde his Bill
For Ven'son, or was owing still
For his two Hornes, and soe did get
Over his Head and Ears in Debt;—
Wherefore he strives to paye his Waye
With his long Legges the while he maye:—
But he is chased, like Silver Dish,
As well as anye Hart wish,
Except that one whose Heart doth beat
So faste it hasteneth his Feet;—   20
And runninge soe, he holdeth Death
Four Feet from him;—till his Breath
Faileth, and slacking Pace at last,
From runninge slow he standeth faste,
With hornie Bayonettes at baye
To baying Dogges around, and they
Pushing him sore, he pusheth sore,
And goreth them that seeke his Gore,—
Whatever Dogge his Horne doth rive
Is dead—as sure as he's alive!   30
Soe that courageous Hart doth fight
With Fate, and calleth up his might,
And standeth stout that he maye fall
Bravelye and be avenged of all,
Nor like a Craven yield his Breath
Under the Jawes of Dogges and Death!

She is far from the land

Cables entangling her,
Shipspars for mangling her,
Ropes, sure of strangling her,
Blocks over-dangling her;
Tiller to batter her,
Topmast to shatter her,
Tobacco to spatter her;
Boreas blustering,
Boatswain quite flustering,
Thunder clouds mustering   10
To blast her with sulphur—
If the deep don't engulf her;
Sometimes fear's scrutiny
Pries out a mutiny,
Sniffs conflagration,
Or hints at starvation:—
All the sea-dangers
Buccaneers, rangers,
Pirates and Sallee-men,
Algerine galleymen,   20
Tornadoes and typhons,
And horrible syphons,
And submarine travels
Thro' roaring sea-navels;
Every thing wrong enough,

She is far from the land

Long-boat not long enough,
Vessel not strong enough;
Pitch marring frippery,
The deck very slippery,
And the cabin—built sloping,   30
The Captain a-toping,
And the Mate a blasphemer,
That names his Redeemer,—
With inward uneasiness;
The cook known, by greasiness,
The victuals beslubber'd,
Her bed—in a cupboard;
Things of strange christening,
Snatch'd in her listening,
Blue lights and red lights   40
And mention of dead-lights,
And shrouds made a theme of,
Things horrid to dream of,—
And *buoys* in the water
To fear all exhort her;
Her friend no Leander,
Herself no sea gander,
And ne'er a cork jacket
On board of the packet;
The breeze still a stiffening,   50
The trumpet quite deafening;
Thoughts of repentance,
And doomsday and sentence;
Every thing sinister,
Not a church minister,—
Pilot a blunderer,
Coral reefs under her,
Ready to sunder her;
Trunks tipsy-topsy,
The ship in a dropsy;   60
Waves oversurging her,
Syrens a-dirgeing her;
Sharks all expecting her,
Sword-fish dissecting her,

Crabs with their hand-vices
Punishing land vices;
Sea-dogs and unicorns,
Things with no puny horns,
Mermen carnivorous—
"Good Lord, deliver us!"   70

Come o'er the sea

Ode on a Distant Prospect of Clapham Academy

Ah me! those old familiar bounds!
That classic house, those classic grounds
   My pensive thought recalls!
What tender urchins now confine,
What little captives now repine,
   Within yon irksome walls!

Ay, that's the very house! I know
Its ugly windows, ten a-row!
   Its chimneys in the rear!
And there's the iron rod so high,   10
That drew the thunder from the sky
   And turn'd our table-beer!

There I was birch'd! there I was bred!
There like a little Adam fed
   From Learning's woeful tree!
The weary tasks I used to con!—
The hopeless leaves I wept upon!—
   Most fruitless leaves to me!—

The summon'd class!—the awful bow!—
I wonder who is master now   20
   And wholesome anguish sheds!
How many ushers now employs,
How many maids to see the boys
   Have nothing in their heads!

And Mrs. S***?—Doth she abet
(Like Pallas in the parlour) yet
   Some favour'd two or three,—
The little Crichtons of the hour,
Her muffin-medals that devour,
   And swill her prize—bohea?   30

Ay, there's the play-ground! there's the lime,
Beneath whose shade in summer's prime
   So wildly I have read!—
Who sits there *now,* and skims the cream
Of young Romance, and weaves a dream
   Of Love and Cottage-bread?

Who struts the Randall of the walk?
Who models tiny heads in chalk?
    Who scoops the light canoe?
What early genius buds apace?   40
Where's Poynter? Harris? Bowers? Chase?
    Hal Baylis? blithe Carew?

Alack! they're gone—a thousand ways!
And some are serving in "the Greys,"
    And some have perish'd young!—
Jack Harris weds his second wife;
Hal Baylis drives the *wane* of life;
    And blithe Carew—is hung!

Grave Bowers teaches A B C
To savages at Owhyee;   50
    Poor Chase is with the worms!—
All, all are gone—the olden breed!—
New crops of mushroom boys succeed,
    "And push us from our *forms!*"

Lo! where they scramble forth, and shout,
And leap, and skip, and mob about,
    At play where we have play'd!
Some hop, some run, (some fall,) some twine
Their crony arms; some in the shine,
    And some are in the shade!   60

Lo there what mix'd conditions run!
The orphan lad; the widow's son;
    And Fortune's favour'd care—
The wealthy born, for whom she hath
Mac-Adamized the future path—
    The Nabob's pamper'd heir!

Some brightly starr'd—some evil born,—
For honour some, and some for scorn,—
    For fair or foul renown!
Good, bad, indiff'rent—none may lack!   70
Look, here's a White, and there's a Black!
    And there's a Creole brown!

75

Some laugh and sing, some mope and weep,
And wish *their* frugal sires would keep
   Their only sons at home;—
Some tease the future tense, and plan
The full-grown doings of the man,
    And pant for years to come!

A foolish wish! There's one at hoop;
And four at *fives!* and five who stoop
   The marble taw to speed!
And one that curvets in and out,
Reining his fellow Cob about,—
    Would I were in his *steed!*

        80

Yet he would gladly halt and drop
That boyish harness off, to swop
   With this world's heavy van—
To toil, to tug. O little fool!
While thou canst be a horse at school
    To wish to be a man!

        90

Perchance thou deem'st it were a thing
To wear a crown,—to be a king!
   And sleep on regal down!
Alas! thou know'st not kingly cares;
Far happier is thy head that wears
    That hat without a crown!

And dost thou think that years acquire
New added joys? Dost think thy sire
   More happy than his son?
That manhood's mirth?—Oh, go thy ways
To Drury-lane when —— *plays,*
    And see how *forced* our fun!

       100

Thy taws are brave!—thy tops are rare!—
Our tops are spun with coils of care,
   Our *dumps* are no delight!—
The Elgin marbles are but tame,

And 'tis at best a sorry game
　To fly the Muse's kite!

Our hearts are dough, our heels are lead,
Our topmost joys fall dull and dead　　　　　　　110
　Like balls with no rebound!
And often with a faded eye
We look behind, and send a sigh
　Towards that merry ground!

Then be contented. Thou hast got
The most of heaven in thy young lot;
　There's sky-blue in thy cup!
Thou'lt find thy Manhood all too fast—
Soon come, soon gone! and Age at last
　A sorry *breaking-up!*　　　　　　　120

Faithless Sally Brown

An Old Ballad

Young Ben he was a nice young man,
   A carpenter by trade;
And he fell in love with Sally Brown,
   That was a lady's maid.

But as they fetch'd a walk one day,
   They met a press-gang crew;
And Sally she did faint away,
   Whilst Ben he was brought to.

The Boatswain swore with wicked words,
   Enough to shock a saint,   10
That though she did seem in a fit,
   'Twas nothing but a feint.

"Come, girl," said he, "hold up your head,
   He'll be as good as me;
For when your swain is in our boat,
   A boatswain he will be."

So when they'd made their game of her,
   And taken off her elf,
She roused, and found she only was
   A coming to herself.   20

"And is he gone, and is he gone?"
   She cried, and wept outright:
"Then I will to the water side,
   And see him out of sight."

A waterman came up to her,—
   "Now, young woman," said he,
"If you weep on so, you will make
   Eye-water in the sea."

"Alas! they've taken my beau, Ben,
   To sail with old Benbow;"   30
And her woe began to run afresh,
   As if she had said Gee woe!

Says he, "they've only taken him
    To the Tender ship, you see;"—
"The Tender-ship," cried Sally Brown,
    "What a hard-ship that must be!

"O! would I were a mermaid now,
    For then I'd follow him;
But, oh! I'm not a fish-woman,
    And so I cannot swim.   40

"Alas! I was not born beneath
    'The virgin and the scales,'
So I must curse my cruel stars,
    And walk about in Wales."

Now Ben had sail'd to many a place
    That's underneath the world;
But in two years the ship came home,
    And all the sails were furl'd.

But when he call'd on Sally Brown,
    To see how she went on,   50
He found she'd got another Ben,
    Whose Christian-name was John.

"O Sally Brown, O Sally Brown,
    How could you serve me so,
I've met with many a breeze before,
    But never such a blow!"

Then reading on his 'bacco box,
    He heaved a heavy sigh,
And then began to eye his pipe,
    And then to pipe his eye.   60

And then he tried to sing "All's Well,"
    But could not, though he tried;
His head was turn'd, and so he chew'd
    His pigtail till he died.

His death, which happen'd in his birth,
    At forty-odd befell:
They went and told the sexton, and
    The sexton toll'd the bell.

Faithless Nelly Gray

A Pathetic Ballad

Ben Battle was a soldier bold,
   And used to war's alarms;
But a cannon-ball took off his legs,
   So he laid down his arms!

Now as they bore him off the field,
   Said he, "Let others shoot,
For here I leave my second leg,
   And the Forty-second Foot!"

The army-surgeons made him limbs:
   Said he,—"They're only pegs: 10
But there's as wooden members quite,
   As represent my legs!"

Now Ben he loved a pretty maid,
   Her name was Nelly Gray;
So he went to pay her his devours,
   When he'd devour'd his pay!

But when he called on Nelly Gray,
   She made him quite a scoff;
And when she saw his wooden legs,
   Began to take them off!   20

"O, Nelly Gray! O, Nelly Gray!
   Is this your love so warm?
The love that loves a scarlet coat,
   Should be more uniform!"

Said she, "I loved a soldier once,
   For he was blythe and brave;
But I will never have a man
   With both legs in the grave!

Before you had those timber toes,
   Your love I did allow,   30
But then, you know, you stand upon
   Another footing now!"

"O, Nelly Gray! O, Nelly Gray!
   For all your jeering speeches,
At duty's call, I left my legs
   In Badajos's *breaches!*"

"Why, then," said she, "you've lost the feet
   Of legs in war's alarms,
And now you cannot wear your shoes
   Upon your feats of arms!"   40

"O, false and fickle Nelly Gray!
   I know why you refuse:—
Though I've no feet—some other man
   Is standing in my shoes!

I wish I ne'er had seen your face;
   But, now, a long farewell!
For you will be my death:—alas!
   You will not be my *Nell!*"

Now when he went from Nelly Gray,
   His heart so heavy got—   50
And life was such a burthen grown,
   It made him take a knot!

So round his melancholy neck,
   A rope he did entwine,
And, for his second time in life,
   Enlisted in the Line!

One end he tied around a beam,
   And then removed his pegs,
And, as his legs were off,—of course,
   He soon was off his legs!   60

And there he hung, till he was dead
   As any nail in town,—
For though distress had cut him up,
   It could not cut him down!

A dozen men sat on his corpse,
   To find out why he died—
And they buried Ben in four cross-roads,
   With a *stake* in his inside!

Mary's Ghost

A Pathetic Ballad

I

'Twas in the middle of the night,
 To sleep young William tried,
When Mary's ghost came stealing in,
 And stood at his bed-side.

II

O William dear! O William dear!
 My rest eternal ceases;
Alas! my everlasting peace
 Is broken into pieces.

III

I thought the last of all my cares
 Would end with my last minute;   10
But tho' I went to my long home,
 I didn't stay long in it.

Gin a body meet a body

IV

The body-snatchers they have come,
    And made a snatch at me;
It's very hard them kind of men
    Won't let a body be!

V

You thought that I was buried deep,
    Quite decent like and chary,
But from her grave in Mary-bone
    They've come and bon'd your Mary.   20

VI

The arm that used to take your arm
    Is took to Dr. Vyse;
And both my legs are gone to walk
    The hospital at Guy's.

VII

I vow'd that you should have my hand,
    But fate gives us denial;
You'll find it there, at Doctor Bell's,
    In spirits and a phial.

VIII

As for my feet, the little feet
    You used to call so pretty,   30
There's one I know, in Bedford Row,
    The t'other's in the city.

IX

I can't tell where my head is gone,
    But Doctor Carpue can:
As for my trunk, it's all pack'd up
    To go by Pickford's van.

X

I wish you'd go to Mr. P.
   And save me such a ride;
I don't half like the outside place,
   They've took for my inside.   40

XI

The cock it crows—I must be gone!
   My William we must part!
But I'll be your's in death, altho'
   Sir Astley has my heart.

XII

Don't go to weep upon my grave,
   And think that there I be;
They haven't left an atom there,
   Of my anatomie.

Tim Turpin

A Pathetic Ballad

Tim Turpin he was gravel blind,
  And ne'er had seen the skies:
For Nature, when his head was made,
  Forgot to dot his eyes.

So, like a Christmas pedagogue,
  Poor Tim was forc'd to do—
Look out for pupils, for he had
  A vacancy for two.

There's some have specs to help their sight
  Of objects dim and small: 10
But Tim had *specks* within his eyes,
  And could not see at all.

Now Tim he woo'd a servant-maid,
  And took her to his arms;
For he, like Pyramus, had cast
  A wall-eye on her charms.

By day she led him up and down
  Where'er he wish'd to jog,
A happy wife, altho' she led
  The life of any dog.   20

But just when Tim had liv'd a month
  In honey with his wife,
A surgeon ope'd his Milton eyes,
  Like oysters, with a knife.

But when his eyes were open'd thus,
  He wish'd them dark again:
For when he look'd upon his wife,
  He saw her very plain.

Her face was bad, her figure worse,
  He couldn't bear to eat: 30
For she was any thing but like
  A Grace before his meat.

Now Tim he was a feeling man:
   For when his sight was thick,
It made him feel for every thing—
   But that was with a stick.

So with a cudgel in his hand—
   It was not light or slim—
He knocked at his wife's head until
   It open'd unto him.   40

And when the corpse was stiff and cold,
   He took his slaughter'd spouse,
And laid her in a heap with all
   The ashes of her house.

But like a wicked murderer,
   He lived in constant fear
From day to day, and so he cut
   His throat from ear to ear.

The neighbours fetch'd a doctor in:
   Said he, this wound I dread   50
Can hardly be sow'd up—his life
   Is hanging on a thread.

But when another week was gone,
   He gave him stronger hope—
Instead of hanging on a thread,
   Of hanging on a rope.

Ah! when he hid his bloody work,
   In ashes round about,
How little he supposed the truth,
   Would soon be sifted out.   60

But when the parish dustman came,
   His rubbish to withdraw,
He found more dust within the heap,
   Than he contracted for!

A dozen men to try the fact,
    Were sworn that very day;
But tho' they all were jurors, yet
    No conjurors were they.

Jurors—not con-jurors

Said Tim unto those jurymen,
    You need not waste your breath,
For I confess myself at once,
    The author of her death.   70

And, oh! when I reflect upon
    The blood that I have spilt,
Just like a button is my soul,
    Inscrib'd with double *guilt!*

Then turning round his head again,
    He saw before his eyes,
A great judge, and a little judge,
    The judges of a-size!   80

The judges of a-size

The great judge took his judgment cap,
  And put it on his head,
And sentenc'd Tim by law to hang,
  'Till he was three times dead.

So he was tried, and he was hung
  (Fit punishment for such)
On Horsham-drop, and none can say
  It was a drop too much.

Death's Ramble

One day the dreary old King of Death
   Inclined for some sport with the carnal,
So he tied a pack of darts on his back,
   And quietly stole from his charnel.

His head was bald of flesh and of hair,
   His body was lean and lank,
His joints at each stir made a crack, and the cur
   Took a gnaw, by the way, at his shank.

And what did he do with his deadly darts,
   This goblin of grisly bone?   10
He dabbled and spill'd man's blood, and he kill'd
   Like a butcher that kills his own.

The first he slaughter'd it made him laugh,
   (For the man was a coffin-maker,)
To think how the mutes, and men in black suits,
   Would mourn for an undertaker.

Death saw two Quakers sitting at church,
   Quoth he, "we shall not differ."
And he led them alone, like figures of stone,
   For he could not make them stiffer.   20

He saw two duellists going to fight,
   In fear they could not smother;
And he shot one through at once—for he knew
   They never would shoot each other.

He saw a watchman fast in his box,
   And he gave a snore infernal;
Said Death, "he may keep his breath, for his sleep
   Can never be more eternal."

He met a coachman driving his coach
   So slow, that his fare grew sick;   30
But he let him stray on his tedious way,
   For Death only wars on the *quick*.

Death saw a toll-man taking a toll,
   In the spirit of his fraternity;
But he knew that sort of man would extort,
   Though summon'd to all eternity.

He found an author writing his life,
   But he let him write no further;
For Death, who strikes whenever he likes,
   Is jealous of all self-murther!   40

Death saw a patient that pull'd out his purse,
   And a doctor that took the sum;
But he let them be—for he knew that the "fee"
   Was a prelude to "faw" and "fum."

He met a dustman ringing a bell,
   And he gave him a mortal thrust;
For himself, by law, since Adam's flaw,
   Is contractor for all our dust.

Dust O!

He saw a sailor mixing his grog,
    And he marked him out for slaughter;   50
For on water he scarcely had cared for Death,
    And never on rum-and-water.

Death saw two players playing at cards,
    But the game wasn't worth a dump,
For he quickly laid them flat with a spade,
    To wait for the final trump!

John Day

A Pathetic Ballad

A Day after the Fair.—Old Proverb

John Day he was the biggest man
   Of all the coachman-kind,
With back too broad to be conceiv'd
   By any narrow mind.

The very horses knew his weight
   When he was in the rear,
And wish'd his box a Christmas box
   To come but once a year.

The box seat

94

Alas! against the shafts of love,
   What armour can avail?   10
Soon Cupid sent an arrow thro'
   His scarlet coat of mail.

The bar-maid of the Crown he lov'd,
   From whom he never ranged,
For though he changed his horses there,
   His love he never changed.

He thought her fairest of all fares,
   So fondly love prefers;
And often, among twelve outsides,
   Deemed no outside like hers.   20

One day as she was sitting down
   Beside the porter-pump—
He came, and knelt with all his fat,
   And made an offer plump.

Said she, my taste will never learn
   To like so huge a man,
So I must beg you will come here
   As little as you can.

But still he stoutly urged his suit,
   With vows, and sighs, and tears,   30
Yet could not pierce her heart, altho'
   He drove the Dart for years.

In vain he wooed, in vain he sued;
   The maid was cold and proud,
And sent him off to Coventry,
   While on his way to Stroud.

He fretted all the way to Stroud,
   And thence all back to town,
The course of love was never smooth,
   So his went up and down.   40

At last her coldness made him pine
   To merely bones and skin,
But still he loved like one resolved
   To love through thick and thin.

Oh Mary, view my wasted back,
   And see my dwindled calf;
Tho' I have never had a wife,
   I've lost my better half.

Alas, in vain he still assail'd,
   Her heart withstood the dint;   50
Though he had carried sixteen stone
   He could not move a flint.

Worn out, at last he made a vow
   To break his being's link;
For he was so reduced in size
   At nothing he could shrink.

Little and Bigamy

Now some will talk in water's praise,
   And waste a deal of breath,
But John, tho' he drank nothing else—
   He drank himself to death.   60

The cruel maid that caused his love,
   Found out the fatal close,
For looking in the butt, she saw,
   The butt-end of his woes.

Some say his spirit haunts the Crown,
   But that is only talk—
For after riding all his life,
   His ghost objects to walk.

Sally Simpkin's Lament; or
John Jones's Kit-Cat-Astrophe

"He left his body to the sea,
And made a shark his legatee."
                    Bryan and Pereene

"Oh! what is that comes gliding in,
    And quite in middling haste?
It is the picture of my Jones,
    And painted to the waist.

"It is not painted to the life,
    For where's the trowsers blue?
Oh Jones, my dear!—Oh dear! my Jones,
    What is become of you?"

"Oh! Sally dear, it is too true,—
    The half that you remark   10
Is come to say my other half
    Is bit off by a shark!

"Oh! Sally, sharks do things by halves,
    Yet most completely do!
A bite in one place seems enough,
    But I've been bit in two.

"You know I once was all your own,
    But now a shark must share!
But let that pass—for now, to you
    I'm neither here nor there.   20

"Alas! death has a strange divorce
    Effected in the sea,
It has divided me from you,
    And even me from me!

"Don't fear my ghost will walk o'nights
    To haunt, as people say;

My ghost *can't* walk, for, oh! my legs
  Are many leagues away!

"Lord! think when I am swimming round,
  And looking where the boat is,   30
A shark just snaps away a *half*,
  Without 'a *quarter's* notice.'

Sea-consumption—waisting away

"One half is here, the other half
  Is near Columbia placed;
Oh! Sally, I have got the whole
  Atlantic for my waist.

99

"But now, adieu—a long adieu!
    I've solved death's awful riddle,
And would say more, but I am doomed
    To break off in the middle!"   40

A centre-bit

A Waterloo Ballad

Fancy portrait: The Duke of Well——— and Prince of Water—

To Waterloo, with sad ado,
    And many a sigh and groan,
Amongst the dead, came Patty Head,
    To look for Peter Stone.

"O prithee tell, good sentinel,
    If I shall find him here?
I'm come to weep upon his corse,
    My Ninety-Second dear!

"Into our town a serjeant came,
    With ribands all so fine,
A-flaunting in his cap—alas!
    His bow enlisted mine!

"They taught him how to turn his toes,
    And stand as stiff as starch;
I thought that it was love and May,
    But it was love and March!

10

101

The ides of March are come

"A sorry March indeed to leave
    The friends he might have kep',—
No March of Intellect it was,
    But quite a foolish step.

"O prithee tell, good sentinel,
    If hereabout he lies?
I want a corpse with reddish hair,
    And very sweet blue eyes."

Her sorrow on the sentinel
    Appear'd to deeply strike:—
"Walk in," he said, "among the dead,
    And pick out which you like."

20

And soon she picked out Peter Stone,
    Half turned into a corse;   30
A cannon was his bolster, and
    His mattress was a horse.

"O Peter Stone, O Peter Stone,
    Lord here has been a skrimmage!
What have they done to your poor breast
    That used to hold my image?"

"O Patty Head, O Patty Head,
    You're come to my last kissing;
Before I'm set in the Gazette
    As wounded, dead, and missing!   40

"Alas! a splinter of a shell
    Right in my stomach sticks;
French mortars don't agree so well
    With stomachs as French bricks.

"This very night a merry dance
    At Brussels was to be;—
Instead of opening a ball,
    A ball has open'd me.

"Its billet every bullet has,
    And well it does fulfil it;—   50
I wish mine hadn't come so straight,
    But been a 'crooked billet.'

"And then there came a cuirassier
    And cut me on the chest;—
He had no pity in his heart,
    For he had *steel'd his breast.*

"Next thing a lancer, with his lance,
    Began to thrust away;
I call'd for quarter, but, alas!
    It was not Quarter-day.   60

"He ran his spear right through my arm,
    Just here above the joint;—
O Patty dear, it was no joke,
    Although it had a point.

"With loss of blood I fainted off,
    As dead as women do—
But soon by charging over me,
    The *Coldstream* brought me to.

"With kicks and cuts, and balls and blows,
    I throb and ache all over;
I'm quite convinc'd the field of Mars
    Is not a field of clover!

70

War dance.—the opening of the ball

"O why did I a soldier turn
    For any royal Guelph?
I might have been a Butcher, and
    In business for myself!

"O why did I the bounty take
   (And here he gasp'd for breath)
My shillingsworth of 'list is nail'd
   Upon the door of death!   80

"Without a coffin I shall lie
   And sleep my sleep eternal:
Not ev'n a *shell*—my only chance
   Of being made a *Kernel!*

"O Patty dear, our wedding bells
   Will never ring at Chester!
Here I must lie in Honour's bed,
   That isn't worth a *tester!*

"Farewell, my regimental mates,
   With whom I used to dress!   90
My corps is changed, and I am now
   In quite another mess.

"Farewell, my Patty dear, I have
   No dying consolations,
Except, when I am dead, you'll go
   And see th' Illuminations."

Firing shells

The Carelesse Nurse Mayd

I sawe a Mayd sitte on a Bank,
Beguild by Wooer fayne and fond;
And whiles His flatterynge Vowes She drank,
Her Nurselynge slipt within a Pond!

As nursemaid, accustomed to the care of children

All Even Tide they Talkde and Kist,
For She was fayre and He was Kinde;
The Sunne went down before She wist
Ane other Sonne had sett behinde!

With angrie Hands and frownynge Browe,
That deemd Her owne the Urchine's Sinne,
She pluckt Him out, but he was nowe
Past being Whipt for fallynge in.

She then beginnes to wayle the Ladde
With Shrikes that Echo answerde round—
O! foolishe Mayd, to be soe sadde
The Momente that her Care was drownd!

10

Domestic Asides;
or,
Truth in Parentheses

I

"I really take it very kind,
This visit, Mrs. Skinner!
I have not seen you such an age—
(The wretch has come to dinner!)

Friends dropping in

II

"Your daughters, too, what loves of girls—
What heads for painters' easels!
Come here and kiss the infant, dears,—
(And give it p'rhaps the measles!)

III

"Your charming boys I see are home
From Reverend Mr. Russel's;   10
'Twas very kind to bring them both,—
(What boots for my new Brussels!)

A moderate income

IV

"What! little Clara left at home?
Well now I call that shabby:
I should have lov'd to kiss her so,—
(A flabby, dabby, babby!)

V

"And Mr. S., I hope he's well,
Ah! though he lives so handy,
He never now drops in to sup,—
(The better for our brandy!)   20

VI

"Come, take a seat—I long to hear
About Matilda's marriage;
You're come of course to spend the day!—
(Thank Heav'n I hear the carriage!)

VII

"What, must you go? next time I hope
You'll give me longer measure;
Nay—I shall see you down the stairs—
(With most uncommon pleasure!)

VIII

"Good bye! good bye! remember all,
Next time you'll take your dinners!   30
(Now, David, mind I'm not at home
In future to the Skinners!")

Domestic Poems

I

Hymeneal Retrospections

O Kate! my dear Partner, through joy and through strife!
  When I look back at Hymen's dear day,
Not a lovelier bride ever chang'd to a wife,
  Though you're now so old, wizen'd, and grey!

How neat she spreads the whacks

Those eyes, then, were stars, shining rulers of fate!
  But as liquid as stars in a pool;
Though now they're so dim, they appear, my dear Kate,
  Just like gooseberries boil'd for a fool!

110

That brow was like marble, so smooth and so fair;
    Though it's wrinkled so crookedly now,   10
As if Time, when those furrows were made by the share,
    Had been tipsy whilst driving his plough!

Your nose, it was such as the sculptors all chose,
    When a Venus demanded their skill;
Though now it can hardly be reckon'd a nose,
    But a sort of Poll-Parroty bill!

Your mouth, it was then quite a bait for the bees,
    Such a nectar there hung on each lip;
Though now it has taken that lemon-like squeeze,
    Not a blue-bottle comes for a sip!   20

Your chin, it was one of Love's favourite haunts,
    From its dimple he could not get loose;
Though now the neat hand of a barber it wants,
    Or a singe, like the breast of a goose!

How rich were those locks, so abundant and full,
    With their ringlets of auburn so deep!
Though now they look only like frizzles of wool,
    By a bramble torn off from a sheep!

That neck, not a swan could excel it in grace,
    While in whiteness it vied with your arms;   30
Though now a grave 'kerchief you properly place,
    To conceal that scrag-end of your charms!

Your figure was tall, then, and perfectly straight,
    Though it now has two twists from upright—
But bless you! still bless you! my Partner! my Kate!
    Though you be such a perfect old fright!

II

Hymeneal Retrospections

The sun was slumbering in the West,
    My daily labours past;

On Anna's soft and gentle breast
  My head reclined at last;—
The darkness clos'd around, so dear
  To fond congenial souls,
And thus she murmur'd at my ear,
  "My love, we're out of coals!"

"That Mister Bond has call'd again,
  Insisting on his rent;   10
And all the Todds are coming up
  To see us, out of Kent;—
I quite forgot to tell you John
  Has had a tipsy fall;—
I'm sure there's something going on
  With that vile Mary Hall!"—

"Miss Bell has bought the sweetest silk,
  And I have bought the rest—
Of course, if we go out of town,
  Southend will be the best.—   20
I really think the Jones's house
  Would be the thing for us;—
I think I told you Mrs. Pope
  Has parted with her *nus*——"

"Cook, by the way, came up to-day,
  To bid me suit myself—
And what d'ye think? the rats have gnawed
  The victuals on the shelf.—
And, lord! there's such a letter come,
  Inviting you to fight!   30
Of course you don't intend to go—
  God bless you, dear, good night!"

III

A Parental Ode to My Son, Aged 3 Years and 5 Months

    Thou happy, happy elf!
(But stop,—first let me kiss away that tear)—

Thou tiny image of myself!
(My love, he's poking peas into his ear!)
Thou merry, laughing sprite!
With spirits feather-light,
Untouch'd by sorrow, and unsoil'd by sin—
(Good heav'ns! the child is swallowing a pin!)

Thou little tricksy Puck!
With antic toys so funnily bestuck,   10
Light as the singing bird that wings the air—
(The door! the door! he'll tumble down the stair!)
Thou darling of thy sire!
(Why, Jane, he'll set his pinafore a-fire!)
Thou imp of mirth and joy!
In Love's dear chain so strong and bright a link,
Thou idol of thy parents—(Drat the boy!
There goes my ink!)

Thou cherub—but of earth;
Fit playfellow for Fays, by moonlight pale,   20
In harmless sport and mirth,
(That dog will bite him if he pulls its tail!)
Thou human humming-bee, extracting honey
From ev'ry blossom in the world that blows,
Singing in Youth's Elysium ever sunny,
(Another tumble!—that's his precious nose!)

Thy father's pride and hope!
(He'll break the mirror with that skipping-rope!)
With pure heart newly stamp'd from Nature's mint—
(Where *did* he learn that squint?)   30
Thou young domestic dove!
(He'll have that jug off, with another shove!)
Dear nurseling of the hymeneal nest!
(Are those torn clothes his best?)
Little epitome of man!
(He'll climb upon the table, that's his plan!)
Touch'd with the beauteous tints of dawning life—
(He's got a knife!)

113

Thou enviable being!
No storms, no clouds, in thy blue sky foreseeing,   40
      Play on, play on,
      My elfin John!
Toss the light ball—bestride the stick—
(I knew so many cakes would make him sick!)
With fancies, buoyant as the thistle-down,
Prompting the face grotesque, and antic brisk,
      With many a lamb-like frisk,
(He's got the scissors, snipping at your gown!)

      Thou pretty opening rose!
(Go to your mother, child, and wipe your nose!)   50
Balmy and breathing music like the South,
(He really brings my heart into my mouth!)
Fresh as the morn, and brilliant as its star,—
(I wish that window had an iron bar!)
Bold as the hawk, yet gentle as the dove,—
      (I'll tell you what, my love,
I cannot write, unless he's sent above!)

IV

A Serenade

    "Lullaby, oh, lullaby!"
Thus I heard a father cry,
    "Lullaby, oh, lullaby!
The brat will never shut an eye;
Hither come, some power divine!
Close his lids, or open mine!"

    "Lullaby, oh, lullaby!
What the devil makes him cry?
    Lullaby, oh, lullaby!
Still he stares—I wonder why,   10
Why are not the sons of earth
Blind, like puppies, from the birth?"

"Lullaby, oh, lullaby!"
Thus I heard the father cry;
  "Lullaby, oh, lullaby!
Mary, you must come and try!—
Hush, oh, hush, for mercy's sake—
The more I sing, the more you wake!"

  "Lullaby, oh, lullaby!
Fie, you little creature, fie!
  Lullaby, oh, lullaby!
Is no poppy-syrup nigh?
Give him some, or give him all,
I am nodding to his fall!"

  "Lullaby, oh, lullaby!
Two such nights, and I shall die!
  Lullaby, oh, lullaby!
He'll be bruised, and so shall I,—
How can I from bedposts keep,
When I'm walking in my sleep?"

  "Lullaby, oh, lullaby!
Sleep his very looks deny—
  Lullaby, oh, lullaby;
Nature soon will stupify—
My nerves relax,—my eyes grow dim—
Who's that fallen—me or him?"

20

30

Stanzas, Composed in a Shower-Bath

"Drip, drip, drip—there's nothing here but dripping."
Remorse, by Coleridge

Trembling, as Father Adam stood
To pull the stalk, before the Fall,
So stand I here, before the Flood,
On my own head the shock to call:
How like our predecessor's luck!
'Tis but to pluck—but needs some pluck!

Still thoughts of gasping like a pup
Will paralyze the nervous pow'r;
Now hoping it will yet hold up,
Invoking now the tumbling show'r;—   10
But, ah! the shrinking body loathes,
Without a parapluie or clothes!

Operation for the cataract

116

"Expect some rain about this time!"
My eyes are seal'd, my teeth are set—
But where's the Stoic so sublime
Can ring, unmov'd, for wringing wet?
Of going hogs some folks talk big—
Just let them try *the whole cold pig*!

The Bachelor's Dream

My pipe is lit, my grog is mix'd,
My curtains drawn and all is snug;
Old Puss is in her elbow-chair,
And Tray is sitting on the rug.
Last night I had a curious dream,
Miss Susan Bates was Mistress Mogg—
What d'ye think of that, my Cat?
What d'ye think of that, my Dog?

She look'd so fair, she sang so well,
I could but woo and she was won,   10
Myself in blue, the bride in white,
The ring was placed, the deed was done!

Predestination and free-will

Away we went in chaise-and-four,
As fast as grinning boys could flog—
What d'ye think of that, my Cat?
What d'ye think of that, my Dog?

What loving tête-à-têtes to come!
But tête-à-têtes must still defer!
When Susan came to live with me,
Her mother came to live with her!   20
With sister Belle she couldn't part,
But all *my* ties had leave to jog—
What d'ye thing of that, my Cat?
What d'ye think of that, my Dog?

The mother brought a pretty Poll—
A monkey too, what work he made!
The sister introduced a Beau—
My Susan brought a favourite maid.
She had a tabby of her own,—
A snappish mongrel christen'd Gog—   30
What d'ye think of that, my Cat?
What d'ye think of that, my Dog?

The Monkey bit—the Parrot scream'd,
All day the sister strumm'd and sung;
The petted maid was such a scold!
My Susan learn'd to use her tongue:
Her mother had such wretched health,
She sate and croak'd like any frog—
What d'ye think of that, my Cat?
What d'ye think of that, my Dog?   40

No longer Deary, Duck, and Love,
I soon came down to simple "M!"
The very servants cross'd my wish,
My Susan let me down to them.
The poker hardly seem'd my own,
I might as well have been a log—
What d'ye think of that, my Cat?
What d'ye think of that, my Dog?

Spirit and water

My clothes they were the queerest shape!
Such coats and hats she never met!   50
My ways they were the oddest ways!
My friends were such a vulgar set!
Poor Tomkinson was snubb'd and huff'd—
She could not bear that Mister Blogg—
What d'ye think of that, my Cat?
What d'ye think of that, my Dog?

At times we had a spar, and then
Mama must mingle in the song—
The sister took a sister's part—
The Maid declared her Master wrong—   60
The Parrot learn'd to call me "Fool!"

My life was like a London fog—
What d'ye think of that, my Cat?
What d'ye think of that, my Dog?

My Susan's taste was superfine,
As proved by bills that had no end—
I never had a decent coat—
I never had a coin to spend!
She forced me to resign my Club,
Lay down my pipe, retrench my grog—   70
What d'ye think of that, my Cat?
What d'ye think of that, my Dog?

Each Sunday night we gave a rout
To fops and flirts, a pretty list;
And when I tried to steal away,
I found my study full of whist!
Then, first to come and last to go,
There always was a Captain Hogg—
What d'ye think of that, my Cat?
What d'ye think of that, my Dog?   80

Now was not that an awful dream
For one who single is and snug—
With Pussy in the elbow-chair
And Tray reposing on the rug?—
If I must totter down the hill,
'Tis safest done without a clog—
What d'ye think of that, my Cat?
What d'ye think of that, my Dog?

No!

No sun—no moon!
No morn—no noon—
No dawn—no dusk—no proper time of day—
No sky—no earthly view—
No distance looking blue—
No road—no street—no "t'other side the way"—
No end to any Row—
No indications where the Crescents go—
No top to any steeple—
No recognitions of familiar people—   10
No courtesies for showing 'em—
No knowing 'em!—
No travelling at all—no locomotion,
No inkling of the way—no notion—
"No go"—by land or ocean—
No mail—no post—
No news from any foreign coast—
No Park—no Ring—no afternoon gentility—
No company—no nobility—
No warmth, no cheerfulness, no healthful ease,   20
No comfortable feel in any member—
No shade, no shine, no butterflies, no bees,
No fruits, no flow'rs, no leaves, no birds,
November!

To Minerva

From the Greek

My temples throb, my pulses boil,
  I'm sick of Song, and Ode, and Ballad—
So, Thyrsis, take the Midnight Oil
  And pour it on a lobster salad.

My brain is dull, my sight is foul,
  I cannot write a verse, or read—
Then, Pallas, take away thine Owl,
  And let us have a Lark instead.

III   Verse Narratives

Bianca's Dream

A Venetian Story

Bianca!—fair Bianca!—who could dwell
  With safety on her dark and hazel gaze,
Nor find there lurk'd in it a witching spell,
  Fatal to balmy nights and blessed days?
The peaceful breath that made the bosom swell,
  She turn'd to gas, and set it in a blaze;
Each eye of hers had Love's Eupyrion in it,
That he could light his link at in a minute.

So that, wherever in her charms she shone,
  A thousand breasts were kindled into flame;   10
Maidens who cursed her looks forgot their own,
  And beaux were turn'd to flambeaux where she came;
All hearts indeed were conquer'd but her own,
  Which none could ever temper down or tame:
In short, to take our haberdasher's hints,
She might have written over it,—"from Flints."

She was, in truth, the wonder of her sex,
  At least in Venice—where with eyes of brown
Tenderly languid, ladies seldom vex
  An amorous gentle with a needless frown;   20
Where gondolas convey guitars by pecks,
  And Love at casements climbeth up and down,
Whom for his tricks and custom in that kind,
Some have considered a Venetian blind.

Howbeit, this difference was quickly taught,
  Amongst more youths who had this cruel jailor,
To hapless Julio—all in vain he sought
  With each new moon his hatter and his tailor;
In vain the richest padusoy he bought,
  And went in bran new beaver to assail her—   30
As if to show that Love had made him *smart*
All over—and not merely round his heart.

In vain he labour'd thro' the sylvan park
    Bianca haunted in—that where she came,
Her learned eyes in wandering might mark
    The twisted cypher of her maiden name,
Wholesomely going thro' a course of bark:
    No one was touched or troubled by his flame,
Except the Dryads, those old maids that grow
In trees,—like wooden dolls in embryo.   40

In vain complaining elegies he writ,
    And taught his tuneful instrument to grieve,
And sang in quavers how his heart was split,
    Constant beneath her lattice with each eve;
She mock'd his wooing with her wicked wit,
    And slash'd his suit so that it matched his sleeve,
Till he grew silent as the vesper star,
And quite despairing, hamstring'd his guitar.

Bianca's heart was coldly frosted o'er
    With snows unmelting—an eternal sheet,   50
But his was red within him, like the core
    Of old Vesuvius, with perpetual heat;
And oft he longed internally to pour
    His flames and glowing lava at her feet,
But when his burnings he began to spout,
She stopp'd his mouth, and put the *crater* out.

Meanwhile he wasted in the eyes of men,
    So thin, he seem'd a sort of skeleton-key
Suspended at death's door—so pale—and then
    He turn'd as nervous as an aspen tree;   60
The life of man is three score years and ten,
    But he was perishing at twenty-three,
For people truly said, as grief grew stronger,
"It could not shorten his poor life—much longer."

For why, he neither slept, nor drank, nor fed,
    Nor relished any kind of mirth below;
Fire in his heart, and frenzy in his head,
    Love had become his universal foe,

Salt in his sugar—nightmare in his bed,
   At last, no wonder wretched Julio,   70
A sorrow-ridden thing, in utter dearth
Of hope,—made up his mind to cut his girth!

For hapless lovers always died of old,
   Sooner than chew reflection's bitter cud;
So Thisbe stuck herself, what time 'tis told,
   The tender-hearted mulberries wept blood;
And so poor Sappho when her boy was cold,
   Drown'd her salt tear drops in a salter flood,
Their fame still breathing, tho' their breath be past,
For those old *suitors* lived beyond their last.   80

So Julio went to drown,—when life was dull,
   But took his corks, and merely had a bath;
And once he pull'd a trigger at his skull,
   But merely broke a window in his wrath;
And once his hopeless being to annul,
   He tied a pack-thread to a beam of lath,
A line so ample, 'twas a query whether
'Twas meant to be a halter or a tether.

Smile not in scorn, that Julio did not thrust
   His sorrows thro'—'tis horrible to die!   90
And come down with our little all of dust,
   That dun of all the duns to satisfy:
To leave life's pleasant city as we must,
   In Death's most dreary spunging-house to lie,
Where even all our personals must go
To pay the debt of nature that we owe!

So Julio liv'd:—'twas nothing but a pet
   He took at life—a momentary spite;
Besides, he hoped that time would some day get
   The better of love's flame, however bright;   100
A thing that time has never compass'd yet,
   For love, we know, is an immortal light.
Like that old fire, that, quite beyond a doubt,
Was always in,—for none have found it out.

Meanwhile, Bianca dream'd—'twas once when Night
  Along the darken'd plain began to creep,
Like a young Hottentot, whose eyes are bright,
  Altho' in skin as sooty as a sweep:
The flow'rs had shut their eyes—the zephyr light
  Was gone, for it had rock'd the leaves to sleep.   110
And all the little birds had laid their heads
Under their wings—sleeping in feather beds.

Lone in her chamber sate the dark ey'd maid,
  By easy stages jaunting thro' her pray'rs,
But list'ning side-long to a serenade,
  That robb'd the saints a little of their shares;
For Julio underneath the lattice play'd
  His Deh Vieni, and such amorous airs,
Born only underneath Italian skies,
Where every fiddle has a Bridge of Sighs.   120

Sweet was the tune—the words were even sweeter
  Praising her eyes, her lips, her nose, her hair,
With all the common tropes wherewith in metre
  The hackney poets overcharge their fair.
Her shape was like Diana's, but completer;
  Her brow with Grecian Helen's might compare:
Cupid, alas! was cruel Sagittarius,
Julio—the weeping water-man Aquarius.

Now, after listing to such laudings rare,
  'Twas very natural indeed to go—   130
What if she did postpone one little pray'r—
  To ask her mirror "if it was not so?"
'Twas a large mirror, none the worse for wear,
  Reflecting her at once from top to toe:
And there she gazed upon that glossy track,
That show'd her front face tho' it "gave her back."

And long her lovely eyes were held in thrall,
  By that dear page where first the woman reads:
That Julio was no flatt'rer, none at all,
  She told herself—and then she told her beads;   140

Meanwhile, the nerves insensibly let fall
   Two curtains fairer than the lily breeds;
For Sleep had crept and kiss'd her unawares,
Just at the half-way milestone of her pray'rs.

Then like a drooping rose so bended she,
   Till her bow'd head upon her hand reposed;
But still she plainly saw, or seem'd to see,
   That fair reflection, tho' her eyes were closed,
A beauty-bright as it was wont to be,
   A portrait Fancy painted while she dozed: 150
'Tis very natural some people say,
To dream of what we dwell on in the day.

Still shone her face—yet not, alas! the same,
   But 'gan some dreary touches to assume,
And sadder thoughts, with sadder changes came—
   Her eyes resigned their light, her lips their bloom,
Her teeth fell out, her tresses did the same,
   Her cheeks were tinged with bile, her eyes with rheum:
There was a throbbing at her heart within,
For, oh, there was a shooting in her chin.   160

And lo! upon her sad desponding brow,
   The cruel trenches of besieging age,
With seams, but most unseemly, 'gan to show
   Her place was booking for the seventh stage;
And where her raven tresses used to flow,
   Some locks that Time had left her in his rage,
And some mock ringlets made her forehead shady,
A compound (like our Psalms) of tête and braidy.

Then for her shape—alas! how Saturn wrecks,
   And bends, and corkscrews all the frame about,   170
Doubles the hams, and crooks the straightest necks,
   Draws in the nape, and pushes forth the snout,
Makes backs and stomachs concave or convex:
   Witness those pensioners called In and Out,
Who all day watching first and second rater,
Quaintly unbend themselves—but grow no straighter.

In-and-out pensioners

So Time with fair Bianca dealt, and made
    Her shape a bow, that once was like an arrow;
His iron hand upon her spine he laid,
    And twisted all awry her "winsome marrow."   180
In truth it was a change!—she had obey'd
    The holy Pope before her chest grew narrow,
But spectacles and palsy seem'd to make her
Something between a Glassite and a Quaker.

Her grief and gall meanwhile were quite extreme,
    And she had ample reason for her trouble;
For what sad maiden can endure to seem
    Set in for singleness, tho' growing double.
The fancy madden'd her; but now the dream,
    Grown thin by getting bigger, like a bubble,   190
Burst,—but still left some fragments of its size,
That, like the soapsuds, smarted in her eyes.

And here—just here—as she began to heed
    The real world, her clock chimed out its score;
A clock it was of the Venetian breed,
    That cried the hour from one to twenty-four;
The works moreover standing in some need
    Of workmanship, it struck some dozens more;

A warning voice that clench'd Bianca's fears,
Such strokes referring doubtless to her years.   200

At fifteen chimes she was but half a nun,
    By twenty she had quite renounced the veil;
She thought of Julio just at twenty-one,
    And thirty made her very sad and pale,
To paint that ruin where her charms would run;
    At forty all the maid began to fail,
And thought no higher, as the late dream cross'd her,
Of single blessedness, than single Gloster.

And so Bianca changed;—the next sweet even,
    With Julio in a black Venetian bark,   210
Row'd slow and stealthily—the hour, eleven,
    Just sounding from the tow'r of old St. Mark,
She sate with eyes turn'd quietly to heav'n,
    Perchance rejoicing in the grateful dark
That veil'd her blushing cheek,—for Julio brought her
Of course—to break the ice upon the water.

But what a puzzle is one's serious mind
    To open;—oysters, when the ice is thick,
Are not so difficult and disinclin'd;
    And Julio felt the declaration stick   220
About his throat in a most awful kind;
    However, he contrived by bits to pick
His trouble forth,—much like a rotten cork
Grop'd from a long-neck'd bottle with a fork.

But love is still the quickest of all readers;
    And Julio spent besides those signs profuse
That English telegraphs and foreign pleaders,
    In help of language, are so apt to use,
Arms, shoulders, fingers, all were interceders,
    Nods, shrugs, and bends,—Bianca could not choose   230
But soften to his suit with more facility,
He told his story with so much agility.

A special pleader

"Be thou my park, and I will be thy dear,
   (So he began at last to speak or quote;)
Be thou my bark, and I thy gondolier,
   (For passion takes this figurative note;)
Be thou my light, and I thy chandelier;
   Be thou my dove, and I will be thy cote:
My lily be, and I will be thy river;
Be thou my life—and I will be thy liver."   240

This, with more tender logic of the kind,
   He pour'd into her small and shell-like ear,
That timidly against his lips inclin'd;
   Meanwhile her eyes glanced on the silver sphere
That even now began to steal behind
   A dewy vapour, which was lingering near,
Wherein the dull moon crept all dim and pale,
Just like a virgin putting on the veil:—

Bidding adieu to all her sparks—the stars,
    That erst had woo'd and worshipp'd in her train,   250
Saturn and Hesperus, and gallant Mars—
    Never to flirt with heavenly eyes again.
Meanwhile, remindful of the convent bars,
    Bianca did not watch these signs in vain,
But turn'd to Julio at the dark eclipse,
With words, like verbal kisses, on her lips.

He took the hint full speedily, and, back'd
    By love, and night, and the occasion's meetness,
Bestow'd a something on her cheek that smack'd
    (Tho' quite in silence) of ambrosial sweetness;   260
That made her think all other kisses lack'd
    Till then, but what she knew not, of completeness:
Being used but sisterly salutes to feel,
Insipid things—like sandwiches of veal.

He took her hand, and soon she felt him wring
    The pretty fingers all instead of one;
Anon his stealthy arm began to cling
    About her waist that had been clasp'd by none;
Their dear confessions I forbear to sing,
    Since cold description would but be outrun;   270
For bliss and Irish watches have the pow'r,
In twenty minutes, to lose half an hour!

The Last Man

'Twas in the year two thousand and one,
A pleasant morning of May,
I sat on the gallows-tree, all alone,
A chaunting a merry lay,—
To think how the pest had spared my life,
To sing with the larks that day!

The last man

When up the heath came a jolly knave,
Like a scarecrow, all in rags:
It made me crow to see his old duds
All abroad in the wind, like flags;—   10
So up he came to the timbers' foot
And pitch'd down his greasy bags.—

Good Lord! how blithe the old beggar was!
At pulling out his scraps,—
The very sight of his broken orts

134

Made a work in his wrinkled chaps:
"Come down," says he, "you Newgate-bird,
And have a taste of my snaps!"—

Then down the rope, like a tar from the mast,
I slided, and by him stood: 20
But I wish'd myself on the gallows again
When I smelt that beggar's food,—
A foul beef-bone and a mouldy crust;—
"Oh!" quoth he, "the heavens are good!"

Then after this grace he cast him down:
Says I, "You'll get sweeter air
A pace or two off, on the windward side"—
For the felons' bones lay there—
But he only laugh'd at the empty skulls,
And offer'd them part of his fare.   30

"I never harm'd *them,* and they won't harm me:
Let the proud and the rich be cravens!"
I did not like that strange beggar man,
He look'd so up at the heavens—
Anon he shook out his empty old poke;—
"There's the crums," saith he, "for the ravens!"

It made me angry to see his face,
It had such a jesting look;
But while I made up my mind to speak,
A small case-bottle he took: 40
Quoth he, "though I gather the green water-cress,
My drink is not of the brook!"

Full manners-like he tender'd the dram;
Oh it came of a dainty cask!
But, whenever it came to his turn to pull,
"Your leave, good sir, I must ask;
But I always wipe the brim with my sleeve,
When a hangman sups at my flask!"

And then he laugh'd so loudly and long,
The churl was quite out of breath;   50
I thought the very Old One was come
To mock me before my death,
And wish'd I had buried the dead men's bones
That were lying about the heath!

But the beggar gave me a jolly clap—
"Come, let us pledge each other,
For all the wide world is dead beside,
And we are brother and brother—
I've a yearning for thee in my heart,
As if we had come of one mother.   60

"I've a yearning for thee in my heart
That almost makes me weep,
For as I pass'd from town to town
The folks were all stone-asleep,—
But when I saw thee sitting aloft,
It made me both laugh and leap!"

Now a curse (I thought) be on his love,
And a curse upon his mirth,—
An' it were not for that beggar man
I'd be the King of the earth,—   70
But I promis'd myself, an hour should come
To make him rue his birth!—

So down we sat and bous'd again
Till the sun was in mid-sky,
When, just as the gentle west-wind came,
We hearken'd a dismal cry:
"Up, up, on the tree," quoth the beggar man,
"Till those horrible dogs go by!"

And, lo! from the forest's far-off skirts,
They came all yelling for gore,   80
A hundred hounds pursuing at once,
And a panting hart before,
Till he sunk adown at the gallows' foot,
And there his haunches they tore!

His haunches they tore, without a horn
To tell when the chase was done;
And there was not a single scarlet coat
To flaunt it in the sun!—
I turn'd, and look'd at the beggar man,
And his tears dropt one by one!   90

And with curses sore he chid at the hounds,
Till the last dropt out of sight,
Anon saith he, "let's down again,
And ramble for our delight,
For the world's all free, and we may choose
A right cozie barn for to-night!"

With that, he set up his staff on end,
And it fell with the point due West;
So we far'd that way to a city great,
Where the folks had died of the pest—   100
It was fine to enter in house and hall,
Wherever it liked me best!—

For the porters all were stiff and cold,
And could not lift their heads;
And when we came where their masters lay,
The rats leapt out of the beds:—
The grandest palaces in the land
Were as free as workhouse sheds.

But the beggar man made a mumping face,
And knocked at every gate: 110
It made me curse to hear how he whined,
So our fellowship turn'd to hate,
And I bade him walk the world by himself,
For I scorn'd so humble a mate!

So *he* turn'd right and *I* turn'd left,
As if we had never met;
And I chose a fair stone house for myself,
For the city was all to let;
And for three brave holydays drank my fill
Of the choicest that I could get.   120

And because my jerkin was coarse and worn,
I got me a properer vest;
It was purple velvet, stitch'd o'er with gold,
And a shining star at the breast,—
'Twas enough to fetch old Joan from her grave
To see me so purely drest!—

But Joan was dead and under the mould,
And every buxom lass;
In vain I watch'd, at the window pane,
For a Christian soul to pass;—   130
But sheep and kine wander'd up the street,
And browz'd on the new-come grass.—

When lo! I spied the old beggar man,
And lustily he did sing!—
His rags were lapp'd in a scarlet cloak,
And a crown he had like a king;
So he stept right up before my gate
And danc'd me a saucy fling!

Heaven mend us all!—but, within my mind,
I had kill'd him then and there;   140
To see him lording so braggart-like
That was born to his beggar's fare,
And how he had stolen the royal crown
His betters were meant to wear.

But God forbid that a thief should die
Without his share of the laws!
So I nimbly whipt my tackle out,
And soon tied up his claws,—
I was judge, myself, and jury, and all,
And solemnly tried the cause.   150

But the beggar man would not plead, but cried
Like a babe without its corals,
For he knew how hard it is apt to go
When the law and a thief have quarrels,—
There was not a Christian soul alive
To speak a word for his morals.

Oh, how gaily I doff'd my costly gear,
And put on my work-day clothes;—
I was tired of such a long Sunday life,
And never was one of the sloths;   160
But the beggar man grumbled a weary deal,
And made many crooked mouths.

So I haul'd him off to the gallows' foot,
And blinded him in his bags;
'Twas a weary job to heave him up,
For a doom'd man always lags;
But by ten of the clock he was off his legs
In the wind and airing his rags!

So there he hung, and there I stood
The LAST MAN left alive,   170
To have my own will of all the earth:
Quoth I, now I shall thrive!
But when was ever honey made
With one bee in a hive!

My conscience began to gnaw my heart
Before the day was done,
For other men's lives had all gone out,
Like candles in the sun!—
But it seem'd as if I had broke, at last,
A thousand necks in one!   180

So I went and cut his body down
To bury it decentlie;—
God send there were any good soul alive
To do the like by me!
But the wild dogs came with terrible speed,
And bay'd me up the tree!

My sight was like a drunkard's sight,
And my head began to swim,
To see their jaws all white with foam,
Like the ravenous ocean brim;—   190
But when the wild dogs trotted away
Their jaws were bloody and grim!

Their jaws were bloody and grim, good Lord!
But the beggar man, where was he?—
There was nought of him but some ribbons of rags
Below the gallows' tree!—
I know the Devil, when I am dead,
Will send his hounds for me!—

I've buried my babies one by one,
And dug the deep hole for Joan,   200
And cover'd the faces of kith and kin,
And felt the old churchyard stone
Go cold to my heart, full many a time,
But I never felt so lone!

For the lion and Adam were company,
And the tiger him beguil'd;
But the simple kine are foes to my life,
And the household brutes are wild.
If the veriest cur would lick my hand,
I could love it like a child!   210

Pigmy and crane

And the beggar man's ghost besets my dreams,
At night, to make me madder,—
And my wretched conscience, within my breast,
Is like a stinging adder;—
I sigh when I pass the gallows' foot,
And look at the rope and ladder!—

For hanging looks sweet,—but, alas! in vain,
My desperate fancy begs,—
I must turn my cup of sorrows quite up,
And drink it to the dregs,—   220
For there is not another man alive,
In the world, to pull my legs!

Jack Hall

'Tis very hard when men forsake
This melancholy world, and make
A bed of turf, they cannot take
        A quiet doze,
But certain rogues will come and break
        Their "bone repose."

'Tis hard we can't give up our breath,
And to the earth our earth bequeath,
Without Death Fetches after death,
        Who thus exhume us;   10
And snatch us from our homes beneath,
        And hearths posthumous.

The tender lover comes to rear
The mournful urn, and shed his tear—
Her glorious dust, he cries, is here!
        Alack! alack!
The while his Sacharissa dear
        Is in a sack!

'Tis hard one cannot lie amid
The mould, beneath a coffin-lid,   20
But thus the Faculty will bid
        Their rogues break thro' it!
If they don't want us there, why did
        They send us to it?

One of these sacrilegious knaves,
Who crave as hungry vulture craves,
Behaving as the ghoul behaves,
        'Neath church-yard wall—
Mayhap because he fed on graves,
        Was nam'd Jack Hall.   30

By day it was his trade to go
Tending the black coach to and fro;
And sometimes at the door of woe,
        With emblems suitable,

He stood with brother Mute, to show
   That life is mutable.

But long before they pass'd the ferry,
The dead that he had help'd to bury,
He sack'd—(he had a sack to carry
   The bodies off in.)   40
In fact, he let them have a very
   Short fit of coffin.

Night after night, with crow and spade,
He drove this dead but thriving trade,
Meanwhile his conscience never weigh'd
   A single horsehair;
On corses of all kinds he prey'd,
   A perfect corsair!

At last—it may be, Death took spite,
Or jesting only meant to fright—   50
He sought for Jack night after night
   The churchyards round;
And soon they met, the man and sprite,
   In Pancras' ground.

Jack, by the glimpses of the moon,
Perceiv'd the bony knacker soon,
An awful shape to meet at noon
   Of night and lonely;
But Jack's tough courage did but swoon
   A minute only.   60

Anon he gave his spade a swing
Aloft, and kept it brandishing,
Ready for what mishaps might spring
   From this conjunction;
Funking indeed was quite a thing
   Beside his function.

"Hollo!" cried Death, "d'ye wish your sands
Run out? the stoutest never stands

A chance with me,—to my commands
                The strongest truckles;   70
But I'm your friend—so let's shake hands,
                I should say—knuckles."

Jack, glad to see th' old sprite so sprightly,
And meaning nothing but uprightly,
Shook hands at once, and, bowing slightly,
                His mull did proffer:
But Death, who had no nose, politely
                Declin'd the offer.

Then sitting down upon a bank,
Leg over leg, shank over shank,   80
Like friends for conversation frank,
                That had no check on:
Quoth Jack unto the Lean and Lank,
                "You're Death, I reckon."

The Jaw-bone grinn'd:—"I am that same,
You've hit exactly on my name;
In truth it has some little fame
                Where burial sod is."
Quoth Jack, (and wink'd,) "of course ye came
                Here after bodies."   90

Death grinn'd again and shook his head:—
"I've little business with the dead;
When they are fairly sent to bed
                I've done my turn;
Whether or not the worms are fed
                Is your concern.

"My errand here, in meeting you,
Is nothing but a 'how-d'ye do;'
I've done what jobs I had—a few
                Along this way;   100
If I can serve a crony too,
                I beg you'll say."

Quoth Jack, "Your Honour's very kind:
And now I call the thing to mind,
This parish very strict I find;
        But in the next 'un
There lives a very well-inclin'd
        Old sort of sexton."

Death took the hint, and gave a wink
As well as eyelet holes can blink;   110
Then stretching out his arm to link
        The other's arm,—
"Suppose," says he, "we have a drink
        Of something warm."

Jack nothing loth, with friendly ease
Spoke up at once:—"Why, what ye please;
Hard by there is the Cheshire Cheese,
        A famous tap."
But this suggestion seem'd to teaze
        The bony chap.   120

"No, no—your mortal drinks are heady,
And only make my hand unsteady;
I do not even care for Deady,
        And loathe your rum;
But I've some glorious brewage ready,
        My drink is—mum!"

And off they set, each right content—
Who knows the dreary way they went?
But Jack felt rather faint and spent,
        And out of breath;   130
At last he saw, quite evident,
        The door of Death.

All other men had been unmann'd
To see a coffin on each hand,
That served a skeleton to stand
        By way of sentry;
In fact, Death has a very grand
        And awful entry.

Death's door

Throughout his dismal sign prevails,
His name is writ in coffin nails, 140
The mortal darts make area rails;
        A scull that mocketh,
Grins on the gloomy gate, and quails
        Whoever knocketh.

And lo! on either side, arise
Two monstrous pillars—bones of thighs;
A monumental slab supplies
        The step of stone,
Where waiting for his master lies
        A dog of bone. 150

The dog leapt up, but gave no yell,
The wire was pull'd, but woke no bell,
The ghastly knocker rose and fell,
        But caused no riot;
The ways of Death, we all know well
        Are very quiet.

Old Bones stept in; Jack stepp'd behind.
Quoth Death, "I really hope you'll find
The entertainment to your mind,
         As I shall treat ye—   160
A friend or two of goblin kind,
         I've asked to meet ye."

And lo! a crowd of spectres tall,
Like jack-a-lanterns on a wall,
Were standing—every ghastly ball
         An eager watcher.
"My friends," says Death—"friends, Mr. Hall,
         The body-snatcher."

Lord, what a tumult it produc'd,
When Mr. Hall was introduced!   170
Jack even, who had long been used
         To frightful things,
Felt just as if his back was sluic'd
         With freezing springs!

Each goblin face began to make
Some horrid mouth—ape—gorgon—snake;
And then a spectre-hag would shake
         An airy thigh-bone;
And cried, (or seem'd to cry,) I'll break
         Your bone, with *my* bone!   180

Some ground their teeth—some seem'd to spit—
(Nothing, but nothing came of it,)
A hundred awful brows were knit
         In dreadful spite.
Thought Jack—I'm sure I'd better quit,
         Without good night.

One skip and hop and he was clear,
And running like a hunted deer,
As fleet as people run by fear
         Well spurr'd and whipp'd,   190

Death, ghosts, and all in that career
               Were quite outstripp'd.

But those who live by death must die;
Jack's soul at last prepar'd to fly;
And when his latter end drew nigh,
               Oh! what a swarm
Of doctors came,—but not to try
               To keep him warm.

No ravens ever scented prey
So early where a dead horse lay,   200
Nor vultures sniff'd so far away
               A last convulse;
A dozen "guests" day after day
               Were "at his pulse."

'Twas strange, altho' they got no fees,
How still they watch'd by twos and threes:
But Jack a very little ease
               Obtain'd from them;
In fact he did not find M. D.s
               Worth one D—M.   210

The passing bell with hollow toll
Was in his thought—the dreary hole!
Jack gave his eyes a horrid roll,
               And then a cough:—
"There's something weighing on my soul
               I wish was off;

"All night it roves about my brains,
All day it adds to all my pains,
It is concerning my remains
               When I am dead;"   220
Twelve wigs and twelve gold-headed canes
               Drew near his bed.

"Alas!" he sighed, "I'm sore afraid,
A dozen pangs my heart invade;

But when I drove a certain trade
   In flesh and bone,
There was a little bargain made
   About my own."

Twelve suits of black began to close,
Twelve pair of sleek and sable hose,   230
Twelve flowing cambric frills in rows,
   At once drew round;
Twelve noses turn'd against his nose,
   Twelve snubs profound.

"Ten guineas did not quite suffice,
And so I sold my body twice;
Twice did not do—I sold it thrice,
   Forgive my crimes!
In short I have received its price
   A dozen times!   240

Twelve brows got very grim and black,
Twelve wishes stretch'd him on the rack,
Twelve pair of hands for fierce attack
   Took up position,
Ready to share the dying Jack
   By long division.

Twelve angry doctors wrangled so,
That twelve had struck an hour ago,
Before they had an eye to throw
   On the departed;   250
Twelve heads turn'd round at once, and lo!
   Twelve doctors started.

Whether some comrade of the dead,
Or Satan took it in his head
To steal the corpse—the corpse had fled!
   'Tis only written,
That "*there was nothing in the bed,*
   But twelve were bitten!"

The Demon-Ship

'Twas off the Wash—the sun went down—the sea look'd
    black and grim,
For stormy clouds, with murky fleece, were mustering
    at the brim;
Titanic shades! enormous gloom!—as if the solid night
Of Erebus rose suddenly to seize upon the light!
It was a time for mariners to bear a wary eye,
With such a dark conspiracy between the sea and sky!

  Down went my helm—close reef'd—the tack held
    freely in my hand—
With ballast snug—I put about, and scudded for the land.
Loud hiss'd the sea beneath her lee—my little boat flew fast,
But faster still the rushing storm came borne upon the
    blast.   10
Lord! what a roaring hurricane beset the straining sail!
What furious sleet, with level drift, and fierce assaults
    of hail!
What darksome caverns yawn'd before! what jagged steeps
    behind!
Like battle-steeds, with foamy manes, wild tossing in
    the wind.
Each after each sank down astern, exhausted in the chase,
But where it sank another rose and gallop'd in its place;
As black as night—they turned to white, and cast against
    the cloud
A snowy sheet, as if each surge upturned a sailor's
    shroud:—
Still flew my boat; alas! alas! her course was nearly run!
Behold yon fatal billow rise—ten billows heap'd in one!   20
With fearful speed the dreary mass came rolling, rolling,
    fast,
As if the scooping sea contain'd one only wave at last!
Still on it came, with horrid roar, a swift pursuing grave;
It seem'd as though some cloud had turned its hugeness
    to a wave!
Its briny sleet began to beat beforehand in my face—
I felt the rearward keel begin to climb its swelling base!
I saw its alpine hoary head impending over mine!

Another pulse—and down it rush'd—an avalanche of
    brine!
Brief pause had I, on God to cry, or think of wife and
    home;
The waters clos'd—and when I shriek'd, I shriek'd
    below the foam!   30
Beyond that rush I have no hint of any after deed—
For I was tossing on the waste, as senseless as a weed.

        *   *   *   *   *

"Where am I? in the breathing world, or in the world
    of death?"
With sharp and sudden pang I drew another birth of
    breath;
My eyes drank in a doubtful light, my ears a doubtful
    sound—
And was that ship a *real* ship whose tackle seem'd around?
A moon, as if the earthly moon, was shining up aloft;
But were those beams the very beams that I had seen
    so oft?
A face, that mock'd the human face, before me watch'd
    alone;
But were those eyes the eyes of man that look'd against
    my own?   40

  Oh! never may the moon again disclose me such a sight
As met my gaze, when first I look'd, on that accursed
    night!
I've seen a thousand horrid shapes begot of fierce
    extremes
Of fever; and most frightful things have haunted
    in my dreams—
Hyenas—cats—blood-loving bats—and apes with hateful
    stare,—
Pernicious snakes, and shaggy bulls—the lion, and
    she-bear—
Strong enemies, with Judas looks, of treachery and
    spite—

Detested features, hardly dimm'd and banish'd by the
  light!
Pale-sheeted ghosts, with gory locks, upstarting from
  their tombs—
All phantasies and images that flit in midnight glooms—   50
Hags, goblins, demons, lemures, have made me all
  aghast,—
But nothing like that GRIMLY ONE who stood beside
  the mast!

  His cheek was black—his brow was black—his eyes
    and hair as dark:
His hand was black, and where it touch'd, it left a sable
    mark;
His throat was black, his vest the same, and when I
    look'd beneath,
His breast was black—all, all, was black except his
    grinning teeth.
His sooty crew were like in hue, as black as Afric
    slaves!
Oh, horror! e'en the ship was black that plough'd the
    inky waves!

  "Alas!" I cried, "for love of truth and blessed
    mercy's sake,
Where am I? in what dreadful ship? upon what dreadful
    lake?   60
What shape is that, so very grim, and black as any coal?
It is Mahound, the Evil One, and he has gain'd my soul!
Oh, mother dear! my tender nurse! dear meadows that
    beguil'd
My happy days, when I was yet a little sinless child,—
My mother dear—my native fields, I never more shall
    see:
I'm sailing in the Devil's Ship, upon the Devil's Sea!"

  Loud laugh'd that SABLE MARINER, and loudly in
    return
His sooty crew sent forth a laugh that rang from stem
    to stern—

A dozen pair of grimly cheeks were crumpled on the
     nonce—
As many sets of grinning teeth came shining out at once: 70
A dozen gloomy shapes at once enjoy'd the merry fit,
With shriek and yell, and oaths as well, like Demons
     of the Pit.
They crow'd their fill, and then the Chief made answer
     for the whole:—
"Our skins," said he, "are black ye see, because we
     carry coal;
You'll find your mother sure enough, and see your
     native fields—
For this here ship has pick'd you up—the Mary Ann
     of Shields!"

The Sea-Spell

"Cauld, cauld, he lies beneath the deep."
                    Old Scotch Ballad

1

It was a jolly mariner!
The tallest man of three,—
He loosed his sail against the wind,
And turned his boat to sea:
The ink-black sky told every eye,
A storm was soon to be!

2

But still that jolly mariner
Took in no reef at all,
For, in his pouch, confidingly,
He wore a baby's caul;   10
A thing, as gossip-nurses know,
That always brings a squall!

3

His hat was new, or newly glaz'd,
Shone brightly in the sun;
His jacket, like a mariner's,
True blue as e'er was spun;
His ample trowsers, like Saint Paul,
Bore forty stripes save one.

4

And now the fretting foaming tide
He steer'd away to cross;   20
The bounding pinnace play'd a game
Of dreary pitch and toss;
A game that, on the good dry land,
Is apt to bring a loss!

5

Good Heaven befriend that little boat,
And guide her on her way!
A boat, they say, has canvas wings,

But cannot fly away!
Though, like a merry singing bird,
She sits upon the spray!   30

6

Still east by east the little boat,
With tawny sail, kept beating:
Now out of sight, between two waves,
Now o'er th' horizon fleeting;
Like greedy swine that feed on mast,—
The waves her mast seem'd eating!

7

The sullen sky grew black above,
The wave as black beneath;
Each roaring billow shew'd full soon
A white and foamy wreath;   40
Like angry dogs that snarl at first,
And then display their teeth.

8

The boatman look'd against the wind,
The mast began to creak,
The wave, per saltum, came and dried,
In salt, upon his cheek!
The pointed wave against him rear'd,
As if it own'd a pique!

9

Nor rushing wind, nor gushing wave,
That boatman could alarm,   50
But still he stood away to sea,
And trusted in his charm;
He thought by purchase he was safe,
And arm'd against all harm!

10

Now thick and fast and far aslant,
The stormy rain came pouring,

De gustibus non est disputandum

He heard upon the sandy bank,
The distant breakers roaring,—
A groaning intermitting sound,
Like Gog and Magog snoring!   6o

11
The seafowl shriek'd around the mast,
Ahead the grampus tumbled,
And far off, from a copper cloud,
The hollow thunder rumbled;
It would have quail'd another heart,
But his was never humbled.

12
For why? he had that infant's caul;
And wherefore should he dread?—

Alas! alas! he little thought,
Before the ebb-tide sped,—   70
That, like that infant, he should die,
And with a watery head!

13

The rushing brine flowed in apace;
His boat had ne'er a deck:
Fate seem'd to call him on, and he
Attended to her beck;
And so he went, still trusting on,
Though reckless—to his wreck!

14

For as he left his helm, to heave
The ballast-bags a-weather,   80
Three monstrous seas came roaring on,
Like lions leagued together.
The two first waves the little boat
Swam over like a feather,—

15

The two first waves were past and gone,
And sinking in her wake;
The hugest still came leaping on,
And hissing like a snake.
Now helm a-lee! for through the midst,
The monster he must take!   90

16

Ah, me! it was a dreary mount!
Its base as black as night,
Its top of pale and livid green,
Its crest of awful white,
Like Neptune with a leprosy,—
And so it rear'd upright!

17

With quaking sails, the little boat
Climb'd up the foaming heap;

With quaking sails it paused awhile,
At balance on the steep;   100
Then, rushing down the nether slope,
Plunged with a dizzy sweep!

18

Look, how a horse, made mad with fear,
Disdains his careful guide;
So now the headlong headstrong boat,
Unmanaged, turns aside,
And straight presents her reeling flank
Against the swelling tide!

19

The gusty wind assaults the sail;
Her ballast lies a-lee!   110
The windward sheet is taut and stiff!
Oh! the Lively—where is she?
Her capsiz'd keel is in the foam,
Her pennon's in the sea!

20

The wild gull, sailing overhead,
Three times beheld emerge
The head of that bold mariner,
And then she screamed his dirge!
For he had sunk within his grave,
Lapp'd in a shroud of surge!   120

21

The ensuing wave, with horrid foam,
Rushed o'er and covered all,—
The jolly boatman's drowning scream
Was smothered by the squall.
Heaven never heard his cry, nor did
The ocean heed his *caul!*

THE

DREAM OF EUGENE ARAM,

The Murderer.

By THOMAS HOOD, Esq.

WITH DESIGNS BY W. HARVEY.

ENGRAVED ON WOOD BY BRANSTON AND WRIGHT.

LONDON:

CHARLES TILT, 86, FLEET STREET.

1831.

Title page of "The Dream of Eugene Aram, The Murderer"

The Dream of Eugene Aram, The Murderer

'Twas in the prime of summer time,
   An evening calm and cool,
And four-and-twenty happy boys
   Came bounding out of school:
There were some that ran and some that leapt,
   Like troutlets in a pool.

Away they sped with gamesome minds,
   And souls untouched by sin;
To a level mead they came, and there
   They drave the wickets in: 10
Pleasantly shone the setting sun
   Over the town of Lynn.

Like sportive deer they cours'd about,
   And shouted as they ran,—
Turning to mirth all things of earth,
   As only boyhood can;
But the Usher sat remote from all,
   A melancholy man!

The usher sat remote from all

160

His hat was off, his vest apart,
  To catch heaven's blessed breeze;   20
For a burning thought was in his brow,
  And his bosom ill at ease:
So he lean'd his head on his hands, and read
  The book between his knees!

Leaf after leaf he turn'd it o'er,
  Nor ever glanc'd aside,
For the peace of his soul he read that book
  In the golden eventide:
Much study had made him very lean,
  And pale, and leaden-ey'd.   30

At last he shut the ponderous tome,
  With a fast and fervent grasp
He strain'd the dusky covers close,
  And fix'd the brazen hasp:
"Oh, God! could I so close my mind,
  And clasp it with a clasp!"

Then leaping on his feet upright,
  Some moody turns he took,—
Now up the mead, then down the mead,
  And past a shady nook,—   40
And, lo! he saw a little boy
  That pored upon a book!

"My gentle lad, what is't you read—
  Romance or fairy fable?
Or is it some historic page,
  Of kings and crowns unstable?"
The young boy gave an upward glance,—
  "It is 'The Death of Abel.'"

The Usher took six hasty strides,
  As smit with sudden pain,—   50
Six hasty strides beyond the place,
  Then slowly back again;

The young boy gave an upward glance

And down he sat beside the lad,
   And talk'd with him of Cain;

And, long since then, of bloody men,
   Whose deeds tradition saves;
Of lonely folk cut off unseen,
   And hid in sudden graves;
Of horrid stabs, in groves forlorn,
   And murders done in caves;   60

And how the sprites of injur'd men
   Shriek upward from the sod,—
Aye, how the ghostly hand will point
   To shew the burial clod;
And unknown facts of guilty acts
   Are seen in dreams from God!

He told how murderers walk the earth
   Beneath the curse of Cain,—
With crimson clouds before their eyes,
   And flames about their brain: 70

For blood has left upon their souls
    Its everlasting stain!

"And well," quoth he, "I know, for truth,
    Their pangs must be extreme,—
Woe, woe, unutterable woe,—
    Who spill life's sacred stream!
For why? Methought, last night, I wrought
    A murder, in a dream!

"One that had never done me wrong—
    A feeble man, and old;   80
I led him to a lonely field,—
    The moon shone clear and cold:
Now here, said I, this man shall die,
    And I will have his gold!

Two sudden blows with a ragged stick and one with a heavy stone

"Two sudden blows with a ragged stick,
    And one with a heavy stone,
One hurried gash with a hasty knife,—
    And then the deed was done:

There was nothing lying at my foot
  But lifeless flesh and bone!   90

"Nothing but lifeless flesh and bone,
  That could not do me ill;
And yet I fear'd him all the more,
  For lying there so still:
There was a manhood in his look,
  That murder could not kill!

"And, lo! the universal air
  Seem'd lit with ghastly flame;—
Ten thousand thousand dreadful eyes
  Were looking down in blame: 100
I took the dead man by his hand,
  And call'd upon his name!

"Oh, God! it made me quake to see
  Such sense within the slain!
But when I touch'd the lifeless clay,
  The blood gushed out amain!
For every clot, a burning spot
  Was scorching in my brain!

"My head was like an ardent coal,
  My heart as solid ice;   110
My wretched, wretched soul, I knew,
  Was at the Devil's price:
A dozen times I groan'd; the dead
  Had never groan'd but twice!

"And now, from forth the frowning sky,
  From the Heaven's topmost height,
I heard a voice—the awful voice
  Of the blood-avenging sprite:—
'Thou guilty man! take up thy dead
  And hide it from my sight!'   120

I took the dreary body up

"I took the dreary body up,
    And cast it in a stream,—
A sluggish water, black as ink,
    The depth was so extreme:—
My gentle Boy, remember this
    Is nothing but a dream!

"Down went the corse with a hollow plunge,
    And vanish'd in the pool;
Anon I cleans'd my bloody hands,
    And wash'd my forehead cool,   130
And sat among the urchins young,
    That evening in the school!

"Oh, Heaven! to think of their white souls,
    And mine so black and grim!
I could not share in childish prayer,
    Nor join in Evening Hymn:
Like a Devil of the Pit I seem'd,
    'Mid holy Cherubim!

"And Peace went with them, one and all,
　　And each calm pillow spread;　　　　　　　　　　140
But Guilt was my grim Chamberlain
　　That lighted me to bed;
And drew my midnight curtains round,
　　With fingers bloody red!

"All night I lay in agony,
　　In anguish dark and deep;
My fever'd eyes I dared not close,
　　But stared aghast at Sleep:
For Sin had render'd unto her
　　The keys of Hell to keep!　　　　　　　　　　150

"All night I lay in agony,
　　From weary chime to chime,
With one besetting horrid hint,
　　That rack'd me all the time;
A mighty yearning, like the first
　　Fierce impulse unto crime!

"One stern tyrannic thought, that made
　　All other thoughts its slave;
Stronger and stronger every pulse
　　Did that temptation crave,—　　　　　　　　　160
Still urging me to go and see
　　The Dead Man in his grave!

"Heavily I rose up, as soon
　　As light was in the sky,
And sought the black accursed pool
　　With a wild misgiving eye;
And I saw the Dead in the river bed,
　　For the faithless stream was dry!

"Merrily rose the lark, and shook
　　The dew-drop from its wing;　　　　　　　　　170
But I never mark'd its morning flight,
　　I never heard it sing:

For I was stooping once again
    Under the horrid thing.

"With breathless speed, like a soul in chase,
    I took him up and ran;—
There was no time to dig a grave
    Before the day began:
In a lonesome wood, with heaps of leaves,
    I hid the murder'd man!   180

"And all that day I read in school,
    But my thought was other where;
As soon as the mid-day task was done,
    In secret I was there:
And a mighty wind had swept the leaves,
    And still the corse was bare!

A mighty wind had swept the leaves

"Then down I cast me on my face,
    And first began to weep,
For I knew my secret then was one
    That earth refused to keep: 190

Or land or sea, though he should be
  Ten thousand fathoms deep.

"So wills the fierce avenging Sprite,
  Till blood for blood atones!
Ay, though he's buried in a cave,
  And trodden down with stones,
And years have rotted off his flesh,—
  The world shall see his bones!

"Oh, God! that horrid, horrid dream
  Besets me now awake!   200
Again—again, with dizzy brain,
  The human life I take;
And my red right hand grows raging hot,
  Like Cranmer's at the stake.

"And still no peace for the restless clay,
  Will wave or mould allow;
The horrid thing pursues my soul,—
  It stands before me now!"

The horrid thing pursues my soul

The fearful Boy look'd up, and saw
  Huge drops upon his brow.   210

That very night, while gentle sleep
  The urchin eyelids kiss'd,
Two stern-faced men set out from Lynn,
  Through the cold and heavy mist;
And Eugene Aram walked between,
  With gyves upon his wrist.

Eugene Aram walked between

The Desert-Born

"Fly to the desert, fly with me."—Lady Hester Stanhope

'Twas in the wilds of Lebanon, amongst its barren hills,—
To think upon it, even now, my very blood it chills!—
My sketch-book spread before me, and my pencil in
   my hand,
I gazed upon the mountain range, the red tumultuous
   sand,
The plumy palms, the sombre firs, the cedars tall and
   proud,—
When lo! a shadow pass'd across the paper like a cloud,
And looking up I saw a form, apt figure for the scene,
Methought I stood in presence of some oriental queen!

The turban on her head was white as any driven snow;
A purple bandalette past o'er the lofty brow below,   10
And thence upon her shoulders fell, by either jewell'd ear;
In yellow folds voluminous she wore her long cachemere;
Whilst underneath, with ample sleeves, a Turkish robe
   of silk
Enveloped her in drapery the colour of new milk;
Yet oft it floated wide in front, disclosing underneath
A gorgeous Persian tunic, rich with many a broider'd
   wreath,
Compelled by clasps of costly pearl around her neck to
   meet—
And yellow as the amber were the buskins on her feet!

Of course I bowed my lowest bow—of all the things on
   earth,
The reverence due to loveliness, to rank, or ancient birth,   20
To pow'r, to wealth, to genius, or to any thing uncommon,
A man should bend the lowest in a *Desert* to a *Woman!*
Yet some strange influence stronger still, though vague
   and undefin'd,
Compell'd me, and with magic might subdued my soul
   and mind;
There was a something in her air that drew the spirit nigh,
Beyond the common witchery that dwells in woman's eye!

170

With reverence deep, like any slave of that peculiar land,
I bowed my forehead to the earth, and kissed the arid sand;
And then I touched her garment's hem, devoutly as a
    Dervish,
Predestinated (so I felt) for ever to her service.   30

Nor was I wrong in auguring thus my fortune from her
    face,
She knew me, seemingly, as well as any of her race;
"Welcome!" she cried, as I uprose submissive to my feet;
"It was ordained that you and I should in this desert
    meet!
Aye, ages since, before thy soul had burst its prison bars,
This interview was promis'd in the language of the stars!"
Then clapping, as the Easterns wont, her all-commanding
    hands,
A score of mounted Arabs came fast spurring o'er the sands,
Nor rein'd they up their foaming steeds till in my very face
They blew the breath impetuous, and panting from the
    race.   40

"Fear nought," exclaimed the radiant one, as I sprang
    off aloof,
"Thy precious frame need never fear a blow from horse's
    hoof!
Thy natal star was fortunate as any orb of birth,
And fate hath held in store for thee the rarest gift of earth."
Then turning to the dusky men, that humbly waited near,
She cried, "Go bring the BEAUTIFUL—for lo! the MAN
    is here!"

Off went th' obsequious train as swift as Arab hoofs could
    flee,
But Fancy fond outraced them all, with bridle loose and
    free,
And brought me back, for love's attack, some fair
    Circassian bride,
Or Georgian girl, the Harem's boast, and fit for sultan's
    side;   50

Methought I lifted up her veil, and saw dark eyes
   beneath,
Mild as gazelle's, a snowy brow, ripe lips, and pearly teeth,
A swanlike neck, a shoulder round, full bosom, and a
   waist
Not too compact, and rounded limbs, to oriental taste;
Methought—but here, alas! alas! the airy dream to blight,
Behold the Arabs leading up a mare of milky white!
To tell the truth, without reserve, evasion, or remorse,
The last of creatures in my love or liking is a horse:
Whether in early youth some kick untimely laid me flat,
Whether from born antipathy, as some dislike a cat,   60
I never yet could bear the kind, from Meux's giant steeds
Down to those little bearish cubs of Shetland's shaggy
   breeds;—
As for a warhorse, he that can bestride one *is* a hero,
Merely to look at such a sight my courage sinks to zero.
With lightning eyes, and thunder mane, and hurricanes
   of legs,
Tempestuous tail—to picture him description vainly begs!
His fiery nostrils send forth clouds of smoke instead of
   breath—
Nay, was it not a Horse that bore the grisly Shape of Death?
Judge then how cold an ague-fit of agony was mine
To see the mistress of my fate, imperious, make a sign   70
To which my own foreboding soul the cruel sense
   supplied:
"Mount, happy man, and *run away* with your Arabian
   bride!"
Grim was the smile, and tremulous the voice with which ⎞
   I spoke,   ⎟
Like any one's when jesting with a subject not a joke, ⎬
So men have trifled with the axe before the fatal stroke. ⎠

"Lady, if mine had been the luck in Yorkshire to be born,
Or any of its *ridings,* this would be a blessed morn;
But, hapless one! I cannot ride—there's something in a
   horse
That I can always honour, but I never could endorse.

To speak still more commercially, in riding I am quite   80
Averse to running long, and apt to be paid off at sight:
In legal phrase, for every class to understand me still,
I never was in stirrups yet a tenant but at will;
Or, if you please, in artist terms, I never went a-straddle
On any horse without 'a want of keeping' in the saddle.
In short," and here I blush'd, abash'd, and held my head
     full low,
"I'm one of those whose infant ears have heard the chimes
     of Bow!"

The lady smiled, as houris smile, adown from Turkish
     skies,
And beams of cruel kindness shone within her hazel eyes;
"Stranger," she said, "or rather say, my nearest, dearest
     friend,   90
There's something in your eyes, your air, and that high
     instep's bend,
That tells me you're of Arab race,—whatever spot of earth
Cheapside, or Bow, or Stepney, had the honour of your
     birth,
The East it is your country! Like an infant changed at
     nurse
By fairies, you have undergone a nurtureship perverse;
But this—these desert sands—these palms, and cedars
     waving wild,
All, all, adopt thee as their own—an oriental child—
The cloud may hide the sun awhile—but soon or late,
     no doubt,
The spirit of your ancestry will burst and sparkle out!
I read the starry characters—and lo! 'tis written there,   100
Thou wert foredoom'd of sons of men to ride upon this
     Mare,
A Mare till now was never back'd by one of mortal mould,
Hark, how she neighs, as if for thee she knew that she
     was foal'd!"

And truly—I devoutly wish'd a blast of the simoom
Had stifled her!—the Mare herself appeared to mock
     my doom;

With many a bound she caper'd round and round me like
  a dance,
I feared indeed some wild caress would end the fearful
  prance,
And felt myself, and saw myself—the phantasy was
  horrid!—
Like old Redgauntlet, with a shoe imprinted on my
  forehead!
On bended knees, with bowing head, and hands uprais'd
  in pray'r,   110
I begg'd the turban'd Sultaness the issue to forbear;
I painted weeping orphan babes, around a widow'd wife,
And drew my death as vividly as others draw from life;
"Behold," I said, "a simple man, for such high feats unfit,
Who never yet has learn'd to know the crupper from
  the bitt,
Whereas the boldest horsemanship, and first equestrian
  skill,
Would well be task'd to bend so wild a creature to the
  will."
Alas! alas! 'twas all in vain, to supplicate and kneel,
The quadruped could not have been more cold to my
  appeal!
"Fear nothing," said the smiling Fate, "when human help
  is vain,   120
Spirits shall by thy stirrups fly, and fairies guide the rein;
Just glance at yonder animal, her perfect shape remark,
And in thy breast at once shall glow the oriental spark!
As for thy spouse and tender babes, no Arab roams the
  wild
But for a mare of such descent, would barter wife and
  child."

"Nay then," cried I—(heav'n shrive the lie!) "to tell
  the secret truth,
'Twas my unhappy fortune once to over-ride a youth!
A playful child,—so full of life!—a little fair-haired boy,
His sister's pet, his father's hope, his mother's darling joy!
Ah me! the frantic shriek she gave! I hear it ringing now!   130
That hour, upon the bloody spot, I made a holy vow;

A solemn compact, deeply sworn, to witness my remorse,
That never more these limbs of mine should mount
  on living horse!"
Good heav'n! to see the angry glance that flashed upon
  me now!
A chill ran all my marrow through—the drops were on
  my brow!
I knew my doom, and stole a glance at that accursed
  Mare,
And there she stood, with nostrils wide, that snuff'd the
  sultry air.
How lion-like she lash'd her flanks with her abundant
  tail;
While on her neck the stormy mane kept tossing to the
  gale!
How fearfully she roll'd her eyes between the earth and
  sky,   140
As if in wild uncertainty to gallop or to fly!
While with her hoof she scoop'd the sand as if before she
  gave
My plunge into eternity she meant to dig my grave!

And I, that ne'er could calmly bear a horse's ears at play
Or hear without a yard of jump his shrill and sudden
  neigh—
Whose foot within a stabledoor had never stood an inch—
Whose hand to pat a living steed would feel an awful
  flinch,—
I that had never thrown a leg across a pony small,
To scour the pathless desert on the tallest of the tall!
For oh! it is no fable, but at ev'ry look I cast,   150
Her restless legs seem'd twice as long as when I saw them
  last!

In agony I shook,—and yet, although congealed by fears,
My blood was boiling fast, to judge from noises in my ears;
I gasp'd as if in vacuo, and thrilling with despair,
Some secret Demon seem'd to pass his fingers through my
  hair.
I could not stir—I could not speak—I could not even see—

A sudden mist rose up between that awful Mare and me,—
I tried to pray, but found no words—tho' ready ripe to
    weep,
No tear would flow,—o'er ev'ry sense a swoon began to
    creep,—
When lo! to bring my horrid fate at once unto the brunt,   160
Two Arabs seized me from behind, two others in the
    front,
And ere a muscle could be strung to try the strife forlorn,
I found myself, Mazeppa-like, upon the Desert-Born!

Terrific was the neigh she gave, the moment that my
    weight
Was felt upon her back, as if exulting in her freight;
Whilst dolefully I heard a voice that set each nerve ajar,—
"Off with the bridle—quick!—and leave his guidance
    to his star!"

"Allah! il Allah!" rose the shout,—and starting with
    a bound,
The dreadful Creature cleared at once a dozen yards of
    ground;
And grasping at her mane with both my cold
    convulsive hands,   170
Away we flew—away! away! across the shifting sands!
My eyes were closed in utter dread of such a fearful race,
But yet by certain signs I knew we went no earthly pace,
For turn whichever way we might, the wind with equal
    force
Rush'd like a torrid hurricane still adverse to our course—
One moment close at hand I heard the roaring Syrian Sea,
The next it only murmur'd like the humming of a bee!
And when I dared at last to glance across the wild
    immense,
Oh ne'er shall I forget the whirl that met the dizzy sense!
What seem'd a little sprig of fern, ere lips could reckon
    twain,   180
A palm of forty cubits high, we passed it on the plain!
What tongue could tell,—what pencil paint,—what pen
    describe the ride?

Now off—now on—now up—now down,—and flung from
    side to side!
I tried to speak, but had no voice, to soothe her with its
    tone—
My scanty breath was jolted out with many a sudden
    groan—
My joints were racked—my back was strained, so firmly
    I had clung—
My nostrils gush'd, and thrice my teeth had bitten
    through my tongue—
When lo!—farewell all hope of life!—she turn'd and
    faced the rocks,
None but a flying horse could clear those monstrous
    granite blocks!
So thought I,—but I little knew the desert pride and fire,   190
Deriv'd from a most deer-like dam, and lion-hearted sire;
Little I guess'd the energy of muscle, blood, and bone,
Bound after bound, with eager springs, she clear'd each
    massive stone;—
Nine mortal leaps were pass'd before a huge grey rock
    at length
Stood planted there as if to dare her utmost pitch of
    strength—
My time was come! that granite heap my monument of
    death!
She paused, she snorted loud and long, and drew a fuller
    breath;
Nine strides and then a louder beat that warn'd me of
    her spring,
I felt her rising in the air like eagle on the wing—
But oh! the crash!—the hideous shock!—the million
    sparks around!   200
Her hindmost hoofs had struck the crest of that
    prodigious mound!
Wild shriek'd the headlong Desert-Born—or else 'twas
    demon's mirth,
One second more, and Man and Mare roll'd breathless
    on the earth!

          *   *   *   *   *   *   *

How long it was I cannot tell ere I revived to sense,
And then but to endure the pangs of agony intense;
For over me lay powerless, and still as any stone,
The Corse that erst had so much fire, strength, spirit,
    of its own.
My heart was still—my pulses stopp'd—midway twixt
    life and death,
With pain unspeakable I fetch'd the fragment of a breath,
Not vital air enough to frame one short and feeble sigh,   210
Yet even that I loath'd because it would not let me die.

Oh! slowly, slowly, slowly on, from starry night till morn,
Time flapp'd along, with leaden wings, across that waste
    forlorn!
I cursed the hour that brought me first within this
    world of strife—
A sore and heavy sin it is to scorn the gift of life—
But who hath felt a horse's weight oppress his labouring
    breast?
Why any who has had, like me, the NIGHT MARE on his
    chest.

The Haunted House

A Romance

"A jolly place, said he, in days of old,
But something ails it now: the spot is curst."
"Hartleap Well," by Wordsworth

Part I

Some dreams we have are nothing else but dreams,
Unnatural, and full of contradictions;
Yet others of our most romantic schemes
Are something more than fictions.

It might be only on enchanted ground;
It might be merely by a thought's expansion;
But in the spirit, or the flesh, I found
An old deserted Mansion.

A residence for woman, child, and man,
A dwelling place,—and yet no habitation;   10
A House,—but under some prodigious ban
Of excommunication.

Unhinged the iron gates half open hung,
Jarr'd by the gusty gales of many winters,
That from its crumbled pedestal had flung
One marble globe in splinters.

No dog was at the threshold, great or small;
No pigeon on the roof—no household creature—
No cat demurely dozing on the wall—
Not one domestic feature.   20

No human figure stirr'd, to go or come,
No face look'd forth from shut or open casement;
No chimney smoked—there was no sign of Home
From parapet to basement.

With shatter'd panes the grassy court was starr'd;
The time-worn coping-stone had tumbled after;

The haunted house

And thro' the ragged roof the sky shone, barr'd
With naked beam and rafter.

O'er all there hung a shadow and a fear;
A sense of mystery the spirit daunted,   30
And said, as plain as whisper in the ear,
The place is Haunted!

The flow'r grew wild and rankly as the weed,
Roses with thistles struggled for espial,
And vagrant plants of parasitic breed
Had overgrown the Dial.

But gay or gloomy, steadfast or infirm,
No heart was there to heed the hour's duration;
All times and tides were lost in one long term
Of stagnant desolation.   40

The wren had built within the Porch, she found
Its quiet loneliness so sure and thorough;
And on the lawn,—within its turfy mound,—
The rabbit made his burrow.

The rabbit wild and gray, that flitted thro'
The shrubby clumps, and frisk'd, and sat, and vanish'd,
But leisurely and bold, as if he knew
His enemy was banish'd.

The wary crow,—the pheasant from the woods—
Lull'd by the still and everlasting sameness,   50
Close to the Mansion, like domestic broods,
Fed with a "shocking tameness."

The coot was swimming in the reedy pond,
Beside the water-hen, so soon affrighted;
And in the weedy moat the heron, fond
Of solitude, alighted.

The moping heron, motionless and stiff,
That on a stone, as silently and stilly,

Stood, an apparent sentinel, as if
To guard the water-lily.   60

No sound was heard except, from far away,
The ringing of the Whitwall's shrilly laughter,
Or, now and then, the chatter of the jay,
That Echo murmur'd after.

But Echo never mock'd the human tongue;
Some weighty crime, that Heaven could not pardon,
A secret curse on that old Building hung,
And its deserted Garden.

The beds were all untouch'd by hand or tool;
No footstep marked the damp and mossy gravel,   70
Each walk as green as is the mantled pool,
For want of human travel.

The vine unprun'd, and the neglected peach,
Droop'd from the wall with which they used to grapple;
And on the canker'd tree, in easy reach,
Rotted the golden apple.

But awfully the truant shunn'd the ground,
The vagrant kept aloof, and daring Poacher;
In spite of gaps that thro' the fences round
Invited the encroacher.   80

For over all there hung a cloud of fear,
A sense of mystery the spirit daunted,
And said, as plain as whisper in the ear,
The place is Haunted!

The pear and quince lay squander'd on the grass;
The mould was purple with unheeded showers
Of bloomy plums—a Wilderness it was
Of fruits, and weeds, and flowers!

The marigold amidst the nettles blew,
The gourd embraced the rose bush in its ramble,   90

The thistle and the stock together grew,
The holly-hock and bramble.

The bear-bine with the lilac interlac'd,
The sturdy bur-dock choked its slender neighbour,
The spicy pink. All tokens were effac'd
Of human care and labour.

The very yew Formality had train'd
To such a rigid pyramidal stature,
For want of trimming had almost regain'd
The raggedness of nature.   100

The Fountain was a-dry—neglect and time
Had marr'd the work of artisan and mason,
And efts and croaking frogs, begot of slime,
Sprawl'd in the ruin'd bason.

The Statue, fallen from its marble base,
Amidst the refuse leaves, and herbage rotten,
Lay like the Idol of some by-gone race,
Its name and rites forgotten.

On ev'ry side the aspect was the same,
All ruin'd, desolate, forlorn, and savage: 110
No hand or foot within the precinct came
To rectify or ravage.

For over all there hung a cloud of fear,
A sense of mystery the spirit daunted,
And said as plain as whisper in the ear,
The place is Haunted!

Part II

O, very gloomy is the House of Woe,
Where tears are falling while the bell is knelling,
With all the dark solemnities which show
That Death is in the dwelling!   120

183

O very, very dreary is the room
Where Love, domestic Love, no longer nestles,
But smitten by the common stroke of doom,
The Corpse lies on the trestles!

But House of Woe, the hearse, and sable pall,
The narrow home of the departed mortal,
Ne'er look'd so gloomy as that Ghostly Hall,
With its deserted portal!

The centipede along the threshold crept,
The cobweb hung across in mazy tangle,   130
And in its winding-sheet the maggot slept,
At every nook and angle.

The keyhole lodg'd the earwig and her brood,
The emmets of the steps had old possession,
And march'd in search of their diurnal food
In undisturb'd procession.

As undisturbed as the prehensile cell
Of moth or maggot, or the spider's tissue,
For never foot upon that threshold fell,
To enter or to issue.   140

O'er all there hung the shadow of a fear,
A sense of mystery the spirit daunted,
And said, as plain as whisper in the ear,
The place is Haunted!

Howbeit, the door I pushed—or so I dream'd—
Which slowly, slowly gaped,—the hinges creaking
With such a rusty eloquence, it seem'd
That Time himself was speaking.

But Time was dumb within that Mansion old,
Or left his tale to the heraldic banners   150
That hung from the corroded walls, and told
Of former men and manners.

Those tatter'd flags, that with the open'd door,
Seem'd the old wave of battle to remember,
While fallen fragments danc'd upon the floor
Like dead leaves in December.

The startled bats flew out—bird after bird—
The screech-owl overhead began to flutter,
And seem'd to mock the cry that she had heard
Some dying victim utter!   160

A shriek that echoed from the joisted roof,
And up the stair, and further still and further,
Till in some ringing chamber far aloof
It ceased its tale of murther!

Meanwhile the rusty armour rattled round,
The banner shudder'd, and the ragged streamer;
All things the horrid tenor of the sound
Acknowledged with a tremor.

The antlers, where the helmet hung and belt,
Stirr'd as the tempest stirs the forest branches,   170
Or as the stag had trembled when he felt
The blood-hound at his haunches.

The window jingled in its crumbled frame,
And thro' its many gaps of destitution
Dolorous moans and hollow sighings came,
Like those of dissolution.

The wood-louse dropped, and rolled into a ball,
Touch'd by some impulse occult or mechanic;
And nameless beetles ran along the wall
In universal panic.   180

The subtle spider, that from overhead
Hung like a spy on human guilt and error,
Suddenly turn'd, and up its slender thread
Ran with a nimble terror.

The very stains and fractures on the wall
Assuming features solemn and terrific,
Hinted some Tragedy of that old Hall,
Lock'd up in hieroglyphic.

Some tale that might, perchance, have solv'd the doubt,
Wherefore amongst those flags so dull and livid,   190
The banner of the BLOODY HAND shone out
So ominously vivid.

Some key to that inscrutable appeal,
Which made the very frame of Nature quiver;
And ev'ry thrilling nerve and fibre feel
So ague-like a shiver.

For over all there hung a cloud of fear,
A sense of mystery the spirit daunted;
And said, as plain as whisper in the ear,
The place is Haunted!   200

If but a rat had lingered in the house,
To lure the thought into a social channel!
But not a rat remain'd, or tiny mouse,
To squeak behind the pannel.

Huge drops roll'd down the walls, as if they wept;
And where the cricket used to chirp so shrilly,
The toad was squatting, and the lizard crept
On that damp hearth and chilly.

For years no cheerful blaze had sparkled there,
Or glanc'd on coat of buff or knightly metal;   210
The slug was crawling on the vacant chair,—
The snail upon the settle.

The floor was redolent of mould and must,
The fungus in the rotten seams had quickened;
While on the oaken table coats of dust
Perennially had thicken'd.

186

No mark of leathern jack or metal can,
No cup—no horn—no hospitable token,—
All social ties between that board and Man
Had long ago been broken.   220

There was so foul a rumour in the air,
The shadow of a Presence so atrocious;
No human creature could have feasted there,
Even the most ferocious.

For over all there hung a cloud of fear,
A sense of mystery the spirit daunted,
And said, as plain as whisper in the ear,
The place is Haunted!

Part III

'Tis hard for human actions to account,
Whether from reason or from impulse only—   230
But some internal prompting bade me mount
The gloomy stairs and lonely.

Those gloomy stairs, so dark, and damp, and cold,
With odours as from bones and relics carnal,
Deprived of rite, and consecrated mould,
The chapel vault, or charnel.

Those dreary stairs, where with the sounding stress
Of ev'ry step so many echoes blended,
The mind, with dark misgivings, fear'd to guess
How many feet ascended.   240

The tempest with its spoils had drifted in,
Till each unwholesome stone was darkly spotted,
As thickly as the leopard's dappled skin,
With leaves that rankly rotted.

The air was thick—and in the upper gloom
The bat—or something in its shape—was winging;

And on the wall, as chilly as a tomb,
The Death's-Head moth was clinging.

That mystic moth, which, with a sense profound
Of all unholy presence, augurs truly;   250
And with a grim significance flits round
The taper burning bluely.

Such omens in the place there seem'd to be,
At ev'ry crooked turn, or on the landing,
The straining eyeball was prepar'd to see
Some Apparition standing.

For over all there hung a cloud of fear,
A sense of mystery the spirit daunted,
And said, as plain as whisper in the ear,
The place is Haunted!   260

Yet no portentous Shape the sight amaz'd;
Each object plain, and tangible, and valid;
But from their tarnish'd frames dark Figures gaz'd,
And Faces spectre-pallid.

Not merely with the mimic life that lies
Within the compass of Art's simulation;
Their souls were looking thro' their painted eyes
With awful speculation.

On ev'ry lip a speechless horror dwelt;
On ev'ry brow the burthen of affliction;   270
The old Ancestral Spirits knew and felt
The House's malediction.

Such earnest woe their features overcast,
They might have stirr'd, or sigh'd, or wept, or spoken;
But, save the hollow moaning of the blast,
The stillness was unbroken.

No other sound or stir of life was there,
Except my steps in solitary clamber,

From flight to flight, from humid stair to stair,
From chamber into chamber.   280

Deserted rooms of luxury and state,
That old magnificence had richly furnish'd
With pictures, cabinets of ancient date,
And carvings gilt and burnish'd.

Rich hangings, storied by the needle's art,
With scripture history, or classic fable;
But all had faded, save one ragged part,
Where Cain was slaying Abel.

The silent waste of mildew and the moth
Had marr'd the tissue with a partial ravage;   290
But undecaying frown'd upon the cloth
Each feature stern and savage.

The sky was pale; the cloud a thing of doubt;
Some hues were fresh, and some decay'd and duller;
But still the BLOODY HAND shone strangely out
With vehemence of colour!

The BLOODY HAND that with a lurid stain
Shone on the dusty floor, a dismal token,
Projected from the casement's painted pane,
Where all beside was broken.   300

The BLOODY HAND significant of crime,
That glaring on the old heraldic banner,
Had kept its crimson unimpair'd by time,
In such a wondrous manner!

O'er all there hung the shadow of a fear,
A sense of mystery the spirit daunted,
And said, as plain as whisper in the ear,
The place is Haunted!

The Death Watch ticked behind the pannel'd oak,
Inexplicable tremors shook the arras,   310

And echoes strange and mystical awoke,
The fancy to embarrass.

Prophetic hints that filled the soul with dread,
But thro' one gloomy entrance pointing mostly,
The while some secret inspiration said,
That Chamber is the Ghostly!

Across the door no gossamer festoon
Swung pendulous—no web—no dusty fringes,
No silky chrysalis or white cocoon
About its nooks and hinges.   320

The spider shunn'd the interdicted room,
The moth, the beetle, and the fly were banish'd,
And where the sunbeam fell athwart the gloom
The very midge had vanish'd.

One lonely ray that glanc'd upon a Bed,
As if with awful aim direct and certain,
To show the BLOODY HAND in burning red
Embroider'd on the curtain.

And yet no gory stain was on the quilt—
The pillow in its place had slowly rotted;   330
The floor alone retain'd the trace of guilt,
Those boards obscurely spotted.

Obscurely spotted to the door, and thence
With mazy doubles to the grated casement—
Oh what a tale they told of fear intense,
Of horror and amazement!

What human creature in the dead of night
Had cours'd like hunted hare that cruel distance?
Had sought the door, the window in his flight,
Striving for dear existence?   340

What shrieking Spirit in that bloody room
Its mortal frame had violently quitted?—

Across the sunbeam, with a sudden gloom,
A ghostly Shadow flitted.

Across the sunbeam, and along the wall,
But painted on the air so very dimly,
It hardly veil'd the tapestry at all,
Or portrait frowning grimly.

O'er all there hung the shadow of a fear,
A sense of mystery the spirit daunted,   350
And said, as plain as whisper in the ear,
The place is Haunted!

Miss Kilmansegg and Her Precious Leg
A Golden Legend

"What is here?
Gold? yellow, glittering, precious gold?"
Timon of Athens

Her Pedigree

To trace the Kilmansegg pedigree,
To the very roots of the family tree,
    Were a task as rash as ridiculous:
Through antediluvian mists as thick
As London fog such a line to pick
Were enough, in truth, to puzzle Old Nick,
    Not to name Sir Harris Nicholas.

It wouldn't require much verbal strain
To trace the Kill-man, perchance, to Cain;
    But waving all such digressions,   10
Suffice it, according to family lore,
A Patriarch Kilmansegg lived of yore,
    Who was famed for his great possessions.

Tradition said he feather'd his nest
Through an Agricultural Interest
    In the Golden Age of Farming;
When golden eggs were laid by the geese,
And Colchian sheep wore a golden fleece,
And golden pippins—the sterling kind
Of Hesperus—now so hard to find—   20
    Made Horticulture quite charming!

A Lord of Land, on his own estate,
He lived at a very lively rate,
    But his income would bear carousing;
Such acres he had of pasture and heath,

With herbage so rich from the ore beneath,
The very ewe's and lambkin's teeth
   Were turn'd into gold by browsing.

He gave, without any extra thrift,
A flock of sheep for a birthday gift   30
   To each son of his loins, or daughter:
And his debts—if debts he had—at will
He liquidated by giving each bill
   A dip in Pactolian water.

'Twas said that even his pigs of lead,
By crossing with some by Midas bred,
   Made a perfect mine of his piggery.
And as for cattle, one yearling bull
Was worth all Smithfield-market full
   Of the Golden Bulls of Pope Gregory.   40

The high-bred horses within his stud,
Like human creatures of birth and blood,
   Had their Golden Cups and flagons:
And as for the common husbandry nags,
Their noses were tied in money-bags,
   When they stopp'd with the carts and waggons.

Moreover, he had a Golden Ass,
Sometimes at stall, and sometimes at grass,
   That was worth his own weight in money—
And a golden hive, on a Golden Bank,   50
Where golden bees, by alchemical prank,
   Gather'd gold instead of honey.

Gold! and gold! and gold without end!
He had gold to lay by, and gold to spend,
Gold to give, and gold to lend,
   And reversions of gold *in futuro*.
In wealth the family revell'd and roll'd,
Himself and wife and sons so bold;—
And his daughters sang to their harps of gold
   "O bella eta del' oro!"   60

Rolling in wealth

Such was the tale of the Kilmansegg Kin,
In golden text on a vellum skin,
Though certain people would wink and grin,
    And declare the whole story a parable—
That the Ancestor rich was one Jacob Ghrimes,
Who held a long lease, in prosperous times,
    Of acres, pasture and arable.

That as money makes money, his golden bees
Were the five per cents, or which you please,
    When his cash was more than plenty—
That the golden cups were racing affairs;
And his daughters, who sang Italian airs,
    Had their golden harps of Clementi.
70

That the Golden Ass, or Golden Bull,
Was English John, with his pockets full,
    Then at war by land and water:
While beef, and mutton, and other meat,
Were almost as dear as money to eat,
And Farmers reaped Golden Harvests of wheat
    At the Lord knows what per quarter!
80

195

Her Birth

What different dooms our birthdays bring!
For instance, one little manikin thing
   Survives to wear many a wrinkle;
While Death forbids another to wake,
And a son that it took nine moons to make
   Expires without even a twinkle!

Into this world we come like ships,
Launch'd from the docks, and stocks, and slips,
   For fortune fair or fatal;
And one little craft is cast away   90
In its very first trip in Babbicome Bay,
   While another rides safe at Port Natal.

What different lots our stars accord!
This babe to be hail'd and woo'd as a Lord!
   And that to be shunn'd like a leper!
One, to the world's wine, honey, and corn,
Another, like Colchester native, born
   To its vinegar, oil, and pepper.

One is litter'd under a roof
Neither wind nor water proof,—   100
   That's the prose of Love in a Cottage,—
A puny, naked, shivering wretch,
The whole of whose birthright would not fetch,
Though Robins himself drew up the sketch,
   The bid of "a mess of pottage."

Born of Fortunatus's kin,
Another comes tenderly usher'd in
   To a prospect all bright and burnish'd:
No tenant he for life's back slums—
He comes to the world as a gentleman comes   110
   To a lodging ready furnish'd.

What wide reverses of fate are there!

And the other sex—the tender—the fair—
What wide reverses of fate are there!
Whilst Margaret, charm'd by the Bulbul rare,
   In a garden of Gul reposes—
Poor Peggy hawks nosegays from street to street,
Till—think of that, who find life so sweet!—
   She hates the smell of roses!

Not so with the infant Kilmansegg!
She was not born to steal or beg,   120
   Or gather cresses in ditches;
To plait the straw, or bind the shoe,
Or sit all day to hem and sew,
As females must, and not a few—
   To fill their insides with stitches!

She was not doom'd, for bread to eat,
To be put to her hands as well as her feet—
  To carry home linen from mangles—
Or heavy-hearted, and weary-limb'd,
To dance on a rope in a jacket trimm'd   130
  With as many blows as spangles.

She was one of those who by Fortune's boon
Are born, as they say, with a silver spoon
  In her mouth, not a wooden ladle:
To speak according to poet's wont,
Plutus as sponsor stood at her font,
  And Midas rock'd the cradle.

At her first *début* she found her head
On a pillow of down, in a downy bed,
  With a damask canopy over.   140
For although by the vulgar popular saw
All mothers are said to be "in the straw,"
  Some children are born in clover.

Her very first draught of vital air
It was not the common chamelion fare
  Of plebeian lungs and noses,—
    No—her earliest sniff
    Of this world was a whiff
Of the genuine Otto of Roses!

When she saw the light—it was no mere ray   150
Of that light so common—so everyday—
  That the sun each morning launches—
But six wax tapers dazzled her eyes,
From a thing—a gooseberry bush for size—
  With a golden stem and branches.

She was born exactly at half-past two,
As witness'd a timepiece in or-molu
  That stood on a marble table—
Shewing at once the time of day,

And a team of *Gildings* running away 160
 As fast as they were able,
With a golden God, with a golden Star,
And a golden Spear, in a golden Car,
 According to Grecian fable.

Like other babes, at her birth she cried;
Which made a sensation far and wide,
 Ay, for twenty miles around her;
For though to the ear 'twas nothing more
Than an infant's squall, it was really the roar
 Of a Fifty-thousand Pounder! 170
  It shook the next heir
  In his library chair,
And made him cry, "Confound her!"

Of signs and omens there was no dearth,
Any more than at Owen Glendower's birth,
 Or the advent of other great people:
  Two bullocks dropp'd dead,
  As if knock'd on the head,
  And barrels of stout
  And ale ran about, 180
  And the village-bells such a peal rang out,
 That they crack'd the village-steeple.

In no time at all, like mushroom spawn,
Tables sprang up all over the lawn;
Not furnish'd scantly or shabbily,
  But on scale as vast
  As that huge repast,
  With its loads and cargoes
  Of drink and botargoes,
At the Birth of the Babe in Rabelais. 190

Hundreds of men were turn'd into beasts,
Like the guests at Circe's horrible feasts,
 By the magic of ale and cider:
And each country lass, and each country lad,

Began to caper and dance like mad,
And even some old ones appear'd to have had
   A bite from the Naples Spider.

   Then as night came on,
   It had scared King John,
Who considered such signs not risible,   200
   To have seen the maroons,
   And the whirling moons,
   And the serpents of flame,
   And wheels of the same,
That according to some were "whizzable."

Oh, happy Hope of the Kilmanseggs!
Thrice happy in head, and body, and legs
   That her parents had such full pockets!
For had she been born of Want and Thrift,
For care and nursing all adrift,   210
It's ten to one she had had to make shift
   With rickets instead of rockets!

And how was the precious Baby drest?
In a robe of the East, with lace of the West,
Like one of Croesus's issue—
   Her best bibs were made
   Of rich gold brocade,
And the others of silver tissue.

And when the Baby inclined to nap
She was lull'd on a Gros de Naples lap,   220
By a nurse in a modish Parish cap,
   Of notions so exalted,
She drank nothing lower than Curaçoa,
Maraschino, or pink Noyau,
   And on principle never malted.

From a golden boat, with a golden spoon,
The babe was fed night, morning, and noon;
   And altho' the tale seems fabulous,

'Tis said her tops and bottoms were gilt,
Like the oats in that Stable-yard Palace built   230
  For the horse of Heliogabalus.

And when she took to squall and kick—
For pain will wring and pins will prick
  E'en the wealthiest nabob's daughter—
They gave her no vulgar Dalby or gin,
But a liquor with leaf of gold therein,
  Videlicet,—Dantzic Water.

In short, she was born, and bred, and nurst,
And drest in the best from the very first,
  To please the genteelest censor—   240
And then, as soon as strength would allow,
Was vaccinated, as babes are now,
With virus ta'en from the best-bred cow
  Of Lord Althorp's—now Earl Spencer.

Her Christening

Though Shakspeare asks us, "What's in a name?"
(As if cognomens were much the same),
  There's really a very great scope in it.
A name?—why, wasn't there Doctor Dodd,
That servant at once of Mammon and God,
Who found four thousand pounds and odd,   250
  A prison—a cart—and a rope in it?

A name?—if the party had a voice,
What mortal would be a Bugg by choice?
As a Hogg, a Grubb, or a Chubb rejoice?
  Or any such nauseous blazon?
Not to mention many a vulgar name,
That would make a doorplate blush for shame,
  If doorplates were not so brazen!

A name?—it has more than nominal worth,
And belongs to good or bad luck at birth—   260
  As dames of a certain degree know,

In spite of his Page's hat and hose,
His Page's jacket, and buttons in rows,
Bob only sounds like a page of prose
   Till turn'd into Rupertino.

My pretty page

Now to christen the infant Kilmansegg,
For days and days it was quite a plague,
   To hunt the list in the Lexicon:
And scores were tried, like coin, by the ring,
Ere names were found just the proper thing   270
   For a minor rich as a Mexican.

Then cards were sent, the presence to beg
Of all the kin of Kilmansegg,
   White, yellow, and brown relations:
Brothers, Wardens of City Hall,
And Uncles—rich as three Golden Balls
   From taking pledges of nations.

Nephews, whom Fortune seem'd to bewitch,
   Rising in life like rockets—
Nieces whose doweries knew no hitch—   280
Aunts as certain of dying rich
   As candles in golden sockets—
Cousins German, and cousin's sons,
All thriving and opulent—some had tons
   Of Kentish hops in their pockets!

For money had stuck to the race through life
(As it did to the bushel when cash so rife
Pozed Ali Baba's brother's wife)—
   And down to the Cousins and Coz-lings,
The fortunate brood of the Kilmanseggs,   290
As if they had come out of golden eggs,
   Were all as wealthy as "Goslings."

It would fill a Court Gazette to name
What East and West End people came
   To the rite of Christianity:
The lofty Lord, and the titled Dame,
   All di'monds, plumes, and urbanity:
His Lordship the May'r with his golden chain,
And two Gold Sticks, and the Sheriffs twain,
Nine foreign Counts, and other great men   300
With their orders and stars, to help M or N
   To renounce all pomp and vanity.

To paint the maternal Kilmansegg
The pen of an Eastern Poet would beg,
   And need an elaborate sonnet;

How she sparkled with gems whenever she stirr'd,
And her head niddle-noddled at every word,
And seem'd so happy, a Paradise Bird
   Had nidificated upon it.

And Sir Jacob the Father strutted and bow'd,   310
And smiled to himself, and laugh'd aloud,
   To think of his heiress and daughter—
And then in his pockets he made a grope,
And then, in the fulness of joy and hope,
Seem'd washing his hands with invisible soap,
   In imperceptible water.

He had roll'd in money like pigs in mud,
Till it seem'd to have enter'd into his blood
   By some occult projection:
And his cheeks, instead of a healthy hue,   320
As yellow as any guinea grew,
Making the common phrase seem true
   About a rich complexion.

And now came the nurse, and during a pause,
Her dead-leaf satin would fitly cause
   A very autumnal rustle—
So full of figure, so full of fuss,
As she carried about the babe to buss,
   She seem'd to be nothing but bustle.

A wealthy Nabob was Godpapa,   330
And an Indian Begum was Godmamma,
   Whose jewels a Queen might covet—
And the Priest was a Vicar, and Dean withal
Of that Temple we see with a Golden Ball,
   And a Golden Cross above it.

The Font was a bowl of American gold,
Won by Raleigh in days of old,
   In spite of Spanish bravado;
And the Book of Pray'r was so overrun
With gilt devices, it shone in the sun   340

Like a copy—a presentation one—
　Of Humboldt's "El Dorado."

Gold! and gold! and nothing but gold!
The same auriferous shine behold
　Wherever the eye could settle!
On the walls—the sideboard—the ceiling-sky—
On the gorgeous footmen standing by,
In coats to delight a miner's eye
　With seams of the precious metal.

Gold! and gold! and besides the gold,　　　　　　350
The very robe of the infant told
A tale of wealth in every fold,
　It lapp'd her like a vapour!
So fine! so thin! the mind at a loss
Could compare it to nothing except a cross
　Of cobweb with bank-note paper.

Then her pearls—'twas a perfect sight, forsooth,
To see them, like "the dew of her youth,"
　In such a plentiful sprinkle.
Meanwhile, the Vicar read through the form,　　　360
And gave her another, not overwarm,
　That made her little eyes twinkle.

Then the babe was cross'd and bless'd amain;
But instead of the Kate, or Ann, or Jane,
　Which the humbler female endorses—
Instead of one name, as some people prefix,
Kilmansegg went at the tails of six,
　Like a carriage of state with its horses.

Oh, then the kisses she got and hugs!
The golden mugs and the golden jugs　　　　　　370
　That lent fresh rays to the midges!
The golden knives, and the golden spoons,
The gems that sparkled like fairy boons,
It was one of the Kilmansegg's own saloons,
　But look'd like Rundell and Bridge's!

Gold! and gold! the new and the old!
The company ate and drank from gold,
   They revell'd, they sang, and were merry;
And one of the Gold Sticks rose from his chair,
And toasted "the Lass with the golden hair"   380
   In a bumper of golden Sherry.

Gold! still gold! it rain'd on the nurse,
Who, unlike Danaë, was none the worse;
There was nothing but guineas glistening!
   Fifty were given to Doctor James,
   For calling the little Baby names,
     And for saying, Amen!
     The Clerk had ten,
And that was the end of the Christening.

The christening

Her Childhood

Our youth! our childhood! that spring of springs!   390
'Tis surely one of the blessedest things
   That nature ever invented!
When the rich are wealthy beyond their wealth,
And the poor are rich in spirits and health,
   And all with their lots contented!

There's little Phelim, he sings like a thrush,
In the selfsame pair of patchwork plush,
   With the selfsame empty pockets,
That tempted his daddy so often to cut
His throat, or jump in the water-butt—   400
But what cares Phelim? an empty nut
   Would sooner bring tears to their sockets.

   Give him a collar without a skirt,
   That's the Irish linen for shirt,
And a slice of bread, with a taste of dirt,
   That's Poverty's Irish butter,
And what does he lack to make him blest?
Some oyster-shells, or a sparrow's nest,
   A candle-end and a gutter.

But to leave the happy Phelim alone,   410
Gnawing, perchance, a marrowless bone,
   For which no dog would quarrel—
Turn we to little Miss Kilmansegg,
Cutting her first little toothy-peg
With a fifty guinea coral—
   A peg upon which
   About poor and rich
Reflection might hang a moral.

Born in wealth, and wealthily nursed,
Capp'd, papp'd, napp'd and lapp'd from the first   420
   On the knees of Prodigality,
Her childhood was one eternal round
Of the game of going on Tickler's ground
   Picking up gold—in reality.

With extempore carts she never play'd,
Or the odds and ends of a Tinker's trade,
Or little dirt pies and puddings made,
   Like children happy and squalid;
The very puppet she had to pet,
Like a bait for the "Nix my Dolly" set,   430
   Was a Dolly of gold—and solid!

Gold! and gold! 'twas the burden still!
To gain the Heiress's early goodwill
There was much corruption and bribery—
 The yearly cost of her golden toys
Woud have given half London's Charity Boys
And Charity Girls the annual joys
 Of a holiday dinner at Highbury.

Bon-bons she ate from the gilt cornet;
And gilded queens on St. Bartlemy's day;   440
 Till her fancy was tinged by her presents—
And first a goldfinch excited her wish,
Then a spherical bowl with its Golden fish,
 And then two Golden Pheasants.

Nay, once she squall'd and scream'd like wild—
And it shews how the bias we give to a child
 Is a thing most weighty and solemn:—
But whence was wonder or blame to spring
If little Miss K.,—after such a swing—
Made a dust for the flaming gilded thing   450
 On the top of the Fish Street column?

Her Education

According to metaphysical creed,
To the earliest books that children read
 For much good or much bad they are debtors—
But before with their A B C they start,
There are things in morals, as well as art,
That play a very important part—
 "Impressions before the letters."

Dame Education begins the pile,
Mayhap in the graceful Corinthian style,   460
 But alas for the elevation!
If the Lady's maid or Gossip the Nurse
With a load of rubbish, or something worse,
 Have made a rotten foundation.

Even thus with little Miss Kilmansegg,
Before she learnt her E for egg,
   Ere her Governess came, or her Masters—
Teachers of quite a different kind
   Had "cramm'd" her beforehand, and put her mind
   In a go-cart on golden castors.   470

Long before her A B and C.
They had taught her by heart her L. S. D.
   And as how she was born a great Heiress;
And as sure as London is built of bricks,
My Lord would ask her the day to fix,
To ride in a fine gilt coach and six,
   Like Her Worship the Lady May'ress.

Instead of stories from Edgeworth's page,
The true golden lore for our golden age,
   Or lessons from Barbauld and Trimmer,   480
Teaching the worth of Virtue and Health,
All that she knew was the Virtue of Wealth,
Provided by vulgar nursery stealth
   With a Book of Leaf Gold for a Primer.

The very metal of merit they told,
And praised her for being as "good as gold!"
   Till she grew as a peacock haughty;
Of money they talk'd the whole day round,
And weigh'd desert like grapes by the pound,
Till she had an idea from the very sound   490
   That people with nought were naughty.

They praised—poor children with nothing at all!
Lord! how you twaddle and waddle and squall
   Like common-bred geese and ganders!
What sad little bad little figures you make
To the rich Miss K., whose plainest seed-cake
   Was stuff'd with corianders!

They praised her falls, as well as her walk,
Flatterers make cream cheese of chalk,

They praised—how they praised—her very small talk,   500
  As if it fell from a Solon;
Or the girl who at each pretty phrase let drop
A ruby comma, or pearl full-stop,
  Or an emerald semi-colon.

They praised her spirit, and now and then,
The Nurse brought her own little "nevy" Ben,
  To play with the future May'ress,
And when he got raps, and taps, and slaps,
Scratches, and pinches, snips, and snaps,
  As if from a Tigress or Bearess,   510
They told him how Lords would court that hand,
And always gave him to understand,
    While he rubb'd, poor soul,
     His carroty poll,
  That his hair had been pull'd by "a *Hairess*."

Such were the lessons from maid and nurse,
A Governess help'd to make still worse,
Giving an appetite so perverse
  Fresh diet whereon to batten—
Beginning with A. B. C. to hold   520
Like a royal playbill printed in gold
  On a square of pearl-white satin.

The books to teach the verbs and nouns,
And those about countries, cities, and towns,
Instead of their sober drabs and browns,
  Were in crimson silk, with gilt edges;—
Her Butler, and Enfield, and Entick—in short
Her "Early Lessons" of every sort,
  Look'd like Souvenirs, Keepsakes, and Pledges.

Old Johnson shone out in as fine array   530
As he did one night when he went to the play;
Chambaud like a beau of King Charles's day—
  Lindley Murray in like conditions—
Each weary, unwelcome, irksome task,

Appear'd in a fancy dress and a mask—
If you wish for similar copies ask
   For Howell and James's Editions.

Novels she read to amuse her mind,
But always the affluent match-making kind
   That ends with Promessi Sposi,   540
And a father-in-law so wealthy and grand,
He could give cheque-mate to Coutts in the Strand;
   So, along with a ring and posy,
He endows the Bride with Golconda off hand,
   And gives the Groom Potosi.

Plays she perused—but she liked the best
Those comedy gentlefolks always possess'd
   Of fortunes so truly romantic—
Of money so ready that right or wrong
It always is ready to go for a song,   550
Throwing it, going it, pitching it strong—
They ought to have purses as green and long
   As the cucumber called the Gigantic.

Then Eastern Tales she loved for the sake
Of the Purse of Oriental make,
   And the thousand pieces they put in it—
But Pastoral scenes on her heart fell cold,
For Nature with her had lost its hold,
No field but the Field of the Cloth of Gold
   Would ever have caught her foot in it.   560

What more? She learnt to sing, and dance,
To sit on a horse, although he should prance,
And to speak a French not spoken in France
   Any more than at Babel's building—
And she painted shells, and flowers, and Turks,
But her great delight was in Fancy Works
   That are done with gold or gilding.

Gold! still gold!—the bright and the dead,
With golden beads, and gold lace, and gold thread

She work'd in gold, as if for her bread;   570
   The metal had so undermined her,
Gold ran in her thoughts and fill'd her brain,
She was golden-headed as Peter's cane
   With which he walk'd behind her.

Miss Kilmansegg and her footman

Her Accident

The horse that carried Miss Kilmansegg,
And a better never lifted leg,
   Was a very rich bay, called Banker—
A horse of a breed and a mettle so rare,—
By Bullion out of an Ingot mare,—
That for action, the best of figures, and air,   580
   It made many good judges hanker.

And when she took a ride in the Park,
Equestrian Lord, or pedestrian Clerk,
   Was thrown in an amorous fever,
To see the Heiress how well she sat,
With her groom behind her, Bob or Nat,
In green, half smother'd with gold, and a hat
   With more gold lace than beaver.

And then when Banker obtain'd a pat,
To see how he arch'd his neck at that!   590
   He snorted with pride and pleasure!
Like the Steed in the fable so lofty and grand,
Who gave the poor Ass to understand,
That *he* didn't carry a bag of sand,
   But a burden of golden treasure.

A load of treasure?—alas! alas!
Had her horse but been fed upon English grass,
   And sheltered in Yorkshire spinneys,
Had he scour'd the sand with the Desart Ass,
   Or where the American whinnies—   600
But a hunter from Erin's turf and gorse,
A regular thorough-bred Irish horse,
Why, he ran away, as a matter of course,
   With a girl worth her weight in guineas!

Mayhap 'tis the trick of such pamper'd nags
To shy at the sight of a beggar in rags,
   But away, like the bolt of a rabbit,
Away went the horse in the madness of fright,
And away went the horsewoman mocking the sight—
Was yonder blue flash a flash of blue light,   610
   Or only the skirt of her habit?

Away she flies, with the groom behind,—
It looks like a race of the Calmuck kind,
   When Hymen himself is the starter:
And the Maid rides first in the fourfooted strife,
Riding, striding, as if for her life,
While the Lover rides after to catch him a wife,
   Although it's catching a Tartar.

But the Groom has lost his glittering hat!
Though he does not sigh and pull up for that—   620
Alas! his horse is a tit for Tat
   To sell to a very low bidder—
His wind is ruin'd, his shoulder is sprung,
Things, though a horse be handsome and young,
   A purchaser *will* consider.

But still flies the Heiress through stones and dust,
Oh, for a fall, if fall she must,
   On the gentle lap of Flora!
But still, thank Heaven! she clings to her seat—
Away! away! she could ride a dead heat   630
With the Dead who ride so fast and fleet,
   In the Ballad of Leonora!

Away she gallops!—it's awful work!
It's faster than Turpin's ride to York,
   On Bess that notable clipper!
She has circled the Ring!—she crosses the Park!
Mazeppa, although he was stripp'd so stark,
   Mazeppa couldn't outstrip her!

The fields seem running away with the folks!
The Elms are having a race for the Oaks!   640
   At a pace that all Jockeys disparages!
All, all is racing! the Serpentine
Seems rushing past like the "arrowy Rhine,"
The houses have got on a railway line,
   And are off like the first-class carriages!

She'll lose her life! she is losing her breath!
A cruel chase, she is chasing Death,
   As female shriekings forewarn her:
And now—as gratis as blood of Guelph—
She clears that gate, which has clear'd itself   650
   Since then, at Hyde Park Corner!

Alas! for the hope of the Kilmanseggs!
For her head, her brains, her body, and legs,
   Her life's not worth a copper!
        Willy-nilly,
        In Piccadilly,
A hundred hearts turn sick and chilly,
   A hundred voices cry, "Stop her!"
And one old gentleman stares and stands,
Shakes his head and lifts his hands,   660
   And says, "How very improper!"

On and on!—what a perilous run!
The iron rails seem all mingling in one,
   To shut out the Green Park scenery!
And now the Cellar its dangers reveals,
She shudders—she shrieks—she's doom'd, she feels,
To be torn by powers of horses and wheels,
   Like a spinner by steam machinery!

Sick with horror she shuts her eyes,
But the very stones seem uttering cries,   670
   As they did to that Persian daughter,
When she climb'd up the steep vociferous hill,
Her little silver flagon to fill
   With the magical Golden Water!

"Batter her! shatter her!
Throw and scatter her!"
Shouts each stony-hearted chatterer—
   "Dash at the heavy Dover!
Spill her! kill her! tear and tatter her!
Smash her! crash her!" (the stones didn't flatter her!)   680
"Kick her brains out! let her blood spatter her!
   Roll on her over and over!"

For so she gather'd the awful sense
Of the street in its past unmacadamized tense,
   As the wild horse overran it,—

His four heels making the clatter of six,
Like a Devil's tattoo, played with iron sticks
   On a kettle-drum of granite!

On! still on! she's dazzled with hints
Of oranges, ribbons, and colour'd prints,   690
A Kaleidoscope jumble of shapes and tints,
   And human faces all flashing,
Bright and brief as the sparks from the flints,
   That the desperate hoof keeps dashing!

On and on! still frightfully fast!
Dover-street, Bond-street, all are past!
But—yes—no—yes!—they're down at last!
   The Furies and Fates have found them!
Down they go with a sparkle and crash,
Like a Bark that's struck by the lightning flash—   700
     There's a shriek—and a sob—
     And the dense dark mob
    Like a billow closes around them!
    *   *   *   *   *
       *   *   *   *

     "She breathes!"
     "She don't!"
     "She'll recover!"
     "She won't!"
   "She's stirring! she's living, by Nemesis!"
Gold, still gold! on counter and shelf!
Golden dishes as plenty as delf!   710
Miss Kilmansegg's coming again to herself
   On an opulent Goldsmith's premises!

Gold! fine gold!—both yellow and red,
Beaten, and molten—polish'd, and dead—
To see the gold with profusion spread
   In all forms of its manufacture!
But what avails gold to Miss Kilmansegg,
When the femoral bone of her dexter leg
   Has met with a compound fracture?

Gold may sooth Adversity's smart;   720
Nay, help to bind up a broken heart;
But to try it on any other part
    Were as certain a disappointment,
As if one should rub the dish and plate,
Taken out of a Staffordshire crate—
In the hope of a Golden Service of State—
    With Singleton's "Golden Ointment."

Her Precious Leg

"As the twig is bent, the tree's inclined,"
Is an adage often recall'd to mind,
    Referring to juvenile bias: 730
And never so well is the verity seen,
As when to the weak, warp'd side we lean,
    While Life's tempests and hurricanes try us.

Even thus with Miss K. and her broken limb,
By a very, very remarkable whim,
    She shew'd her early tuition:
While the buds of character came into blow
With a certain tinge that served to show
The nursery culture long ago,
    As the graft is known by fruition!   740

For the King's Physician, who nursed the case,
His verdict gave with an awful face,
    And three others concurr'd to egg it;
That the Patient to give old Death the slip,
Like the Pope, instead of a personal trip,
    Must send her Leg as a Legate.

The limb was doom'd—it couldn't be saved!
And like other people the patient behaved,
Nay, bravely that cruel parting braved,
    Which makes some persons so falter,   750
They rather would part, without a groan,
With the flesh of their flesh, and bone of their bone,
    They obtain'd at St. George's altar.

217

But when it came to fitting the stump
With a proxy limb—then flatly and plump
   She spoke, in the spirit olden;
She couldn't—she shouldn't—she wouldn't have wood!
Nor a leg of cork, if she never stood,
And she swore an oath, or something as good,
   The proxy limb should be golden! 760

A wooden leg! what, a sort of peg,
   For your common Jockeys and Jennies!
No, no, her mother might worry and plague—
Weep, go down on her knees, and beg,
But nothing would move Miss Kilmansegg!
She could—she would have a Golden Leg,
   If it cost ten thousand guineas!

Wood indeed, in Forest or Park,
With its sylvan honours and feudal bark,
   Is an aristocratical article: 770
But split and sawn, and hack'd about town,
Serving all needs of pauper or clown,
Trod on! stagger'd on! Wood cut down
   Is vulgar—fibre and particle!

And Cork!—when the noble Cork Tree shades
A lovely group of Castilian maids,
   'Tis a thing for a song or sonnet!—
But cork, as it stops the bottle of gin,
Or bungs the beer—the *small* beer—in,
It pierced her heart like a corking-pin, 780
   To think of standing upon it!

A Leg of Gold—solid gold throughout,
Nothing else, whether slim or stout,
   Should ever support her, God willing!
She must—she could—she would have her whim,
Her father, she turn'd a deaf ear to him—
   He might kill her—she didn't mind killing!
He was welcome to cut off her other limb—
   He might cut her all off with a shilling!

All other promised gifts were in vain,   790
Golden Girdle, or Golden Chain,
She writhed with impatience more than pain,
    And utter'd "pshaws!" and "pishes!"
But a Leg of Gold! as she lay in bed,
It danced before her—it ran in her head!
    It jump'd with her dearest wishes!

"Gold—gold—gold! Oh, let it be gold!"
Asleep or awake that tale she told,
    And when she grew delirious:
Till her parents resolved to grant her wish,   800
If they melted down plate, and goblet, and dish,
    The case was getting so serious.

So a Leg was made in a comely mould,
Of Gold, fine virgin glittering gold,
    As solid as man could make it—
Solid in foot, and calf, and shank,
A prodigious sum of money it sank;
In fact 'twas a Branch of the family Bank,
    And no easy matter to break it.

All sterling metal—not half-and-half,   810
The Goldsmith's mark was stamp'd on the calf—
    'Twas pure as from Mexican barter!
And to make it more costly, just over the knee,
Where another ligature used to be,
Was a circle of jewels, worth shillings to see,
    A new-fangled Badge of the Garter!

'Twas a splendid, brilliant, beautiful Leg,
Fit for the Court of Scander-Beg,
That Precious Leg of Miss Kilmansegg!
    For, thanks to parental bounty,   820
Secure from Mortification's touch,
She stood on a member that cost as much
    As a Member for all the County!

Her Fame

To gratify stern ambition's whims,
With hundreds and thousands of precious limbs
   On a field of battle we scatter!
Sever'd by sword, or bullet, or saw,
Off they go, all bleeding and raw,—
But the public seems to get the lock-jaw,
    So little is said on the matter!   830

Legs, the tightest that ever were seen,
The tightest, the lightest, that danced on the green,
   Cutting capers to sweet Kitty Clover;
Shatter'd, scatter'd, cut, and bowl'd down,
Off they go, worse off for renown,
A line in the *Times,* or a talk about town,
    Than the leg that a fly runs over!

But the Precious Leg of Miss Kilmansegg,
That gowden, goolden, golden leg,
   Was the theme of all conversation!   840
Had it been a Pillar of Church and State,
Or a prop to support the whole Dead Weight,
It could not have furnish'd more debate
    To the heads and tails of the nation!

East and west, and north and south,
Though useless for either hunger or drouth,—
The Leg was in every body's mouth,
   To use a poetical figure;
Rumour, in taking her ravenous swim,
Saw, and seized on the tempting limb,   850
    Like a shark on the leg of a nigger.

Wilful murder fell very dead;
Debates in the House were hardly read;
In vain the Police Reports were fed
   With Irish riots and *rumpuses*—
The Leg! the Leg! was the great event,
Through every circle of life it went,
    Like the leg of a pair of compasses.

The last new Novel seem'd tame and flat,
The Leg, a novelty newer than that, 860
   Had tripp'd up the heels of Fiction!
It Burked the very essays of Burke,
And, alas! how Wealth over Wit plays the Turk!
As a regular piece of goldsmith's work,
   Got the better of Goldsmith's diction.

"A leg of gold! what of solid gold?"
Cried rich and poor, and young and old,—
   And Master and Miss and Madam—
'Twas the talk of 'Change—the Alley—the Bank—
And with men of scientific rank, 870
It made as much stir as the fossil shank
   Of a Lizard coeval with Adam!

Of course with Greenwich and Chelsea elves,
Men who had lost a limb themselves,
   Its interest did not dwindle—
But Bill, and Ben, and Jack, and Tom,
Could hardly have spun more yarns therefrom,
   If the leg had been a spindle.

Meanwhile the story went to and fro,
Till, gathering like the ball of snow, 880
By the time it got to Stratford-le-Bow,
   Through Exaggeration's touches,
The Heiress and Hope of the Kilmanseggs
Was propp'd on *two* fine Golden Legs,
   And a pair of Golden Crutches!

Never had Leg so great a run!
'Twas the "go" and the "Kick" thrown into one!
The mode—the new thing under the sun,
   The rage—the fancy—the passion!
Bonnets were named, and hats were worn, 890
A la Golden Leg instead of Leghorn,
     And stockings and shoes,
       Of golden hues,
   Took the lead in the walks of fashion!

The Golden Leg had a vast career,
It was sung and danced—and to show how near
   Low Folly to lofty approaches,
Down to society's very dregs,
The Belles of Wapping wore "Kilmanseggs,"
And St. Giles's Beaux sported Golden Legs
   In their pinchbeck pins and brooches!

900

Her First Step

Supposing the Trunk and Limbs of Man
Shared, on the allegorical plan,
   By the Passions that mark Humanity,
Whichever might claim the head, or heart,
The stomach, or any other part,
   The Legs would be seized by Vanity.

There's Bardus, a six-foot column of fop,
A lighthouse without any light atop,
   Whose height would attract beholders,
If he had not lost some inches clear
By looking down at his kerseymere,
Ogling the limbs he holds so dear,
   Till he got a stoop in his shoulders.

910

Talk of Art, of Science, or Books,
And down go the everlasting looks,
   To his crural beauties so wedded!
Try him, wherever you will, you find
His mind in his legs, and his legs in his mind,
All prongs and folly—in short a kind
   Of Fork—that is Fiddle-headed.

920

What wonder, then, if Miss Kilmansegg,
With a splendid, brilliant, beautiful leg,
Fit for the court of Scander Beg,
Disdain'd to hide it like Joan or Meg,
   In petticoats stuff'd or quilted?
Not she! 'twas her convalescent whim
To dazzle the world with her precious limb,—
   Nay, to go a little high-kilted.

So cards were sent for that sort of mob   930
Where Tartars and Africans hob-and-nob,
And the Cherokee talks of his cab and cob
  To Polish or Lapland lovers—
Cards like that hieroglyphical call
To a geographical Fancy Ball
  On the recent Post-Office covers.

For if Lion-hunters—and great ones too—
Would mob a savage from Latakoo,
Or squeeze for a glimpse of Prince Le Boo,
  That unfortunate Sandwich scion—   940
Hundreds of first-rate people, no doubt,
Would gladly, madly, rush to a rout,
  That promised a Golden Lion!

Her Fancy Ball

Of all the spirits of evil fame
That hurt the soul, or injure the frame,
  And poison what's honest and hearty,
There's none more needs a Mathew to preach
A cooling, antiphlogistic speech,
      To praise and enforce
        A temperate course,   950
  Than the Evil Spirit of Party.

Go to the House of Commons, or Lords,
And they seem to be busy with simple words
  In their popular sense or pedantic—
But, alas! with their cheers, and sneers, and jeers,
They're really busy, whatever appears,
Putting peas in each other's ears,
  To drive their enemies frantic!

Thus Tories love to worry the Whigs,
Who treat them in turn like Schwalbach pigs,   960
Giving them lashes, thrashes, and digs,
  With their writhing and pain delighted—
But after all that's said, and more,

The malice and spite of Party are poor
To the malice and spite of a party next door,
    To a party not invited.

On with the cap and out with the light,
Weariness bids the world good night,
    At least for the usual season;
But hark! a clatter of horses' heels;   970
And Sleep and Silence are broken on wheels,
    Like Wilful Murder and Treason!

Another crash—and the carriage goes—
Again poor Weariness seeks the repose
    That Nature demands imperious;
But Echo takes up the burden now,
With a rattling chorus of row-de-dow-dow,
Till Silence herself seems making a row,
    Like a Quaker gone delirious!

'Tis night—a winter night—and the stars   980
Are shining like winkin'—Venus and Mars
Are rolling along in their golden cars
    Through the sky's serene expansion—
But vainly the stars dispense their rays,
Venus and Mars are lost in the blaze
    Of the Kilmanseggs' luminous mansion!

Up jumps Fear in a terrible fright!
His bedchamber windows look so bright,
    With light all the Square is glutted!
Up he jumps, like a sole from the pan,   990
And a tremor sickens his inward man,
For he feels as only a gentleman can,
    Who thinks he's being "gutted."

Again Fear settles, all snug and warm;
But only to dream of a dreadful storm
From Autumn's sulphurous locker;
    But the only electric body that falls,

Wears a negative coat, and positive smalls,
And draws the peal that so appals
　　From the Kilmansegg's brazen knocker!　　　　　1000

'Tis Curiosity's Benefit night—
And perchance 'tis the English Second-Sight,
　　But whatever it be, so be it—
As the friends and guests of Miss Kilmansegg
Crowd in to look at her Golden Leg,
　　　　As many more
　　　　Mob round the door,
　　To see them going to see it!

In they go—in jackets, and cloaks,
Plumes, and bonnets, turbans, and toques,　　　　1010
　　As if to a Congress of Nations:
Greeks and Malays, with daggers and dirks,
Spaniards, Jews, Chinese, and Turks—
Some like original foreign works,
　　But mostly like bad translations.

In they go, and to work like a pack,
Juan, Moses, and Shacabac,
　　Tom, and Jerry, and Springheel'd Jack,
For some of low Fancy are lovers—
Skirting, zigzagging, casting about,　　　　　　1020
Here and there, and in and out,
With a crush, and a rush, for a full-bodied rout
　　Is one of the stiffest of covers.

In they went, and hunted about,
Open mouth'd like chub and trout,
And some with the upper lip thrust out,
　　Like that fish for routing, a barbel—
While Sir Jacob stood to welcome the crowd,
And rubb'd his hands, and smiled aloud,
And bow'd, and bow'd, and bow'd, and bow'd,　　　1030
　　Like a man who is sawing marble.

For Princes were there, and Noble Peers;
Dukes descended from Norman spears;
Earls that dated from early years;
   And Lords in vast variety—
Besides the Gentry both new and old—
For people who stand on legs of gold,
   Are sure to stand well with society.

"But where—where—where?" with one accord
Cried Moses and Mufti, Jack and my Lord,   1040
   Wang-Fong and Il Bondocani—
When slow, and heavy, and dead as a dump,
They heard a foot begin to stump,
        Thump! lump!
        Lump! thump!
  Like the Spectre in "Don Giovanni!"

And lo! the Heiress, Miss Kilmansegg,
With her splendid, brilliant, beautiful leg,
   In the garb of a Goddess olden—
Like chaste Diana going to hunt,   1050
With a golden spear—which of course was blunt,
And a tunic loop'd up to a gem in front,
   To shew the Leg that was Golden!

Gold! still gold! her Crescent behold,
That should be silver, but would be gold;
   And her robe's auriferous spangles!
Her golden stomacher—how she would melt!
Her golden quiver, and golden belt,
   Where a golden bugle dangles!

And her jewell'd Garter? Oh, Sin! Oh, Shame!   1060
Let Pride and Vanity bear the blame,
That bring such blots on female fame!
   But to be a true recorder,
Besides its thin transparent stuff,
The tunic was loop'd quite high enough
   To give a glimpse of the Order!

But what have sin or shame to do
With a Golden Leg—and a stout one too?
   Away with all Prudery's panics!
That the precious metal, by thick and thin,   1070
Will cover square acres of land or sin,
     Is a fact made plain
     Again and again,
  In Morals as well as Mechanics.

A few, indeed, of her proper sex,
Who seem'd to feel her foot on their necks,
And fear'd their charms would meet with checks
   From so rare and splendid a blazon—
A few cried "fie!"—and "forward"—and "bold!"
And said of the Leg it might be gold,   1080
   But to them it looked like brazen!

'Twas hard they hinted for flesh and blood,
Virtue, and Beauty, and all that's good,
   To strike to mere dross their topgallants—
But what were Beauty, or Virtue, or Worth,
Gentle manners, or gentle birth,
Nay, what the most talented head on earth
   To a Leg worth fifty Talents!

But the men sang quite another hymn
Of glory and praise to the precious Limb—   1090
Age, sordid Age, admired the whim,
   And its indecorum pardon'd—
While half of the young—ay, more than half—
Bow'd down and worshipp'd the Golden Calf,
   Like the Jews when their hearts were harden'd.

A Golden Leg! what fancies it fired!
What golden wishes and hopes inspired!
   To give but a mere abridgement—
What a leg to leg-bail Embarrassment's serf!
What a leg for a Leg to take on the turf!   1100
   What a leg for a marching regiment!

A Golden Leg!—whatever Love sings,
'Twas worth a bushel of "Plain Gold Rings"
   With which the Romantic wheedles.
'Twas worth all the legs in stockings and socks—
'Twas a leg that might be put in the Stocks,
   N.B.—Not the parish beadle's!

And Lady K. nid-nodded her head,
Lapp'd in a turban fancy-bred,
Just like a love-apple, huge and red,   1110
   Some Mussul-womanish mystery;
     But whatever she meant
        To represent,
  She talk'd like the Muse of History.

She told how the filial leg was lost;
And then how much the gold one cost;
   With its weight to a Trojan fraction:
And how it took off, and how it put on;
And call'd on Devil, Duke, and Don,
Mahomet, Moses, and Prester John,   1120
   To notice its beautiful action.

And then of the Leg she went in quest;
And led it where the light was best;
And made it lay itself up to rest
   In postures for painters' studies:
It cost more tricks and trouble by half,
Than it takes to exhibit a Six-Legg'd Calf
To a boothful of country Cuddies.

Nor yet did the Heiress herself omit
The arts that help to make a hit,   1130
  And preserve a prominent station.
She talk'd and laugh'd far more than her share;
And took a part in "Rich and Rare
Were the gems she wore"—and the gems were there,
   Like a Song with an Illustration.

She even stood up with a Count of France
To dance—alas! the measures we dance
   When Vanity plays the Piper!
Vanity, Vanity, apt to betray,
And lead all sorts of legs astray,
Wood, or metal, or human clay,—
   Since Satan first play'd the Viper!

1140

Vanity, vanity, apt to betray

But first she doff'd her hunting gear,
And favour'd Tom Tug with her golden spear,
   To row with down the river—
A Bonze had her golden bow to hold;
A Hermit her belt and bugle of gold;
   And an Abbot her golden quiver.

And then a space was clear'd on the floor,
And she walk'd the Minuet de la Cour,   1150
With all the pomp of a Pompadour,
   But although she began *andante,*
Conceive the faces of all the Rout,
When she finish'd off with a whirligig bout,
And the Precious Leg stuck stiffly out
   Like the leg of a *Figurantè!*

So the courtly dance was goldenly done,
And golden opinions, of course, it won
   From all different sorts of people—
Chiming, ding-dong, with flattering phrase,   1160
In one vociferous peal of praise,
Like the peal that rings on Royal days
   From Loyalty's parish-steeple.

And yet, had the leg been one of those
That dance for bread in flesh-colour'd hose,
   With Rosina's pastoral bevy,
The jeers it had met,—the shouts! the scoff!
The cutting advice to "take itself off,"
   For sounding but half so heavy.

Had it been a leg like those, perchance,   1170
That teach little girls and boys to dance,
To set, poussette, recede, and advance,
   With the steps and figures most proper,—
Had it hopp'd for a weekly or quarterly sum,
How little of praise or grist would have come
   To a mill with such a hopper!

But the Leg was none of those limbs forlorn—
Bartering capers and hops for corn—
That meet with public hisses and scorn,
   Or the morning journal denounces—   1180
Had it pleas'd to caper from morn till dusk,
There was all the music of "Money Musk"
   In its ponderous bangs and bounces.

But hark!—as slow as the strokes of a pump,
    Lump, thump!
    Thump, lump!
As the Giant of Castle Otranto might stump
  To a lower room from an upper—
Down she goes with a noisy dint,
For taking the crimson turban's hint,   1190
A noble Lord at the Head of the Mint
  Is leading the Leg to supper!

Leading the leg to supper

But the supper, alas! must rest untold,
With its blaze of light and its glitter of gold,
  For to paint that scene of glamour,

It would need the Great Enchanter's charm,
Who waves over Palace, and Cot, and Farm,
An arm like the Goldbeater's Golden Arm
   That wields a Golden Hammer.

He—only **HE**—could fitly state   1200
THE MASSIVE SERVICE OF GOLDEN PLATE,
   With the proper phrase and expansion—
The Rare Selection of **FOREIGN WINES**—
The **ALPS OF ICE** and **MOUNTAINS OF PINES,**
The punch in **OCEANS** and sugary shrines,
The **TEMPLE OF TASTE** from **GUNTER'S DESIGNS**—
In short, all that **WEALTH** with **A FEAST** combines,
   In a **SPLENDID FAMILY MANSION.**

Suffice it each mask'd outlandish guest
Ate and drank of the very best,   1210
   According to critical conners—
And then they pledged the Hostess and Host,
But the Golden Leg was the standing toast,
     And as somebody swore,
     Walk'd off with more
   Than its share of the "Hips!" and honours!

     "Miss Kilmansegg!—
     Full glasses I beg!—
Miss Kilmansegg and her Precious Leg!"
   And away went the bottle careering!   1220
Wine in bumpers! and shouts in peals!
Till the Clown didn't know his head from his heels,
The Mussulman's eyes danced two-some reels,
   And the Quaker was hoarse with cheering!

Her Dream

Miss Kilmansegg took off her leg,
And laid it down like a cribbage-peg,
   For the Rout was done and the riot:
The Square was hush'd; not a sound was heard;
The sky was gray, and no creature stirr'd,
Except one little precocious bird,   1230
   That chirp'd—and then was quiet.

So still without,—so still within;—
    It had been a sin
    To drop a pin—
So intense is silence after a din,
  It seem'd like Death's rehearsal!
To stir the air no eddy came;
And the taper burnt with as still a flame,
As to flicker had been a burning shame,
  In a calm so universal.   1240

The time for sleep had come at last;
And there was the bed, so soft, so vast,
  Quite a field of Bedfordshire clover;
Softer, cooler, and calmer, no doubt,
From the piece of work just ravell'd out,
For one of the pleasures of having a rout
  Is the pleasure of having it over.

No sordid pallet, or truckle mean,
Of straw, and rug, and tatters unclean;
But a splendid, gilded, carved machine,   1250
  That was fit for a Royal Chamber.
On the top was a gorgeous golden wreath;
And the damask curtains hung beneath,
  Like clouds of crimson and amber.

Curtains, held up by two little plump things,
With golden bodies and golden wings,—
  Mere fins for such solidities—
    Two Cupids, in short,
    Of the regular sort,
But the housemaid call'd them "Cupidities."   1260

No patchwork quilt, all seams and scars,
But velvet, powder'd with golden stars,
  A fit mantle for *Night*-Commanders!
And the pillow, as white as snow undimm'd,
And as cool as the pool that the breeze has skimm'd,
Was cased in the finest cambric, and trimm'd
With the costliest lace of Flanders.

And the bed—of the Eider's softest down,
'Twas a place to revel, to smother, to drown
   In a bliss inferr'd by the Poet;   1270
For if Ignorance be indeed a bliss,
What blessed ignorance equals this,
   To sleep—and not to know it?

Oh, bed! oh, bed! delicious bed!
That heaven upon earth to the weary head;
But a place that to name would be ill-bred,
   To the head with a wakeful trouble—
'Tis held by such a different lease!
To one, a place of comfort and peace,
All stuff'd with the down of stubble geese,   1280
   To another with only the stubble!

To one, a perfect Halcyon nest,
All calm, and balm, and quiet, and rest,
   And soft as the fur of the cony—
To another, so restless for body and head,
That the bed seems borrow'd from Nettlebed,
   And the pillow from Stratford the Stony!

To the happy, a first-class carriage of ease,
To the Land of Nod, or where you please;
   But alas! for the watchers and weepers,   1290
Who turn, and turn, and turn again,
But turn, and turn, and turn in vain,
      With an anxious brain,
      And thoughts in a train
    That does not run upon *sleepers!*

Wide awake as the mousing owl,
Night-hawk, or other nocturnal fowl,—
   But more profitless vigils keeping,—
Wide awake in the dark they stare,
Filling with phantoms the vacant air,   1300
As if that Crook-Back'd Tyrant Care
   Had plotted to kill them sleeping.

And oh! when the blessed diurnal light
Is quench'd by the providential night,
   To render our slumber more certain,
Pity, pity the wretches that weep,
For they must be wretched who cannot sleep
   When God himself draws the curtain!

The careful Betty the pillow beats,
And airs the blankets, and smoothes the sheets,   1310
   And gives the mattress a shaking—
But vainly Betty performs her part,
If a ruffled head and a rumpled heart
   As well as the couch want making.

There's Morbid, all bile, and verjuice, and nerves,
Where other people would make preserves,
   He turns his fruits into pickles:
Jealous, envious, and fretful by day,
At night, to his own sharp fancies a prey,
He lies like a hedgehog rolled up the wrong way,   1320
   Tormenting himself with his prickles.

But a child—that bids the world good night,
In downright earnest and cuts it quite—
   A Cherub no Art can copy,—
'Tis a perfect picture to see him lie
As if he had supp'd on dormouse pie,
(An ancient classical dish by the by)
   With a sauce of syrup of poppy.

Oh, bed! bed! bed! delicious bed!
That heav'n upon earth to the weary head,   1330
   Whether lofty or low its condition!
But instead of putting our plagues on shelves,
In our blankets how often we toss ourselves,
Or are toss'd by such allegorical elves
   As Pride, Hate, Greed, and Ambition!

The independent Miss Kilmansegg
Took off her independent Leg
   And laid it beneath her pillow,

And then on the bed her frame she cast,
The time for repose had come at last,   1340
But long, long, after the storm is past
   Rolls the turbid, turbulent billow.

No part she had in vulgar cares
That belong to common household affairs—
Nocturnal annoyances such as theirs
   Who lie with a shrewd surmising
That while they are couchant (a bitter cup!)
Their bread and butter are getting up,
   And the coals,—confound them!—are rising.

No fear she had her sleep to postpone,   1350
Like the crippled Widow who weeps alone,
And cannot make a doze her own,
   For the dread that mayhap on the morrow,
The true and Christian reading to balk,
A broker will take up her bed and walk,
   By way of curing her sorrow.

No cause like these she had to bewail:
But the breath of applause had blown a gale,
And winds from that quarter seldom fail
   To cause some human commotion;   1360
But whenever such breezes coincide
     With the very spring-tide
     Of human pride,
   There's no such swell on the ocean!

Peace, and ease, and slumber lost,
She turn'd, and roll'd, and tumbled, and toss'd,
   With a tumult that would not settle:
A common case, indeed, with such
As have too little, or think too much,
   Of the precious and glittering metal.   1370

Gold!—she saw at her golden foot
The Peer whose tree had an olden root,
The Proud, the Great, the Learned to boot,
   The handsome, the gay, and the witty—

The Man of Science—of Arms—of Art,
The man who deals but at Pleasure's mart,
   And the man who deals in the City.

Gold, still gold—and true to the mould!
In the very scheme of her dream it told;
   For, by magical transmutation,   1380
From her Leg through her body it seem'd to go,
Till, gold above, and gold below,
She was gold, all gold, from her little gold toe
   To her organ of Veneration!

And still she retain'd, through Fancy's art,
The Golden Bow, and the Golden Dart,
With which she had played a Goddess's part
   In her recent glorification.
And still, like one of the self-same brood,
On a Plinth of the selfsame metal she stood   1390
   For the whole world's adoration.

Worship of the leg

And hymns and incense around her roll'd,
From Golden Harps and Censers of Gold,—
For Fancy in dreams is as uncontroll'd
   As a horse without a bridle:
What wonder, then, from all checks exempt,
If, inspired by the Golden Leg, she dreamt
   She was turn'd to a Golden Idol?

Her Courtship

When leaving Eden's happy land
The grieving Angel led by the hand   1400
   Our banish'd Father and Mother,
Forgotten amid their awful doom,
The tears, the fears, and the future's gloom,
On each brow was a wreath of Paradise bloom,
   That our Parents had twined for each other.

It was only while sitting like figures of stone,
For the grieving Angel had skyward flown,
As they sat, those Two, in the world alone,
   With disconsolate hearts nigh cloven,
That scenting the gust of happier hours,   1410
They look'd around for the precious flow'rs,
And lo!—a last relic of Eden's dear bow'rs—
   The chaplet that Love had woven!

And still, when a pair of Lovers meet,
There's a sweetness in air, unearthly sweet,
That savours still of that happy retreat
   Where Eve by Adam was courted:
Whilst the joyous Thrush, and the gentle Dove,
Woo'd their mates in the boughs above,
   And the Serpent, as yet, only sported.   1420

Who hath not felt that breath in the air,
A perfume and freshness strange and rare,
A warmth in the light, and a bliss every where,
   When young hearts yearn together?
All sweets below, and all sunny above,

Oh! there's nothing in life like making love,
   Save making hay in fine weather!

Who hath not found amongst his flow'rs
A blossom too bright for this world of ours,
   Like a rose among snows of Sweden?   1430
But to turn again to Miss Kilmansegg,
Where must Love have gone to beg,
If such a thing as a Golden Leg
   Had put its foot in Eden!

Where must love have gone to beg

And yet—to tell the rigid truth—
Her favour was sought by Age and Youth—
   For the prey will find a prowler!

She was follow'd, flatter'd, courted, address'd,
Woo'd, and coo'd, and wheedled, and press'd,
By suitors from North, South, East, and West,   1440
   Like the Heiress, in song, Tibbie Fowler!

But, alas! alas! for the Woman's fate,
Who has from a mob to choose a mate!
   'Tis a strange and painful mystery!
But the more the eggs, the worse the hatch;
The more the fish, the worse the catch;
The more the sparks, the worse the match;
   Is a fact in Woman's history.

Give her between a brace to pick,
And, mayhap, with luck to help the trick,   1450
She will take the Faustus, and leave the Old Nick—
   But her future bliss to baffle,
Amongst a score let her have a voice,
And she'll have as little cause to rejoice,
As if she had won the "Man of her choice"
   In a matrimonial raffle!

Thus, even thus, with the Heiress and Hope,
Fulfilling the adage of too much rope,
   With so ample a competition,
She chose the least worthy of all the group,   1460
Just as the vulture makes a stoop,
And singles out from the herd or troop
   The beast of the worst condition.

A Foreign Count—who came incog.,
Not under a cloud, but under a fog,
   In a Calais packet's fore-cabin,
To charm some lady British-born,
With his eyes as black as the fruit of the thorn,
And his hooky nose, and his beard half-shorn,
   Like a half-converted Rabbin.   1470

And because the Sex confess a charm
In the man who has slash'd a head or arm,
   Or has been a throat's undoing,

The foreign count

He was dress'd like one of the glorious trade,
At least when Glory is off parade,
With a stock, and a frock, well trimm'd with braid,
   And frogs—that went a-wooing.

Moreover, as Counts are apt to do,
On the left-hand side of his dark surtout,
At one of those holes that buttons go through,   1480
   (To be a precise recorder)
A ribbon he wore, or rather a scrap,
About an inch of ribbon mayhap,
That one of his rivals, a whimsical chap,
   Described as his "Retail Order."

And then—and much it help'd his chance—
He could sing, and play first fiddle, and dance,
Perform charades, and Proverbs of France—
    Act the tender, and do the cruel;
For amongst his other killing parts,   1490
He had broken a brace of female hearts,
    And murder'd three men in duel!

Savage at heart, and false of tongue,
Subtle with age, and smooth to the young,
    Like a snake in his coiling and curling—
Such was the Count—to give him a niche—
Who came to court that Heiress rich,
And knelt at her foot—one needn't say which—
    Besieging her Castle of *Sterling*.

With pray'rs and vows he open'd his trench,   1500
And plied her with English, Spanish, and French,
    In phrases the most sentimental:
And quoted poems in High and Low Dutch,
With now and then an Italian touch,
Till she yielded, without resisting much,
    To homage so continental.

And then the sordid bargain to close,
With a miniature sketch of his hooky nose,
And his dear dark eyes, as black as sloes,
And his beard and whiskers as black as those,   1510
    The lady's consent he requited—
And instead of the lock that lovers beg,
The Count received from Miss Kilmansegg
A model, in small, of her Precious Leg—
    And so the couple were plighted!

But, oh! the love that gold must crown!
Better—better, the love of the clown,
Who admires his lass in her Sunday gown,
    As if all the fairies had dress'd her!
Whose brain to no crooked thought gives birth,   1520
Except that he never will part on earth
    With his true love's crooked tester!

Alas! for the love that's link'd with gold!
Better—better a thousand times told—
   More honest, happy, and laudable,
The downright loving of pretty Cis,
Who wipes her lips, though there's nothing amiss,
And takes a kiss, and gives a kiss,
   In which her heart is audible!

Pretty Cis, so smiling and bright,   1530
Who loves as she labours, with all her might,
   And without any sordid leaven!
Who blushes as red as haws and hips,
Down to her very finger-tips,
For Roger's blue ribbons—to her, like strips
   Cut out of the azure of Heaven!

Her Marriage

'Twas morn—a more auspicious one!
From the Golden East, the Golden Sun
Came forth his glorious race to run,
   Through clouds of most splendid tinges;   1540
Clouds that lately slept in shade,
      But now seem'd made
      Of gold brocade,
   With magnificent golden fringes.

Gold above, and gold below,
The earth reflected the golden glow,
   From river, and hill, and valley;
Gilt by the golden light of morn,
The Thames—it look'd like the Golden Horn,
And the Barge, that carried coal or corn,   1550
   Like Cleopatra's Galley!

Bright as clusters of Golden-rod,
Suburban poplars began to nod,
   With extempore splendour furnish'd;
While London was bright with glittering clocks,

Golden dragons, and Golden cocks,
    And above them all,
      The dome of St. Paul,
With its Golden Cross and its Golden ball,
   Shone out as if newly burnish'd!   1560

And lo! for Golden Hours and Joys,
Troops of glittering Golden Boys
Danced along with a jocund noise,
   And their gilded emblems carried!
In short, 'twas the year's most Golden Day,
By mortals call'd the First of May,
      When Miss Kilmansegg,
        Of the Golden Leg,
   With a Golden Ring was married!

And thousands of children, women, and men,   1570
Counted the clock from eight till ten,
   From St. James's sonorous steeple;
For next to that interesting job,
The hanging of Jack, or Bill, or Bob,
There's nothing so draws a London mob
   As the noosing of very rich people.

And a treat it was for a mob to behold
The Bridal Carriage that blazed with gold!
And the Footmen tall, and the Coachman bold,
   In liveries so resplendent—   1580
Coats you wonder'd to see in place,
They seem'd so rich with golden lace,
   That they might have been independent.

Coats that made those menials proud
Gaze with scorn on the dingy crowd,
   From their gilded elevations;
Not to forget that saucy lad
(Ostentation's favourite cad),
The Page, who look'd, so splendidly clad,
   Like a Page of the "Wealth of Nations."   1590

But the Coachman carried off the state,
With what was a Lancashire body of late
   Turn'd into a Dresden Figure;
With a bridal Nosegay of early bloom,
About the size of a birchen broom,
And so huge a White Favour, had Gog been Groom
   He need not have worn a bigger.

And then to see the Groom! the Count!
With Foreign Orders to such an amount,
   And whiskers so wild—nay, bestial;   1600
He seem'd to have borrow'd the shaggy hair
As well as the Stars of the Polar Bear,
   To make him look celestial!

And then—Great Jove!—the struggle, the crush,
The screams, the heaving, the awful rush,
   The swearing, the tearing, and fighting,
The hats and bonnets smash'd like an egg—
To catch a glimpse of the Golden Leg,
Which, between the steps and Miss Kilmansegg,
   Was fully display'd in alighting!   1610

From the Golden Ankle up to the Knee
There it was for the mob to see!
A shocking act had it chanced to be
   A crooked leg or a skinny:
But although a magnificent veil she wore,
Such as never was seen before,
In case of blushes, she blush'd no more
   Than George the First on a guinea!

Another step, and lo! she was launch'd!
All in white, as Brides are *blanch'd*,   1620
   With a wreath of most wonderful splendour—
Diamonds, and pearls, so rich in device,
That, according to calculation nice,
Her head was worth as royal a price
   As the head of the Young Pretender.

Bravely she shone—and shone the more
As she sail'd through the crowd of squalid and poor,
   Thief, beggar, and tatterdemalion—
Led by the Count, with his sloe-black eyes
Bright with triumph, and some surprise,   1630
Like Anson on making sure of his prize,
   The famous Mexican Galleon!

Anon came Lady K., with her face
Quite made up to act with grace,
   But she cut the performance shorter;
For instead of pacing stately and stiff,
At the stare of the vulgar she took a miff,
And ran, full speed, into Church, as if
   To get married before her daughter.

But Sir Jacob walk'd more slowly, and bow'd   1640
Right and left to the gaping crowd,
   Wherever a glance was seizable;
For Sir Jacob thought he bow'd like a Guelph,
And therefore bow'd to imp and elf,
And would gladly have made a bow to himself,
   Had such a bow been feasible.

And last—and not the least of the sight,
Six "Handsome Fortunes," all in white,
Came to help in the marriage rite,—
   And rehearse their own hymeneals;   1650
And then the bright procession to close,
They were followed by just as many Beaux
   Quite fine enough for Ideals.

Glittering men, and splendid dames,
Thus they enter'd the porch of St. James',
   Pursued by a thunder of laughter:
For the Beadle was forced to intervene,
For Jim the Crow, and his Mayday Queen,
With her gilded ladle, and Jack i' the Green,
   Would fain have follow'd after!   1660

Beadle-like he hush'd the shout;
But the temple was full "inside and out,"
And a buzz kept buzzing all round about
 Like bees when the day is sunny—
A buzz universal that interfered
With the rite that ought to have been revered,
As if the couple already were smear'd
 With Wedlock's treacle and honey!

Yet Wedlock's a very awful thing!
'Tis something like that feat in the ring   1670
 Which requires good nerve to do it—
When one of a "Grand Equestrian Troop"
Makes a jump at a gilded hoop,
  Not certain at all
  Of what may befall
 After his getting through it!

But the Count he felt the nervous work
No more than any polygamous Turk,
 Or bold piratical schipper,
Who, during his buccaneering search,   1680
Would as soon engage "a hand" in church
 As a hand on board his clipper!

And how did the Bride perform her part?
Like any Bride who is cold at heart,
 Mere snow with the ice's glitter;
What but a life of winter for her!
Bright but chilly, alive without stir,
So splendidly comfortless,—just like a Fir
 When the frost is severe and bitter.

Such were the future man and wife!   1690
Whose bale or bliss to the end of life
 A few short words were to settle—
  Wilt thou have this woman?
   I will—and then,
  Wilt thou have this man?
   I will, and Amen—

247

And those Two were one Flesh, in the Angels' ken,
Except one Leg—that was metal.

Wilt thou have this woman?

Then the names were sign'd—and kiss'd the kiss:
And the Bride, who came from her coach a Miss,   1700
   As a Countess walk'd to her carriage—
Whilst Hymen preen'd his plumes like a dove,
And Cupid flutter'd his wings above,
In the shape of a fly—as little a Love
   As ever look'd in at a marriage!

Another crash—and away they dash'd,
And the gilded carriage and footmen flash'd
   From the eyes of the gaping people—

Who turn'd to gaze at the toe-and-heel
Of the Golden Boys beginning a reel,   1710
To the merry sound of a wedding-peal
   From St. James's musical steeple.

Those wedding-bells! those wedding-bells!
How sweetly they sound in pastoral dells
   From a tow'r in an ivy-green jacket!
But town-made joys how dearly they cost;
And after all are tumbled and tost,
Like a peal from a London steeple, and lost
   In town-made riot and racket.

The wedding-peal, how sweetly it peals   1720
With grass or heather beneath our heels,—
   For bells are Music's laughter!—
But a London peal, well mingled, be sure,
With vulgar noises and voices impure,
What a harsh and discordant overture
   To the Harmony meant to come after!

But hence with Discord—perchance, too soon
To cloud the face of the honeymoon
   With a dismal occultation!
Whatever Fate's concerted trick,   1730
The Countess and Count, at the present nick,
Have a chicken and not a crow to pick
   At a sumptuous Cold Collation.

A Breakfast—no unsubstantial mess,
But one in the style of Good Queen Bess,
   Who,—hearty as hippocampus,—
Broke her fast with ale and beef,
Instead of toast and the Chinese leaf,
   And in lieu of anchovy—grampus!

A breakfast of fowl, and fish, and flesh,   1740
Whatever was sweet, or salt, or fresh;
   With wines the most rare and curious—

Wines, of the richest flavour and hue;
With fruits from the worlds both Old and New;
And fruits obtain'd before they were due
   At a discount most usurious.

For wealthy palates there be, that scout
What is *in* season, for what is *out,*
   And prefer all precocious savour:
For instance, early green peas, of the sort   1750
That costs some four or five guineas a quart;
   Where the *Mint* is the principal flavour.

And many a wealthy man was there,
Such as the wealthy City could spare,
   To put in a portly appearance—
Men whom their fathers had help'd to gild:
And men who had had their fortunes to build
And—much to their credit—had richly fill'd
   Their purses by *pursy-verance.*

Men, by popular rumour at least,   1760
Not the last to enjoy a feast!
   And truly they were not idle!
Luckier far than the chestnut tits,
Which, down at the door, stood champing their bitts,
   At a different sort of bridle.

For the time was come—and the whisker'd Count
Help'd his Bride in the carriage to mount,
   And fain would the Muse deny it,
But the crowd, including two butchers in blue,
(The regular killing Whitechapel hue,)   1770
Of her Precious Calf had as ample a view,
   As if they had come to buy it!

Then away! away! with all the speed
That golden spurs can give to the steed,—
Both Yellow Boys and Guineas, indeed,
   Concurr'd to urge the cattle—

Away they went, with favours white,
Yellow jackets, and pannels bright,
And left the mob, like a mob at night,
   Agape at the sound of a rattle.   1780

Away! away! they rattled and roll'd,
The Count, and his Bride, and her Leg of Gold—
   That fated charm to the charmer!
Away,—through Old Brentford rang the din,
Of wheels and heels, on their way to win
That hill, named after one of her kin,
   The Hill of the Golden Farmer!

Gold, still gold—it flew like dust!
It tipp'd the post-boy, and paid the trust;
In each open palm it was freely thrust;   1790
   There was nothing but giving and taking!
And if gold could ensure the future hour,
What hopes attended that Bride to her bow'r,
But alas! even hearts with a four-horse pow'r
   Of opulence end in breaking!

Her Honeymoon

The moon—the moon, so silver and cold,
Her fickle temper has oft been told,
   Now shady—now bright and sunny—
But of all the lunar things that change,
The one that shews most fickle and strange,   1800
And takes the most eccentric range
   Is the moon—so called—of honey!

To some a full-grown orb reveal'd,
As big and as round as Norval's shield,
   And as bright as a burner Bude-lighted;
To others as dull, and dingy, and damp,
As any oleaginous lamp,
Of the regular old parochial stamp,
   In a London fog benighted.

To the loving, a bright and constant sphere,   1810
That makes earth's commonest scenes appear
    All poetic, romantic, and tender:
Hanging with jewels a cabbage-stump,
And investing a common post, or a pump,
A currant-bush, or a gooseberry-clump,
    With a halo of dreamlike splendour.

A sphere such as shone from Italian skies,
In Juliet's dear, dark, liquid eyes,
    Tipping trees with its argent braveries—
And to couples not favour'd with Fortune's boons,   1820
One of the most delightful of moons,
For it brightens their pewter platters and spoons
    Like a silver service of Savory's!

For all is bright, and beauteous, and clear,
And the meanest thing most precious and dear,
    When the magic of love is present:
Love, that lends a sweetness and grace
To the humblest spot and the plainest face—
That turns Wilderness Row into Paradise Place,
    And Garlick Hill to Mount Pleasant!   1830

Love that sweetens sugarless tea,
And makes contentment and joy agree
    With the coarsest boarding and bedding:
Love that no golden ties can attach,
But nestles under the humblest thatch,
And will fly away from an Emperor's match
    To dance at a Penny Wedding!

Oh, happy, happy, thrice happy state,
When such a bright Planet governs the fate
    Of a pair of united lovers!   1840
'Tis theirs, in spite of the Serpent's hiss,
To enjoy the pure primeval kiss,
With as much of the old original bliss
    As mortality ever recovers!

Love for dinner

There's strength in double joints, no doubt,
In double X Ale, and Dublin Stout,
That the single sorts know nothing about
    And a fist is strongest when doubled—
And double aqua-fortis, of course,
And double soda-water, perforce,   1850
    Are the strongest that ever bubbled!

There's double beauty whenever a Swan
Swims on a Lake, with her double thereon;
And ask the gardener, Luke or John,
    Of the beauty of double-blowing—
A double dahlia delights the eye;
And it's far the loveliest sight in the sky
When a double rainbow is glowing!

There's warmth in a pair of double soles;
As well as a double allowance of coals—   1860
    In a coat that is double-breasted—
In double windows and double doors;
And a double U wind is blest by scores
    For its warmth to the tender-chested.

There's a twofold sweetness in double pipes;
And a double barrel and double snipes
　　Give the sportsman a duplicate pleasure:
There's double safety in double locks;
And double letters bring cash for the box;
And all the world knows that double knocks　　　　　1870
　　Are gentility's double measure.

There's a double sweetness in double rhymes,
And a double at Whist and a double Times
　　In profit are certainly double—
By doubling, the Hare contrives to escape:
And all seamen delight in a doubled Cape,
　　And a double-reef'd topsail in trouble.

There's a double chuck at a double chin,
And of course there's a double pleasure therein,
　　If the parties were brought to telling:　　　　　1880
And however our Dennises take offence,
A double meaning shews double sense;
　　　　And if proverbs tell truth,
　　　　　A double tooth
　　Is Wisdom's adopted dwelling!

But double wisdom, and pleasure, and sense,
Beauty, respect, strength, comfort, and thence
　　Through whatever the list discovers,
They are all in the double blessedness summ'd,
Of what was formerly double-drumm'd,　　　　　1890
　　The Marriage of two true Lovers!

Now the Kilmansegg Moon—it must be told—
Though instead of silver it tipp'd with gold—
Shone rather wan, and distant, and cold,
　　And before its days were at thirty,
Such gloomy clouds began to collect,
With an ominous ring of ill effect,
As gave but too much cause to expect
　　Such weather as seamen call dirty!

And yet the moon was the "Young May Moon," 1900
And the scented hawthorn had blossom'd soon,
   And the thrush and the blackbird were singing—
The snow-white lambs were skipping in play,
And the bee was humming a tune all day
To flowers as welcome as flowers in May,
   And the trout in the stream was springing!

But what were the hues of the blooming earth,
Its scents—its sounds—or the music and mirth
   Of its furr'd or its feather'd creatures,
To a Pair in the world's last sordid stage, 1910
Who had never look'd into Nature's page,
And had strange ideas of a Golden Age,
   Without any Arcadian features?

And what were joys of the pastoral kind
To a Bride—town-made—with a heart and mind
   With simplicity ever at battle?
A bride of an ostentatious race,
Who, thrown in the Golden Farmer's place,
Would have trimm'd her shepherds with golden lace,
   And gilt the horns of her cattle. 1920

She could not please the pigs with her whim,
And the sheep wouldn't cast their eyes at a limb
   For which she had been such a martyr:
The deer in the park, and the colts at grass,
And the cows unheeded let it pass;
And the ass on the common was such an ass,
     That he wouldn't have swapp'd
     The thistle he cropp'd
   For her Leg, including the Garter!

She hated lanes, and she hated fields— 1930
She hated all that the country yields—
   And barely knew turnips from clover;
She hated walking in any shape,
And a country stile was an awkward scrape,
Without the bribe of a mob to gape
   At the Leg in clambering over!

O blessed nature, "O rus! O rus!"
Who cannot sigh for the country thus,
    Absorbed in a worldly torpor—
Who does not yearn for its meadow-sweet breath,   1940
Untainted by care, and crime, and death,
And to stand sometimes upon grass or heath—
    That soul, spite of gold, is a pauper!

But to hail the pearly advent of morn,
And relish the odour fresh from the thorn,
    She was far too pamper'd a madam—
Or to joy in the daylight waxing strong,
While, after ages of sorrow and wrong,
The scorn of the proud, the misrule of the strong,
And all the woes that to man belong,   1950
The lark still carols the self-same song
    That he did to the uncurst Adam!

The Lark! she had given all Leipsic's flocks
For a Vauxhall tune in a musical box;
    And as for the birds in the thicket,
Thrush or ousel in leafy niche,
The linnet or finch, she was far too rich
To care for a Morning Concert to which
    She was welcome without any ticket.

Gold, still gold, her standard of old,   1960
All pastoral joys were tried by gold,
    Or by fancies golden and crural—
Till ere she had pass'd one week unblest,
As her agricultural Uncle's guest,
Her mind was made up and fully imprest
    That felicity could not be rural!

And the Count?—to the snow-white lambs at play,
And all the scents and the sights of May,
    And the birds that warbled their passion,
His ears, and dark eyes, and decided nose,   1970
Were as deaf and as blind and as dull as those
That overlook the Bouquet de Rose,

The Huile Antique,
And Parfum Unique,
In a Barber's Temple of Fashion.

To tell, indeed, the true extent
Of his rural bias so far it went
   As to covet estates in ring fences—
And for rural lore he had learn'd in town
That the country was green, turn'd up with brown,   1980
And garnish'd with trees that a man might cut down
   Instead of his own expenses.

And yet had that fault been his only one,
The Pair might have had few quarrels or none,
   For their tastes thus far were in common;
But faults he had that a haughty bride
With a Golden Leg could hardly abide—
Faults that would even have roused the pride
   Of a far less metalsome woman!

It was early days indeed for a wife,   1990
In the very spring of her married life,
   To be chill'd by its wintry weather—
But instead of sitting as Love-Birds do,
Or Hymen's turtles that bill and coo—
Enjoying their "moon and honey for two"
   They were scarcely seen together!

In vain she sat with her Precious Leg
A little exposed, *à la* Kilmansegg,
   And roll'd her eyes in their sockets!
He left her in spite of her tender regards,   2000
And those loving murmurs described by bards,
For the rattling of dice and the shuffling of cards,
   And the poking of balls into pockets!

Moreover he loved the deepest stake
And the heaviest bets the players would make;
   And he drank—the reverse of sparely,—

And he used strange curses that made her fret;
And when he play'd with herself at piquet,
    She found, to her cost,
    For she always lost,   2010
  That the Count did not count quite fairly.

And then came dark mistrust and doubt,
Gather'd by worming his secrets out,
  And slips in his conversations—
Fears, which all her peace destroy'd,
That his title was null—his coffers were void—
And his French Château was in Spain, or enjoy'd
  The most airy of situations.

But still his heart—if he had such a part—
She—only she—might possess his heart,   2020
  And hold his affections in fetters—
Alas! that hope, like a crazy ship,
Was forced its anchor and cable to slip
When, seduced by her fears, she took a dip
  In his private papers and letters.

Letters that told of dangerous leagues;
And notes that hinted as many intrigues
  As the Count's in the "Barber of Seville"—
In short such mysteries came to light,
That the Countess-Bride, on the thirtieth night,   2030
Woke and started up in affright,
And kick'd and scream'd with all her might,
And finally fainted away outright,
  For she dreamt she had married the Devil!

Her Misery

Who hath not met with home-made bread,
A heavy compound of putty and lead—
And home-made wines that rack the head,
  And home-made liqueurs and waters?
Home-made pop that will not foam,
And home-made dishes that drive one from home,   2040

Not to name each mess,
For the face or dress,
Home-made by the homely daughters?

Home-made physic, that sickens the sick;
Thick for thin and thin for thick;—
In short each homogeneous trick
For poisoning domesticity?
And since our Parents, called the First,
A little family squabble nurst,
Of all our evils the worst of the worst   2050
Is home-made infelicity.

There's a Golden Bird that claps its wings,
And dances for joy on its perch, and sings
With a Persian exaltation:
For the Sun is shining into the room,
And brightens up the carpet-bloom,
As if it were new, bran new from the loom,
Or the lone Nun's fabrication.

And thence the glorious radiance flames
On pictures in massy gilded frames—   2060
Enshrining, however, no painted Dames,
But portraits of colts and fillies—
Pictures hanging on walls which shine,
In spite of the bard's familiar line,
With clusters of "gilded lilies."

And still the flooding sunlight shares
Its lustre with gilded sofas and chairs,
That shine as if freshly burnish'd—
And gilded tables, with glittering stocks
Of gilded china, and golden clocks,   2070
Toy, and trinket, and musical box,
That Peace and Paris have furnish'd.

And lo! with the brightest gleam of all
The glowing sunbeam is seen to fall
On an object as rare as splendid—

The golden foot of the Golden Leg
Of the Countess—once Miss Kilmansegg—
    But there all sunshine is ended.

Her cheek is pale, and her eye is dim,
And downward cast, yet not at the limb,   2080
    Once the centre of all speculation;
But downward drooping in comfort's dearth,
As gloomy thoughts are drawn to the earth—
Whence human sorrows derive their birth—
    By a moral gravitation.

Her golden hair is out of its braids,
And her sighs betray the gloomy shades
    That her evil planet revolves in—
And tears are falling that catch a gleam
So bright as they drop in the sunny beam,   2090
That tears of *aqua regia* they seem,
    The water that gold dissolves in!

Yet, not in filial grief were shed
    Those tears for a mother's insanity;
Nor yet because her father was dead,
For the bowing Sir Jacob had bow'd his head
    To Death—with his usual urbanity;
The waters that down her visage rill'd
Were drops of unrectified spirit distill'd
    From the limbeck of Pride and Vanity.   2100

Tears that fell alone and uncheckt,
Without relief, and without respect,
Like the fabled pearls that the pigs neglect,
    When pigs have that opportunity—
And of all the griefs that mortals share,
The one that seems the hardest to bear
    Is the grief without community.

How bless'd the heart that has a friend
A sympathising ear to lend
    To troubles too great to smother!   2110

260

For as ale and porter, when flat, are restored
Till a sparkling bubbling head they afford,
So sorrow is cheer'd by being pour'd
   From one vessel into another.

But friend or gossip she had not one
To hear the vile deeds that the Count had done,
   How night after night he rambled;
And how she had learn'd by sad degrees
That he drank, and smoked, and worse than these,
   That he "swindled, intrigued, and gambled."   2120

How he kiss'd the maids, and sparr'd with John;
And came to bed with his garments on;
   With other offences as heinous—
And brought *strange* gentlemen home to dine,
That he said were in the Fancy Line,
And they fancied spirits instead of wine,
   And call'd her lap-dog "Wenus."

He brought strange gentlemen home to dine

Of "making a book" how he made a stir,
But never had written a line to her,
   Once his idol and Cara Sposa: 2130
And how he had storm'd, and treated her ill,
Because she refused to go down to a mill,
She didn't know where, but remember'd still
   That the Miller's name was Mendoza.

How often he waked her up at night,
And oftener still by the morning light,
   Reeling home from his haunts unlawful;
Singing songs that shouldn't be sung,
Except by beggars and thieves unhung—
Or volleying oaths, that a foreign tongue   2140
   Made still more horrid and awful!

How oft, instead of otto of rose,
With vulgar smells he offended her nose,
   From gin, tobacco, and onion!
And then how wildly he used to stare!
And shake his fist at nothing, and swear,—
And pluck by the handful his shaggy hair,
Till he look'd like a study of Giant Despair
   For a new Edition of Bunyan!

For dice will run the contrary way,   2150
As well is known to all who play,
   And cards will conspire as in treason:
And what with keeping a hunting-box,
        Following fox—
        Friends in flocks,
        Burgundies, Hocks,
        From London Docks;
        Stultz's frocks,
        Manton and Nock's
        Barrels and locks,   2160
        Shooting blue rocks,
        Trainers and jocks,
        Buskins and socks,

Pugilistical knocks,
And fighting-cocks,
If he found himself short in funds and stocks,
   These rhymes will furnish the reason!

His friends, indeed, were falling away—
Friends who insist on play or pay—
And he fear'd at no very distant day   2170
   To be cut by Lord and by cadger,
As one who was gone or going to smash,
For his checks no longer drew the cash,
Because, as his comrades explain'd in flash,
   "He had overdrawn his badger."

Gold, gold—alas! for the gold
Spent where souls are bought and sold,
   In Vice's Walpurgis revel!
Alas! for muffles, and bulldogs, and guns,
The leg that walks, and the leg that runs,   2180
All real evils, though Fancy ones,
When they lead to debt, dishonour, and duns,
   Nay, to death, and perchance the devil!

Alas! for the last of a Golden race!
Had she cried her wrongs in the market-place,
   She had warrant for all her clamour—
For the worst of rogues, and brutes, and rakes,
Was breaking her heart by constant aches,
With as little remorse as the Pauper who breaks
   A flint with a parish hammer!   2190

Her Last Will

Now the Precious Leg while cash was flush,
Or the Count's acceptance worth a rush,
   Had never excited dissension;
But no sooner the stocks began to fall,
Than, without any ossification at all,
The limb became what people call
   A perfect bone of contention.

For alter'd days brought alter'd ways,
And instead of the complimentary phrase,
　　So current before her bridal—　　　　　　2200
The Countess heard, in language low,
That her Precious Leg was precious slow,
A good 'un to look at but bad to go,
　　And kept quite a sum lying idle.

That instead of playing musical airs,
Like Colin's foot in going up-stairs—
　　As the wife in the Scottish ballad declares—
　　It made an infernal stumping.
Whereas a member of cork, or wood,
Would be lighter and cheaper and quite as good,　　2210
　　Without the unbearable thumping.

P'rhaps she thought it a decent thing
To shew her calf to cobbler and king,
　　But nothing could be absurder—
While none but the crazy would advertise
Their gold before their servants' eyes,
Who of course some night would make it a prize,
　　By a Shocking and Barbarous Murder.

But spite of hint, and threat, and scoff,
　　The Leg kept its situation:　　　　　　2220
For legs are not to be taken off
　　By a verbal amputation.

And mortals when they take a whim,
The greater the folly the stiffer the limb
　　That stands upon it or by it—
So the Countess, then Miss Kilmansegg,
At her marriage refused to stir a peg,
Till the Lawyers had fastened on her Leg,
　　As fast as the Law could tie it.

Firmly then—and more firmly yet—　　　　　2230
With scorn for scorn, and with threat for threat,
　　The Proud One confronted the Cruel:

And loud and bitter the quarrel arose,
Fierce and merciless—one of those,
With spoken daggers, and looks like blows,
   In all but the bloodshed a duel!

Rash, and wild, and wretched, and wrong,
Were the words that came from Weak and Strong,
   Till madden'd for desperate matters,
Fierce as tigress escaped from her den,   2240
She flew to her desk—'twas open'd—and then,
In the time it takes to try a pen,
Or the clerk to utter his slow Amen,
   Her Will was in fifty tatters!

Where there's a *will* there's a way

But the Count, instead of curses wild,
Only nodded his head and smiled,
As if at the spleen of an angry child;
   But the calm was deceitful and sinister!

A lull like the lull of the treacherous sea—
For Hate in that moment had sworn to be   2250
The Golden Leg's sole Legatee,
  And that very night to administer!

Her Death

'Tis a stern and startling thing to think
How often mortality stands on the brink
  Of its grave without any misgiving:
And yet in this slippery world of strife,
In the stir of human bustle so rife,
There are daily sounds to tell us that Life
  Is dying, and Death is living!

Ay, Beauty the Girl, and Love the Boy,   2260
Bright as they are with hope and joy,
  How their souls would sadden instanter,
To remember that one of those wedding bells,
Which ring so merrily through the dells,
      Is the same that knells
      Our last farewells,
  Only broken into a canter!

But breath and blood set doom at nought—
How little the wretched Countess thought,
  When at night she unloosed her sandal,   2270
That the Fates had woven her burial-cloth,
And that Death, in the shape of a Death's Head Moth,
  Was fluttering round her candle!

As she look'd at her clock of or-molu,
For the hours she had gone so wearily through
  At the end of a day of trial—
How little she saw in her pride of prime
The Dart of Death in the Hand of Time—
  That hand which moved on the dial!

As she went with her taper up the stair,   2280
How little her swollen eye was aware
  That the Shadow which follow'd was double!
Or when she closed her chamber door,

It was shutting out, and for evermore,
　　The world—and its worldly trouble.

Little she dreamt, as she laid aside
Her jewels—after one glance of pride—
　　They were solemn bequests to Vanity—
Or when her robes she began to doff,
That she stood so near to the putting off　　　　　　　2290
　　Of the flesh that clothes humanity.

And when she quench'd the taper's light,
How little she thought as the smoke took flight,
That her day was done—and merged in a night
　　Of dreams and duration uncertain—
　　　　　Or, along with her own,
　　　　　That a Hand of Bone
　　Was closing mortality's curtain!

But life is sweet, and mortality blind,
And youth is hopeful, and Fate is kind　　　　　　2300
　　In concealing the day of sorrow;
And enough is the present tense of toil—
For this world is, to all, a stiffish soil—
And the mind flies back with a glad recoil
　　From the debts not due till to-morrow.

Wherefore else does the Spirit fly
And bid its daily cares good-bye,
　　Along with its daily clothing?
Just as the felon condemned to die—
　　With a very natural loathing—　　　　　　2310
Leaving the Sheriff to dream of ropes,
From his gloomy cell in a vision elopes,
To caper on sunny greens and slopes,
　　Instead of the dance upon nothing.

Thus, even thus, the Countess slept,
While Death still nearer and nearer crept,
　　Like the Thane who smote the sleeping—
But her mind was busy with early joys,
Her golden treasures and golden toys,

That flash'd a bright   2320
    And golden light
Under lids still red with weeping.

The golden doll that she used to hug!
Her coral of gold, and the golden mug!
    Her godfather's golden presents!
The golden service she had at her meals,
The golden watch, and chain, and seals,
Her golden scissors, and thread, and reels,
    And her golden fishes and pheasants!

The golden guineas in silken purse—   2330
And the Golden Legends she heard from her nurse,
    Of the Mayor in his gilded carriage—
And London streets that were paved with gold—
And the Golden Eggs that were laid of old—
        With each golden thing
        To the golden ring
    At her own auriferous Marriage!

And still the golden light of the sun
Through her golden dream appear'd to run,
Though the night that roar'd without was one   2340
    To terrify seamen or gipsies—
While the moon, as if in malicious mirth,
Kept peeping down at the ruffled earth,
As though she enjoyed the tempest's birth,
    In revenge of her old eclipses.

But vainly, vainly, the thunder fell,
For the soul of the Sleeper was under a spell
    That time had lately embitter'd—
The Count, as once at her foot he knelt—
That Foot which now he wanted to melt!   2350
But—hush!—'twas a stir at her pillow she felt—
    And some object before her glitter'd.

'Twas the Golden Leg!—she knew its gleam!
And up she started, and tried to scream,—
    But ev'n in the moment she started—

Down came the limb with a frightful smash,
And, lost in the universal flash
That her eyeballs made at so mortal a crash,
    The Spark, called Vital, departed!

        *   *   *   *

Gold, still gold! hard, yellow, and cold,   2360
For gold she had lived, and she died for gold—
By a golden weapon—not oaken;
In the morning they found her all alone—
Stiff, and bloody, and cold as stone—
But her Leg, the Golden Leg was gone,
    And the "Golden Bowl was broken!"

Gold—still gold! it haunted her yet—
At the Golden Lion the Inquest met—
    Its foreman, a carver and gilder—
And the Jury debated from twelve till three   2370
What the Verdict ought to be,
And they brought it in as Felo de Se,
    "Because her own Leg had killed her!"

Bed time

Her Moral

Gold! Gold! Gold! Gold!
Bright and yellow, hard and cold,
Molten, graven, hammer'd, and roll'd;
Heavy to get, and light to hold;
Hoarded, barter'd, bought, and sold,
Stolen, borrow'd, squander'd, doled:
Spurn'd by the young, but hugg'd by the old   2380
To the very verge of the churchyard mould;
Price of many a crime untold;
Gold! Gold! Gold! Gold:
Good or bad a thousand-fold!
   How widely its agencies vary—
To save—to ruin—to curse—to bless—
As even its minted coins express,
Now stamp'd with the image of Good Queen Bess,
   And now of a Bloody Mary!

Going to settle

V   Poems of Social Protest

Ode to H. Bodkin, Esq.

Secretary to the Society for the Suppression of Mendicity

"This is your charge—you shall comprehend all vagrom men."
Much Ado About Nothing

1

Hail, King of Shreds and Patches, hail,
  Disperser of the Poor!
Thou Dog in office, set to bark
  All beggars from the door!

2

Great overseer of overseers,
  And Dealer in old rags!
Thy public duty never fails,
  Thy ardour never flags!

3

Oh, when I take my walks abroad,
  How many Poor I *miss!*   10
Had Doctor Watts walk'd now a days
  He would have written this!

4

So well thy Vagrant catchers prowl,
  So clear thy caution keeps
The path—O, Bodkin, sure thou hast
  The eye that never sleeps!

5

No Belisarius pleads for alms,
  No Benbow lacketh legs;
The pious man in black is now
  The only man that begs!   20

6

Street-Handels are disorganiz'd,
  Disbanded every band!—
The silent *scraper* at the door
  Is scarce allow'd to stand!

7

The Sweeper brushes with his broom,
  The Carstairs with his chalk
Retires,—the Cripple leaves his stand,
  But cannot sell his walk.

8

The old Wall-blind resigns the wall,
  The Camels hide their humps,   30
The Witherington without a leg
  Mayn't beg upon his stumps!

9

Poor Jack is gone, that used to doff
  His batter'd tatter'd hat,
And show his dangling sleeve, alas!
  There seem'd no arm in that!

10

Oh! was it such a sin to air
  His true blue naval rags,
Glory's own trophy, like St. Paul,
  Hung round with holy flags!   40

11

Thou knowest best. I meditate,
  My Bodkin, no offence!
Let us, henceforth, but guard our pounds,
  Thou dost protect our pence!

12

Well art thou pointed 'gainst the Poor,
  For, when the Beggar Crew

Bring their petitions, thou art paid,
   Of course, to "run them through."

13

Doubtless thou art what Hamlet meant—
   To wretches the last friend;   50
What ills can mortals have, they can't
   "With a bare *Bodkin*" end?

Ode to Mr. Malthus

A child's *call* to be disposed of

My dear, do pull the bell,
    And pull it well,
And send those noisy children all up stairs,
    Now playing here like bears—
You George, and William, go into the grounds,
Charles, James, and Bob are there,—and take your string,
    Drive horses, or fly kites, or any thing,
You're quite enough to play at hare and hounds,—
    You little May, and Caroline, and Poll,
        Take each your doll,   10
    And go, my dears, into the two-back pair,
        Your sister Margaret's there—
Harriet and Grace, thank God, are both at school,
        At far off Ponty Pool—
I want to read, but really can't get on—
Let the four twins, Mark, Matthew, Luke, and John,
    Go—to their nursery—go—I never can
    Enjoy my Malthus among such a clan!

    Oh, Mr. Malthus, I agree
    In every thing I read with thee!   20
    The world's too full, there is no doubt,

And wants a deal of thinning out,—
It's plain—as plain as Harrow's Steeple—
And I agree with some thus far,
Who say the King's too popular,
That is,—he has too many people.

There are too many of all trades,
   Too many bakers,
Too many every-thing-makers,
But not too many undertakers,—   30
   Too many boys,—
Too many hobby-de-hoys,—
Too many girls, men, widows, wives, and maids,—
There is a dreadful surplus to demolish,
   And yet some Wrongheads,
   With thick not long heads,
   Poor metaphysicians!
   Sign petitions
Capital punishment to abolish;
And in the face of censuses such vast ones   40
   New hospitals contrive,
   For keeping life alive,
Laying first stones, the dolts! instead of last ones!—
Others, again, in the same contrariety,
Deem that of all Humane Society
   They really deserve the thanks,
Because the two banks of the Serpentine,
   By their design,
   Are Saving Banks.

Oh! were it given but to me to weed,   50
   The human breed,
And root out here and there some cumbering elf,
   I think I could go through it,
   And really do it
With profit to the world and to myself,—
For instance, the unkind among the Editors,
   My debtors, those I mean to say
   Who cannot or who will not pay,
   And all my creditors.

Laying the first stone of a hospital

These, for my own sake, I'd destroy;   60
But for the world's, and every one's,
I'd hoe up Mrs. G——'s two sons,
And Mrs. B——'s big little boy,
Call'd only by herself an "only joy."
As Mr. Irving's chapel's not too full,
    Himself alone I'd pull—
But for the peace of years that have to run,
I'd make the Lord Mayor's a perpetual station,
    And put a period to rotation,
    By rooting up all Aldermen but one,—   70
These are but hints what good might thus be done!
    But ah! I fear the public good
    Is little by the public understood,—

For instance—if with flint, and steel, and tinder,
Great Swing, for once a philanthropic man,
Proposed to throw a light upon thy plan,
No doubt some busy fool would hinder
His burning all the Foundling to a cinder.

Or, if the Lord Mayor, on an Easter Monday,
    That wine and bun-day, 80
Proposed to poison all the little Blue-coats,
Before they died by bit or sup,
Some meddling Marplot would blow up,
    Just at the moment critical,
    The economy political
Of saving their fresh yellow plush and new coats.

    Equally 'twould be undone,
    Suppose the Bishop of London,
      On that great day
      In June or May, 90
When all the large small family of charity,
    Brown, black, or carrotty,
Walk in their dusty parish shoes,
In too, too many two-and-twos,
To sing together till they scare the walls
    Of old St. Paul's,
Sitting in red, grey, green, blue, drab, and white,
    Some say a gratifying sight,
    Tho' I think sad—but that's a schism—
    To witness so much pauperism— 100
Suppose, I say, the Bishop then, to make
In this poor overcrowded world more room,
    Proposed to shake
Down that immense extinguisher, the dome—
Some humane Martin in the charity *Gal*-way
    I fear would come and interfere,
    Save beadle, brat, and overseer,
    To walk back in their parish shoes,
    In too, too many two-and-twos,
Islington—Wapping—or Pall Mall way! 110

Fancy portrait—Mr. Malthus

Thus, people hatch'd from goose's egg,
Foolishly think a pest, a plague,
And in its face their doors all shut,
On hinges oil'd with cajeput—
Drugging themselves with drams well spiced and cloven,
    And turning pale as linen rags
    At hoisting up of yellow flags,
While you and I are crying "Orange Boven!"
Why should we let precautions so absorb us,
Or trouble shipping with a quarantine—   120
When if I understand the thing you mean,
We ought to *import* the Cholera Morbus!

A rocking horse

Answer to Pauper

Don't tell *me* of buds and blossoms,
Or with rose and vi'let wheedle—
Nosegays grow for other bosoms,
Churchwarden and Beadle.
What have you to do with streams?
What with sunny skies, or garish
Cuckoo-song, or pensive dreams?—
Nature's not your Parish!

What right have such as you to dun
For sun or moon-beams, warm or bright?   10
Before you talk about the sun,
Pay for window-light!
Talk of passions—amorous fancies?
While your betters' flames miscarry—
If *you* love your Dolls and Nancys,
Don't we *make* you marry?

Talk of wintry chill and storm,
Fragrant winds, that blanch your bones!
You poor can always keep you warm,—
An't there breaking stones?   20
Suppose you don't enjoy the spring,
Roses fair and vi'lets meek—
You cannot look for everything
On eighteen-pence a week!

With seasons what have you to do?—
If corn doth thrive, or wheat is harm'd?—
What's weather to the cropless? You
Don't farm—but you are farm'd!
Why everlasting murmurs hurl'd,
With hardship for the text?—   30
If such as you don't like this world—
We'll pass you to the next.
                              Overseer

A Lay of Real Life

"Some are born with a wooden spoon in their mouths, and some with a golden ladle."
Goldsmith

"Some are born with tin rings in their noses, and some with silver ones."
Silversmith

Who ruined me ere I was born,
Sold every acre, grass or corn,
And left the next heir all forlorn?
                    My Grandfather.

Who said my mother was no nurse,
And physicked me and made me worse,
Till infancy became a curse?
                    My Grandmother.

Who left me in my seventh year,
A comfort to my mother dear,   10
And Mr. Pope, the overseer?
                    My Father.

Who let me starve, to buy her gin,
Till all my bones came through my skin,
Then called me "ugly little sin?"
                    My Mother.

Who said my mother was a Turk,
And took me home—and made me work,
But managed half my meals to shirk?
                    My Aunt.   20

Who "of all earthly things" would boast,
"He hated others' brats the most,"
And therefore made me feel my post?
                    My Uncle.

Who got in scrapes, an endless score,
And always laid them at my door,
Till many a bitter bang I bore?
                    My Cousin.

Who took me home when mother died,
Again with father to reside,   30
Black shoes, clean knives, run far and wide?
              My Stepmother.

Who marred my stealthy urchin joys,
And when I played cried "What a noise!"—
Girls always hector over boys—
              My Sister.

Who used to share in what was mine,
Or took it all, did he incline,
'Cause I was eight, and he was nine?
              My Brother.   40

Who stroked my head, and said "Good lad,"
And gave me sixpence, "all he had;"
But at the stall the coin was bad?
              My Godfather.

Who, gratis, shared my social glass,
But when misfortune came to pass,
Referr'd me to the pump? Alas!
              My Friend.

Through all this weary world, in brief,
Who ever sympathised with grief,   50
Or shared my joy—my sole relief?
              Myself.

Ode to Rae Wilson, Esquire

Close, close your eyes with holy dread,
And weave a circle round him thrice;
For he on honey-dew hath fed,
And drunk the milk of Paradise!   —*Coleridge*

It's very hard them kind of men
Won't let a body be.   —*Old Ballad*

A wanderer, Wilson, from my native land,
Remote, O Rae, from godliness and thee,
Where rolls between us the eternal sea,
Besides some furlongs of a foreign sand,—
Beyond the broadest Scotch of London Wall;
Beyond the loudest Saint that has a call;
Across the wavy waste between us stretch'd,
A friendly missive warns me of a stricture,
Wherein my likeness you have darkly etch'd,
And tho' I have not seen the shadow sketch'd,   10
Thus I remark prophetic on the picture.

I guess the features:—in a line to paint
Their moral ugliness, I'm not a saint.
Not one of those self-constituted saints,
Quacks—not physicians—in the cure of souls,
Censors who sniff out mortal taints,
And call the devil over his own coals—
Those pseudo Privy Councillors of God,
Who write down judgments with a pen hard-nibb'd;
     Ushers of Beelzebub's Black Rod,   20
Commending sinners, not to ice thick-ribb'd,
But endless flames, to scorch them up like flax,—
Yet sure of heav'n themselves, as if they'd cribb'd
Th' impression of St. Peter's keys in wax!

Of such a character no single trace
Exists, I know, in my fictitious face;
There wants a certain cast about the eye;
A certain lifting of the nose's tip;
A certain curling of the nether lip,
In scorn of all that is, beneath the sky;   30
In brief it is an aspect deleterious,

A face decidedly not serious,
A face profane, that would not do at all
To make a face at Exeter Hall,—
That Hall where bigots rant, and cant, and pray,
And laud each other face to face,
Till ev'ry farthing-candle *ray*
Conceives itself a great gas-light of grace!

Well!—be the graceless lineaments confest!
I do enjoy this bounteous beauteous earth;   40
    And dote upon a jest
"Within the limits of becoming mirth;"—
No solemn sanctimonious face I pull,
Nor think I'm pious when I'm only bilious—
Nor study in my sanctum supercilious
To frame a Sabbath Bill or forge a Bull.
I pray for grace—repent each sinful act—
Peruse, but underneath the rose, my Bible;
And love my neighbour, far too well, in fact,
To call and twit him with a godly tract   50
That's turn'd by application to a libel.
My heart ferments not with the bigot's leaven,
All creeds I view with toleration thorough,
And have a horror of regarding heaven
    As anybody's rotten borough.

What else? no part I take in party fray,
With tropes from Billingsgate's slang-whanging tartars,
I fear no Pope—and let great Ernest play
At Fox and Goose with Fox's Martyrs!
I own I laugh at over-righteous men,   60
I own I shake my sides at ranters,
And treat sham-Abr'am saints with wicked banters,
I even own, that there are times—but then
It's when I've got my wine—I say d —— canters!

I've no ambition to enact the spy
On fellow souls, a Spiritual Pry—
'Tis said that people ought to guard their noses

Who thrust them into matters none of theirs;
And, tho' no delicacy discomposes
Your Saint, yet I consider faith and pray'rs   70
Amongst the privatest of men's affairs.

I do not hash the Gospel in my books,
And thus upon the public mind intrude it,
As if I thought, like Otaheitan cooks,
No food was fit to eat till I had chew'd it.
On Bible stilts I don't affect to stalk;
Nor lard with Scripture my familiar talk,—
    For man may pious texts repeat,
And yet religion have no inward seat;
'Tis not so plain as the old Hill of Howth,   80
A man has got his bellyfull of meat
Because he talks with victuals in his mouth!

Mere verbiage,—it is not worth a carrot!
Why, Socrates or Plato—where's the odds?—
Once taught a jay to supplicate the Gods,
And made a Polly-theist of a Parrot!

A mere professor, spite of all his cant, is
    Not a whit better than a Mantis,—
An insect, of what clime I can't determine,
That lifts its paws most parson-like, and thence,   90
By simple savages—thro' sheer pretence—
Is reckon'd quite a saint amongst the vermin.

But where's the reverence, or where the *nous*,
To ride on one's religion thro' the lobby,
    Whether as stalking-horse or hobby,
To show its pious paces to "the House"?

I honestly confess that I would hinder
The Scottish member's legislative rigs,
    That spiritual Pinder,
Who looks on erring souls as straying pigs,   100
That must be lash'd by law, wherever found,

And driv'n to church as to the parish pound.
I do confess, without reserve or wheedle,
I view that grovelling idea as one
Worthy some parish clerk's ambitious son,
A charity-boy who longs to be a beadle.

On such a vital topic sure 'tis odd
How much a man can differ from his neighbour:
One wishes worship freely giv'n to God,
Another wants to make it statute-labour—   110
The broad distinction in a line to draw,
As means to lead us to the skies above,
You say—Sir Andrew and his love of law,
And I—the Saviour with his law of love.

Spontaneously to God should tend the soul,
Like the magnetic needle to the Pole;
But what were that intrinsic virtue worth,
Suppose some fellow, with more zeal than knowledge,
    Fresh from St. Andrew's College,
Should nail the conscious needle to the north?   120

I do confess that I abhor and shrink
From schemes, with a religious willy-nilly,
That frown upon St. Giles's sins, but blink
The peccadilloes of all Piccadilly—
My soul revolts at such a bare hypocrisy,
And will not, dare not, fancy in accord
The Lord of Hosts with an Exclusive Lord
    Of this world's aristocracy.
It will not own a notion so unholy,
As thinking that the rich by easy trips   130
May go to heav'n, whereas the poor and lowly
Must work their passage, as they do in ships.

One place there is—beneath the burial sod
Where all mankind are equalized by death;
Another place there is—the Fane of God,
Where all are equal who draw living breath;—
Juggle who will *elsewhere* with his own soul,

Playing the Judas with a temporal dole—
He who can come beneath that awful cope,
In the dread presence of a Maker just,   140
Who metes to ev'ry pinch of human dust
One even measure of immortal hope—
He who can stand within that holy door,
With soul unbow'd by that pure spirit-level,
And frame unequal laws for rich and poor,—
Might sit for Hell and represent the Devil!

Such are the solemn sentiments, O Rae,
In your last Journey-Work, perchance, you ravage,
Seeming, but in more courtly terms, to say
I'm but a heedless, creedless, godless, savage;   150
A very Guy, deserving fire and faggots,—
     A Scoffer, always on the grin,
And sadly given to the mortal sin
Of liking Mawworms less than merry maggots!

The humble records of my life to search,
I have not herded with mere pagan beasts;
But sometimes I have "sat at good men's feasts,"
And I have been "where bells have knoll'd to church."
Dear bells! how sweet the sounds of village bells
When on the undulating air they swim!   160
Now loud as welcomes! faint, now, as farewells!
And trembling all about the breezy dells,
As flutter'd by the wings of Cherubim.
Meanwhile the bees are chaunting a low hymn;
And lost to sight th' extatic lark above
Sings, like a soul beatified, of love,—
With, now and then, the coo of the wild pigeon;—
O Pagans, Heathens, Infidels, and Doubters!
If such sweet sounds can't woo you to religion,
Will the harsh voices of church cads and touters?   170

A man may cry Church! Church! at ev'ry word,
With no more piety than other people—
A daw's not reckon'd a religious bird
Because it keeps a-cawing from a steeple.

The Temple is a good, a holy place,
But quacking only gives it an ill savour;
While saintly mountebanks the porch disgrace,
And bring religion's self into disfavour!

Behold yon servitor of God and Mammon,
Who, binding up his Bible with his Ledger,   180
    Blends Gospel texts with trading gammon,
A black-leg saint, a spiritual hedger,
Who backs his rigid Sabbath, so to speak,
Against the wicked remnant of the week,
A saving bet against his sinful bias—
"Rogue that I am," he whispers to himself,
"I lie—I cheat—do anything for pelf,
But who on earth can say I am not pious?"

In proof how over-righteousness re-acts,
Accept an anecdote well bas'd on facts.   190

One Sunday morning—(at the day don't fret)—
In riding with a friend to Ponder's End
Outside the stage, we happen'd to commend
A certain mansion that we saw To Let.
"Aye," cried our coachman, with our talk to grapple,
"You're right! no house along the road comes nigh it!
'Twas built by the same man as built yon chapel,
    And master wanted once to buy it,—
But t'other driv the bargain much too hard—
    He ax'd sure-*ly* a sum purdigious!   200
But being so particular religious,
Why, *that,* you see, put master on his guard!"

    Church is "a little heav'n below,
  I have been there and still would go,"—
Yet I am none of those who think it odd
    A man can pray unbidden from the cassock,
      And, passing by the customary hassock,
Kneel down remote upon the simple sod,
And sue in formâ pauperis to God.

As for the rest,—intolerant to none,   210
Whatever shape the pious rite may bear,
Ev'n the poor Pagan's homage to the Sun
I would not harshly scorn, lest even there
I spurn'd some elements of Christian pray'r—
An aim, tho' erring, at a "world ayont"—
Acknowledgment of good—of man's futility,
A sense of need, and weakness, and indeed
That very thing so many Christians want—
          Humility.

Such, unto Papists, Jews, or turban'd Turks,   220
Such is my spirit—(I don't mean my wraith!)
Such, may it please you, is my humble faith;
I know, full well, you do not like my *works!*

I have not sought, 'tis true, the Holy Land,
As full of texts as Cuddie Headrigg's mother,
          The Bible in one hand,
And my own common-place-book in the other—
But you have been to Palestine—alas!
Some minds improve by travel, others, rather,
          Resemble copper wire, or brass,   230
Which gets the narrower by going farther!
Worthless are all such Pilgrimages—very!
If Palmers at the Holy Tomb contrive
The human heats and rancour to revive
That at the Sepulchre they ought to bury.
A sorry sight it is to rest the eye on,
To see a Christian creature graze at Sion,
Then homeward, of the saintly pasture full,
Rush bellowing, and breathing fire and smoke,
At crippled Papistry to butt and poke,   240
Exactly as a skittish Scottish bull
Hunts an old woman in a scarlet cloke?

Why leave a serious, moral, pious home,
Scotland, renown'd for sanctity of old,
Far distant Catholics to rate and scold

For—doing as the Romans do at Rome?
With such a bristling spirit wherefore quit
The Land of Cakes for any land of wafers,
About the graceless images to flit,
And buzz and chafe importunate as chafers,   250
Longing to carve the carvers to Scotch collops—?
People who hold such absolute opinions
Should stay at home, in Protestant dominions,
   Not travel like male Mrs. Trollopes.

   Gifted with noble tendency to climb,
     Yet weak at the same time,
Faith is a kind of parasitic plant,
That grasps the nearest stem with tendril-rings;
And as the climate and the soil may grant,
So is the sort of tree to which it clings.   260
Consider, then, before, like Hurlothrumbo,
You aim your club at any creed on earth,
That, by the simple accident of birth,
You might have been High Priest to Mumbo Jumbo.

For me—thro' heathen ignorance perchance,
Not having knelt in Palestine,—I feel
None of that griffinish excess of zeal,
Some travellers would blaze with here in France.
Dolls I can see in Virgin-like array,
Nor for a scuffle with the idols hanker   270
Like crazy Quixotte at the puppets' play,
If their "offence be rank," should mine be *rancour?*
Mild light, and by degrees, should be the plan
To cure the dark and erring mind;
But who would rush at a benighted man,
And give him two black eyes for being blind?

Suppose the tender but luxuriant hop
Around a canker'd stem should twine,
What Kentish boor would tear away the prop
So roughly as to wound, nay kill the bine?   280

The images, 'tis true, are strangely dress'd,
With gauds and toys extremely out of season;
The carving nothing of the very best,
The whole repugnant to the eye of reason,
Shocking to Taste, and to Fine Arts a treason—
Yet ne'er o'erlook in bigotry of sect
One truly *Catholic,* one common form,
       At which uncheck'd
All Christian hearts may kindle or keep warm.

Say, was it to my spirit's gain or loss,   290
One bright and balmy morning, as I went
From Liège's lovely environs to Ghent,
If hard by the wayside I found a cross,
That made me breathe a pray'r upon the spot—
While Nature of herself, as if to trace
The emblem's use, had trail'd around its base
The blue significant Forget-Me-Not?
Methought, the claims of charity to urge
More forcibly, along with Faith and Hope,
The pious choice had pitch'd upon the verge   300
       Of a delicious slope,
Giving the eye much variegated scope;—
"Look round," it whisper'd, "on that prospect rare,
Those vales so verdant, and those hills so blue;
Enjoy the sunny world, so fresh, and fair,
But"—(how the simple legend pierc'd me thro'!)
       "Priez pour les Malheureux."

With sweet kind natures, as in honey'd cells,
Religion lives, and feels herself at home;
But only on a formal visit dwells   310
Where wasps instead of bees have form'd the comb.

Shun pride, O Rae!—whatever sort beside
You take in lieu, shun spiritual pride!
A pride there is of rank—a pride of birth,
A pride of learning, and a pride of purse,

A London pride—in short, there be on earth
A host of prides, some better and some worse;
But of all prides, since Lucifer's attaint,
The proudest swells a self-elected Saint.

To picture that cold pride so harsh and hard,   320
Fancy a peacock in a poultry yard.
Behold him in conceited circles sail,
Strutting and dancing, and now planted stiff,
In all his pomp of pageantry, as if
He felt "the eyes of Europe" on his tail!
As for the humble breed retain'd by man,
     He scorns the whole domestic clan—
     He bows, he bridles,
     He wheels, he sidles,
At last, with stately dodgings, in a corner   330
He pens a simple russet hen, to scorn her
Full in the blaze of his resplendent fan!
    "Look here," he cries, (to give him words,)
    "Thou feather'd clay,—thou scum of birds!"
Flirting the rustling plumage in her eyes,—
"Look here, thou vile predestin'd sinner,
    Doom'd to be roasted for a dinner,
Behold these lovely variegated dyes!
These are the rainbow colours of the skies,
That heav'n has shed upon me *con amore*—   340
A Bird of Paradise?—a pretty story!
I am that Saintly Fowl, thou paltry chick!
    Look at my crown of glory!
Thou dingy, dirty, dabbled, draggled jill!"
And off goes Partlet, wriggling from a kick,
With bleeding scalp laid open by his bill!

That little simile exactly paints
How sinners are despis'd by saints.
By saints!—the Hypocrites that ope heav'n's door
Obsequious to the sinful man of riches—   350
But put the wicked, naked, barelegg'd poor,
    In parish stocks instead of breeches.

The Saints!—the Bigots that in public spout,
Spread phosphorus of zeal on scraps of fustian,
And go like walking "Lucifers" about
    Mere living bundles of combustion.

The Saints!—the aping Fanatics that talk
All cant and rant and rhapsodies highflown—
    That bid you baulk
    A Sunday walk,   360
And shun God's work as you should shun your own.

The Saints!—the Formalists, the extra pious,
Who think the mortal husk can save the soul,
By trundling, with a mere mechanic bias,
To church, just like a lignum-vitæ bowl!

The Saints!—the Pharisees, whose beadle stands
    Beside a stern coercive kirk,
    A piece of human mason-work,
Calling all sermons contrabands,
In that great Temple that's not made with hands!   370

Thrice blessed, rather, is the man with whom
The gracious prodigality of nature,
The balm, the bliss, the beauty, and the bloom,
The bounteous providence in ev'ry feature,
Recall the good Creator to his creature,
Making all earth a fane, all heav'n its dome!
To *his* tun'd spirit the wild heather-bells
    Ring Sabbath knells;
The jubilate of the soaring lark
    Is chaunt of clerk;   380
For Choir, the thrush and the gregarious linnet;
The sod's a cushion for his pious want;
And, consecrated by the heav'n within it,
    The sky-blue pool, a font.
Each cloud-capp'd mountain is a holy altar;
    An organ breathes in every grove;
    And the full heart's a Psalter,
Rich in deep hymns of gratitude and love!

Sufficiently by stern necessitarians
Poor Nature, with her face begrim'd by dust,   390
Is stok'd, cok'd, smok'd, and almost chok'd; but must
Religion have its own Utilitarians,
Labell'd with evangelical phylacteries,
To make the road to heav'n a railway trust,
And churches—that's the naked fact—mere factories?

Oh! simply open wide the Temple door,
And let the solemn, swelling, organ greet,
    With *Voluntaries* meet,
The *willing* advent of the rich and poor!
And while to God the loud Hosannas soar,   400
With rich vibrations from the vocal throng—
From quiet shades that to the woods belong,
    And brooks with music of their own,
Voices may come to swell the choral song
With notes of praise they learn'd in musings lone.

How strange it is while on all vital questions,
That occupy the House and public mind,
We always meet with some humane suggestions
Of gentle measures of a healing kind,
Instead of harsh severity and vigour,   410
The Saint alone his preference retains
    For bills of penalties and pains,
And marks his narrow code with legal rigour!
Why shun, as worthless of affiliation,
What men of all political persuasion
Extol—and even use upon occasion—
That Christian principle, conciliation?
But possibly the men who make such fuss
With Sunday pippins and old Trots infirm,
Attach some other meaning to the term,   420
       As thus:

One market morning, in my usual rambles,
Passing along Whitechapel's ancient shambles,

Where meat was hung in many a joint and quarter,
I had to halt awhile, like other folks,
    To let a killing butcher coax
A score of lambs and fatted sheep to slaughter.
A sturdy man he look'd to fell an ox,
Bull-fronted, ruddy, with a formal streak
Of well-greas'd hair down either cheek,   430
As if he dee-dash-dee'd some other flocks
Besides those woolly-headed stubborn blocks
That stood before him, in vexatious huddle—
Poor little lambs, with bleating wethers group'd,
While, now and then, a thirsty creature stoop'd
And meekly snuff'd, but did not taste the puddle.

Fierce bark'd the dog, and many a blow was dealt,
That loin, and chump, and scrag and saddle felt,
Yet still, that fatal step they all declin'd it,—
And shunn'd the tainted door as if they smelt   440
Onions, mint sauce, and lemon juice behind it.
At last there came a pause of brutal force,
    The cur was silent, for his jaws were full
    Of tangled locks of tarry wool,
The man had whoop'd and bellow'd till dead hoarse,
The time was ripe for mild expostulation,
And thus it stammer'd from a stander-by—
"Zounds!—my good fellow,—it quite makes me—why,
It really—my dear fellow—do just try
        Conciliation!"   450

    Stringing his nerves like flint,
The sturdy butcher seiz'd upon the hint,—
At least he seiz'd upon the foremost wether,—
And hugg'd and lugg'd and tugg'd him neck and crop
Just *nolens volens* thro' the open shop—
If tails come off he didn't care a feather,—
Then walking to the door, and smiling grim,
He rubb'd his forehead and his sleeve together—
    "There!—I've *con*ciliated him!"

Again—good-humouredly to end our quarrel—   460
    (Good humour should prevail!)
    I'll fit you with a tale
    Whereto is tied a moral.

Once on a time a certain English lass
Was seiz'd with symptoms of such deep decline,
Cough, hectic flushes, ev'ry evil sign,
That, as their wont is at such desperate pass,
The Doctors gave her over—to an ass.
Accordingly, the grisly Shade to bilk,
Each morn the patient quaff'd a frothy bowl   470
    Of asinine new milk,
Robbing a shaggy suckling of a foal
Which got proportionably spare and skinny—
Meanwhile the neighbours cried "poor Mary Ann!
She can't get over it! she never can!"
When lo! to prove each prophet was a ninny
The one that died was the poor wetnurse Jenny.

    To aggravate the case,
There were but two grown donkeys in the place;
And most unluckily for Eve's sick daughter,   480
The other long-ear'd creature was a male,
Who never in his life had given a pail
    Of milk, or even chalk and water.
No matter: at the usual hour of eight
Down trots a donkey to the wicket-gate,
With Mister Simon Gubbins on its back,—
"Your sarvant, Miss,—a werry spring-like day,—
Bad time for hasses tho'! good lack! good lack!
Jenny be dead, Miss,—but I'ze brought ye Jack,
He doesn't give no milk—but he can bray."   490

    So runs the story,
And, in vain self-glory,
Some Saints would sneer at Gubbins for his blindness—
But what the better are their pious saws
To ailing souls, than dry hee-haws,
    Without the milk of human kindness?

A Plain Direction

"Do you never deviate?"
John Bull

In London once I lost my way
In faring to and fro,
And ask'd a little ragged boy
The way that I should go;
He gave a nod, and then a wink,
And told me to get there
"Straight down the Crooked Lane,
And all round the Square."

Does your mother know you're out?

I box'd his little saucy ears,
And then away I strode;
But since I've found that weary path   10

297

Is quite a common road.
Utopia is a pleasant place,
But how shall I get there?
"Straight down the Crooked Lane,
And all round the Square."

I've read about a famous town
That drove a famous trade,
Where Whittington walk'd up and found
A fortune ready made.   20
The very streets are paved with gold;
But how shall I get there?
"Straight down the Crooked Lane,
And all round the Square."

I've read about a Fairy Land,
In some romantic tale,
Where Dwarfs if good are sure to thrive
And wicked Giants fail.
My wish is great, my shoes are strong,
But how shall I get there?   30
"Straight down the Crooked Lane,
And all round the Square."

I've heard about some happy Isle,
Where ev'ry man is free,
And none can lie in bonds for life
For want of L. S. D.
Oh that's the land of Liberty!
But how shall I get there?
"Straight down the Crooked Lane,
And all round the Square."   40

I've dreamt about some blessed spot,
Beneath the blessed sky,
Where Bread and Justice never rise
Too dear for folks to buy.
It's cheaper than the Ward of Cheap,
But how shall I get there?
"Straight down the Crooked Lane,
And all round the Square."

They say there is an ancient House,
As pure as it is old,   50
Where Members always speak their minds,
And votes are never sold.
I'm fond of all antiquities,
But how shall I get there?
"Straight down the Crooked Lane,
And all round the Square."

They say there is a Royal Court
Maintain'd in noble state,
Where ev'ry able man, and good,
Is certain to be great!   60
I'm very fond of seeing sights,
But how shall I get there?
"Straight down the Crooked Lane,
And all round the Square."

They say there is a Temple too,
Where Christians come to pray;
But canting knaves and hypocrites,
And bigots keep away.
O! that's the parish church for me!
But how shall I get there?   70
"Straight down the Crooked Lane,
And all round the Square."

They say there is a Garden fair,
That's haunted by the dove,
Where love of gold doth ne'er eclipse
The golden light of love—
The place must be a Paradise,
But how shall I get there?
"Straight down the Crooked Lane,
And all round the Square."   80

I've heard there is a famous Land
For public spirit known—
Whose Patriots love its interests
Much better than their own.

The Land of Promise sure it is!
But how shall I get there?
"Straight down the Crooked Lane,
And all round the Square."

I've read about a fine Estate,
A Mansion large and strong;   90
A view all over Kent and back,
And going for a song.
George Robins knows the very spot,
But how shall I get there?
"Straight down the Crooked Lane,
And all round the Square."

I've heard there is a Company
All formal and enroll'd,
Will take your smallest silver coin
And give it back in gold.   100
Of course the office door is mobb'd,
But how shall I get there?
"Straight down the Crooked Lane,
And all round the Square."

I've heard about a pleasant land,
Where omelettes grow on trees,
And roasted pigs run crying out,
"Come eat me, if you please."
My appetite is rather keen,
But how shall I get there?   110
"Straight down the Crooked Lane,
And all round the Square."

A Drop of Gin!

Gin! Gin! a Drop of Gin!
What magnified Monsters circle therein!
Ragged, and stained with filth and mud,
Some plague-spotted, and some with blood!
Shapes of Misery, Shame, and Sin!
Figures that make us loathe and tremble,
Creatures scarce human, that more resemble
Broods of diabolical kin,
Ghoule and Vampyre, Demon and Jin!

Gin! Gin! a Drop of Gin! 10
The dram of Satan! the liquor of Sin!—
    Distill'd from the fell
    Alembics of Hell,
By Guilt and Death, his own brother and twin!
    That Man might fall
    Still lower than all
The meanest creatures with scale and fin.
But hold—we are neither Barebones nor Prynne,
    Who lash'd with such rage
    The sins of the age; 20
Then, instead of making too much of a din,
    Let Anger be mute,
    And sweet Mercy dilute,
With a Drop of Pity, the Drop of Gin!

Gin! Gin! a Drop of Gin!—
When darkly Adversity's day's set in,
    And the friends and peers
    Of earlier years
Prove warm without, but cold within,—
    And cannot retrace 30
    A familiar face
That's steep'd in poverty up to the chin;—
But snub, neglect, cold-shoulder and cut
The ragged pauper, misfortune's butt,
Hardly acknowledg'd by kith and kin—
    Because, poor rat!
    He has no cravat;
A seedy coat, and a hole in that!—

The gin drop

No sole to his shoe, and no brim to his hat;
Nor a change of linen—except his skin:— 40
    No gloves—no vest,
    Either second or best;
And what is worse than all the rest,
No light heart, tho' his breeches are thin,—
    While Time elopes
    With all golden hopes,
And even with those of pewter and tin,—
    The brightest dreams,
    And the best of schemes,
All knock'd down, like a wicket by Mynn,— 50
    Each castle in air
    Seized by Giant Despair,
No prospect in life worth a minikin pin,—
    No credit—no cash,
    No cold mutton to hash,
    No bread—not even potatoes to mash;
No coal in the cellar, no wine in the binn,—
    Smash'd, broken to bits,
    With judgments and writs,
Bonds, bills, and cognovits, distracting the wits, 60
In the webs that the spiders of Chancery spin,—
    Till weary of life, its worry and strife;
    Black visions are rife of a razor, a knife,
Of poison—a rope—"louping over a linn."—
Gin! Gin! a Drop of Gin!
Oh! then its tremendous temptations begin,
    To take, alas!
    To the fatal glass,—
And happy the wretch that it does not win
    To change the black hue 70
    Of his ruin to blue—
While Angels sorrow, and Demons grin—
    And lose the rheumatic
    Chill of his attic
By plunging into the Palace of Gin!

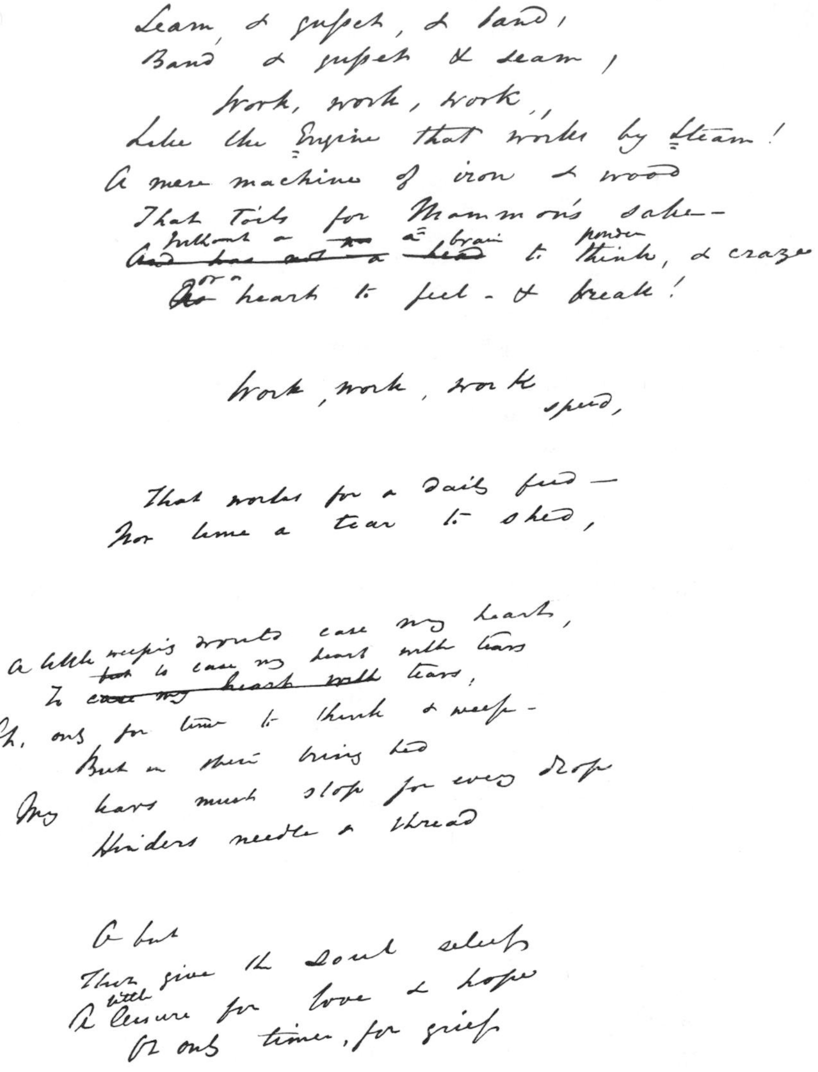

Facsimile of part of the manuscript of "The Song of the Shirt"

The Song of the Shirt

With fingers weary and worn,
  With eyelids heavy and red,
A Woman sat, in unwomanly rags,
  Plying her needle and thread—
    Stitch! stitch! stitch!
In poverty, hunger, and dirt,
  And still with a voice of dolorous pitch
She sang the "Song of the Shirt!"

  "Work! work! work!
While the cock is crowing aloof!   10
  And work—work—work,
Till the stars shine through the roof!
It's O! to be a slave
  Along with the barbarous Turk,
Where woman has never a soul to save,
  If this is Christian work!

  "Work—work—work
Till the brain begins to swim;
  Work—work—work
Till the eyes are heavy and dim!   20
Seam, and gusset, and band,
  Band, and gusset, and seam,
    Till over the buttons I fall asleep,
  And sew them on in a dream!

"O! Men, with Sisters dear!
  O! Men! with Mothers and Wives!
It is not linen you're wearing out,
  But human creatures' lives!
    Stitch—stitch—stitch,
  In poverty, hunger, and dirt,   30
Sewing at once, with a double thread,
  A Shroud as well as a Shirt.

"But why do I talk of Death?
  That Phantom of grisly bone,
I hardly fear his terrible shape,
  It seems so like my own—

It seems so like my own,
　　Because of the fasts I keep,
Oh! God! that bread should be so dear,
　　And flesh and blood so cheap!　　　　　　　　　　40

　　"Work—work—work!
　　My labour never flags;
And what are its wages? A bed of straw,
　　A crust of bread—and rags.
That shatter'd roof—and this naked floor—
　　A table—a broken chair—
And a wall so blank, my shadow I thank
　　For sometimes falling there!

　　"Work—work—work!
From weary chime to chime,　　　　　　　　　　　　50
　　Work—work—work—
As prisoners work for crime!
　　Band, and gusset, and seam,
　　Seam, and gusset, and band,
Till the heart is sick, and the brain benumb'd,
　　As well as the weary hand.

　　"Work—work—work,
In the dull December light,
　　And work—work—work,
When the weather is warm and bright—　　　　　　60
While underneath the eaves
　　The brooding swallows cling
As if to show me their sunny backs
　　And twit me with the spring.

　　"Oh! but to breathe the breath
Of the cowslip and primrose sweet—
　　With the sky above my head,
And the grass beneath my feet,
For only one short hour
　　To feel as I used to feel,　　　　　　　　　　　70
Before I knew the woes of want
　　And the walk that costs a meal!

"Oh but for one short hour!
 A respite however brief!
No blessed leisure for Love or Hope,
 But only time for Grief!
A little weeping would ease my heart,
 But in their briny bed
My tears must stop, for every drop
 Hinders needle and thread!"   80

With fingers weary and worn,
 With eyelids heavy and red,
A Woman sate in unwomanly rags,
 Plying her needle and thread—
  Stitch! stitch! stitch!
 In poverty, hunger, and dirt,
And still with a voice of dolorous pitch,
Would that its tone could reach the Rich!
 She sang this "Song of the Shirt!"

The Pauper's Christmas Carol

Full of drink and full of meat,
On our SAVIOUR's natal day,
CHARITY's perennial treat;
Thus I heard a Pauper say:—
"Ought not I to dance and sing
Thus supplied with famous cheer?
  Heigho!
  I hardly know—
Christmas comes but once a year!

"After labour's long turmoil,   10
Sorry fare and frequent fast,
Two-and-fifty weeks of toil,
Pudding-time is come at last!
But are raisins high or low,
Flour and suet cheap or dear?
  Heigho!
  I hardly know—
Christmas comes but once a year.

"Fed upon the coarsest fare
Three hundred days and sixty-four   20
But for *one* on viands rare,
Just as if I wasn't poor!
Ought not I to bless my stars,
Warden, clerk, and overseer?
  Heigho!
  I hardly know—
Christmas comes but once a year.

"Treated like a welcome guest,
 One of Nature's social chain,
Seated, tended on, and press'd—   30
But when shall I be press'd again,
Twice to pudding, thrice to beef,
A dozen times to ale and beer?
  Heigho!
  I hardly know,
Christmas comes but once a year!

"Come to-morrow how it will;
Diet scant and usage rough,
Hunger once has had its fill,
Thirst for once has had enough,   40
But shall I ever dine again?
Or see another feast appear?
          Heigho!
          I only know
Christmas comes but once a year.

"Frozen cares begin to melt,
Hopes revive and spirits flow—
Feeling as I have not felt
Since a dozen months ago—
Glad enough to sing a song—   50
To-morrow shall I volunteer?
          Heigho!
          I hardly know—
Christmas comes but once a year.

"Bright and blessed is the time,
Sorrows end and joys begin,
While the bells with merry chime
Ring the Day of Plenty in!
But the happy tide to hail
With a sigh or with a tear,   60
          Heigho!
          I hardly know—
Christmas comes but once a year!"

The modern Belinda

The Lady's Dream

The lady lay in her bed,
  Her couch so warm and soft,
But her sleep was restless and broken still;
  For turning often and oft
From side to side, she mutter'd and moan'd,
  And toss'd her arms aloft.

At last she startled up,
  And gaz'd on the vacant air,
With a look of awe, as if she saw
  Some dreadful phantom there—   10
And then in the pillow she buried her face
  From visions ill to bear.

The very curtain shook,
  Her terror was so extreme;
And the light that fell on the broider'd quilt
  Kept a tremulous gleam;
And her voice was hollow, and shook as she cried:—
  "Oh me! that awful dream!

"That weary, weary walk,
  In the churchyard's dismal ground!   20
And those horrible things, with shady wings,
  That came and flitted round,—
Death, death, and nothing but death,
  In every sight and sound!

"And oh! those maidens young,
  Who wrought in that dreary room,
With figures drooping and spectres thin,
  And cheeks without a bloom;—
And the Voice that cried, 'For the pomp of pride,
  We haste to an early tomb!   30

" 'For the pomp and pleasure of Pride,
  We toil like Afric slaves,
And only to earn a home at last,
  Where yonder cypress waves;'—
And then they pointed—I never saw
  A ground so full of graves!

"And still the coffins came,
  With their sorrowful trains and slow;
Coffin after coffin still,
  A sad and sickening show;   40
From grief exempt, I never had dreamt
  Of such a World of Woe!

"Of the hearts that daily break,
  Of the tears that hourly fall,
Of the many, many troubles of life,
  That grieve this earthly ball—
Disease and Hunger, and Pain, and Want,
  But now I dreamt of them all!

"For the blind and the cripple were there,
  And the babe that pined for bread,   50
And the houseless man, and the widow poor
  Who begged—to bury the dead;
The naked, alas, that I might have clad,
  The famished I might have fed!

"The sorrow I might have soothed,
  And the unregarded tears;
For many a thronging shape was there,
  From long forgotten years,
Aye, even the poor rejected Moor,
  Who rais'd my childish fears!   60

"Each pleading look, that long ago
  I scann'd with a heedless eye,
Each face was gazing as plainly there,
  As when I passed it by:
Woe, woe for me if the past should be
  Thus present when I die!

"No need of sulphureous lake,
  No need of fiery coal,
But only that crowd of human kind
  Who wanted pity and dole—   70

In everlasting retrospect—
　　Will wring my sinful soul!

"Alas! I have walked through life
　　Too heedless where I trod;
Nay, helping to trample my fellow worm,
　　And fill the burial sod—
Forgetting that even the sparrow falls
　　Not unmark'd of God!

"I drank the richest draughts;
　　And ate whatever is good—　　　　　　　　　　80
Fish, and flesh, and fowl, and fruit,
　　Supplied my hungry mood;
But I never remembered the wretched ones
　　That starve for want of food!

"I dressed as the noble dress,
　　In cloth of silver and gold,
With silk, and satin, and costly furs,
　　In many an ample fold;
But I never remembered the naked limbs
　　That froze with winter's cold.　　　　　　　　90

"The wounds I might have heal'd!
　　The human sorrow and smart!
And yet it never was in my soul
　　To play so ill a part:
But evil is wrought by want of Thought,
　　As well as want of Heart!"

She clasp'd her fervent hands,
　　And the tears began to stream;
Large, and bitter, and fast they fell,
　　Remorse was so extreme;　　　　　　　　　　100
And yet, oh yet, that many a Dame
　　Would dream the Lady's Dream!

313

The Workhouse Clock

An Allegory

There's a murmur in the air,
And noise in every street—
The murmur of many tongues,
The noise of numerous feet—
While round the Workhouse door
The Labouring Classes flock,
For why? the Overseer of the Poor
Is setting the Workhouse Clock.

Who does not hear the tramp
Of thousands speeding along   10
Of either sex and various stamp,
Sickly, crippled, or strong,
Walking, limping, creeping
From court, and alley, and lane,
But all in one direction sweeping
Like rivers that seek the main?

Who does not see them sally
From mill, and garret, and room,
In lane, and court and alley,
From homes in poverty's lowest valley,   20
Furnished with shuttle and loom—
Poor slaves of Civilization's galley—
And in the road and footways rally,
As if for the Day of Doom?
Some, of hardly human form,
Stunted, crooked, and crippled by toil;
Dingy with smoke and dust and oil,
And smirch'd besides with vicious soil,
Clustering, mustering, all in a swarm.
Father, mother, and careful child,   30
Looking as if it had never smiled—
The Sempstress, lean, and weary, and wan,
With only the ghosts of garments on—
The Weaver, her sallow neighbour,
The grim and sooty Artisan;
Every soul—child, woman, or man,
Who lives—or dies—by labour.

314

Stirred by an overwhelming zeal,
And social impulse, a terrible throng!
Leaving shuttle, and needle, and wheel,   40
Furnace, and grindstone, spindle, and reel,
Thread, and yarn, and iron, and steel—
Yea, rest and the yet untasted meal—
Gushing, rushing, crushing along,
A very torrent of Man!
Urged by the sighs of sorrow and wrong,
Grown at last to a hurricane strong,
Stop its course who can!
Stop who can its onward course
And irresistible moral force;   50
O! vain and idle dream!
For surely as men are all akin,
Whether of fair or sable skin,
According to Nature's scheme,
That Human Movement contains within
A Blood-Power stronger than Steam.

Onward, onward, with hasty feet,
They swarm—and westward still—
Masses born to drink and eat,
But starving amidst Whitechapel's meat,   60
And famishing down Cornhill!
Through the Poultry—but still unfed—
Christian Charity, hang your head!
Hungry—passing the Street of Bread;
Thirsty—the street of Milk;
Ragged—beside the Ludgate Mart,
So gorgeous, through Mechanic-Art,
With cotton, and wool, and silk!

At last, before that door
That bears so many a knock   70
Ere ever it opens to Sick or Poor,
Like sheep they huddle and flock—
And would that all the Good and Wise
Could see the Million of hollow eyes,

With a gleam deriv'd from Hope and the skies,
Upturn'd to the Workhouse Clock!

Oh! that the Parish Powers,
Who regulate Labour's hours,
The daily amount of human trial,
Weariness, pain, and self-denial   80
Would turn from the artificial dial
That striketh ten or eleven,
And go, for once, by that older one
That stands in the light of Nature's sun,
And takes its time from Heaven!

The Bridge of Sighs

"Drown'd! drown'd!"   —*Hamlet*

One more Unfortunate,
Weary of breath,
Rashly importunate,
Gone to her death!

Take her up tenderly,
Lift her with care;
Fashion'd so slenderly,
Young, and so fair!

Look at her garments
Clinging like cerements;   10
Whilst the wave constantly
Drips from her clothing;
Take her up instantly,
Loving, not loathing.—

Touch her not scornfully;
Think of her mournfully,
Gently and humanly;
Not of the stains of her,
All that remains of her
Now is pure womanly.   20

Make no deep scrutiny
Into her mutiny
Rash and undutiful:
Past all dishonour,
Death has left on her
Only the beautiful.

Still, for all slips of hers,
One of Eve's family—
Wipe those poor lips of hers
Oozing so clammily.   30

Loop up her tresses
Escaped from the comb,

Her fair auburn tresses;
Whilst wonderment guesses
Where was her home?

Who was her father?
Who was her mother?
Had she a sister?
Had she a brother?
Or was there a dearer one   40
Still, and a nearer one
Yet, than all other?

Alas! for the rarity
Of Christian charity
Under the sun!
Oh! it was pitiful!
Near a whole city full,
Home she had none.

Sisterly, brotherly,
Fatherly, motherly   50
Feelings had changed:
Love, by harsh evidence,
Thrown from its eminence;
Even God's providence
Seeming estranged.

Where the lamps quiver
So far in the river,
With many a light
From window and casement,
From garret to basement,   60
She stood, with amazement,
Houseless by night.

The bleak wind of March
Made her tremble and shiver;
But not the dark arch,
Or the black flowing river:

Mad from life's history,
Glad to death's mystery,
Swift to be hurl'd—
Any where, any where   70
Out of the world!

In she plunged boldly,
No matter how coldly
The rough river ran,—
Over the brink of it,
Picture it—think of it,
Dissolute Man!
Lave in it, drink of it,
Then, if you can!

Take her up tenderly,   80
Lift her with care;
Fashion'd so slenderly,
Young, and so fair!

Ere her limbs frigidly
Stiffen too rigidly,
Decently,—kindly,—
Smoothe, and compose them;
And her eyes, close them,
Staring so blindly!

Dreadfully staring   90
Thro' muddy impurity,
As when with the daring
Last look of despairing
Fix'd on futurity.

Perishing gloomily,
Spurr'd by contumely,
Cold inhumanity,
Burning insanity,
Into her rest.—
Cross her hands humbly,   100

As if praying dumbly,
Over her breast!

Owning her weakness,
Her evil behaviour,
And leaving, with meekness,
Her sins to her Saviour!

The Lay of the Labourer

A spade! a rake! a hoe!
  A pickaxe, or a bill!
A hook to reap, or a scythe to mow,
  A flail, or what ye will—
And here's a ready hand
  To ply the needful tool,
And skill'd enough, by lessons rough,
  In Labour's rugged school.

To hedge, or dig the ditch,
  To lop or fell the tree,   10
To lay the swarth on the sultry field,
  Or plough the stubborn lea;
The harvest stack to bind,
  The wheaten rick to thatch,
And never fear in my pouch to find
  The tinder or the match.

To a flaming barn or farm
  My fancies never roam;
The fire I yearn to kindle and burn
  Is on the hearth of Home;   20
Where children huddle and crouch
  Through dark long winter days,
Where starving children huddle and crouch,
  To see the cheerful rays,
A-glowing on the haggard cheek,
  And not in the haggard's blaze!

To Him who sends a drought
  To parch the fields forlorn,
The rain to flood the meadows with mud,
  The blight to blast the corn,   30
To Him I leave to guide
  The bolt in its crooked path,
To strike the miser's rick, and show
  The skies blood-red with wrath.

A spade! a rake! a hoe!
  A pickaxe, or a bill!

A hook to reap, or a scythe to mow,
   A flail, or what ye will—
The corn to thrash, or the hedge to plash,
   The market-team to drive,   40
Or mend the fence by the cover side,
   And leave the game alive.

Ay, only give me work,
   And then you need not fear
That I shall snare his worship's hare,
   Or kill his grace's deer;
Break into his lordship's house,
   To steal the plate so rich;
Or leave the yeoman that had a purse
   To welter in a ditch.   50

Wherever Nature needs,
   Wherever Labour calls,
No job I'll shirk of the hardest work,
   To shun the workhouse walls;
Where savage laws begrudge
   The pauper babe its breath,
And doom a wife to a widow's life,
   Before her partner's death.

My only claim is this,
   With labour stiff and stark,   60
By lawful turn, my living to earn,
   Between the light and dark;
My daily bread, and nightly bed,
   My bacon, and drop of beer—
But all from the hand that holds the land,
   And none from the overseer!

No parish money, or loaf,
   No pauper badges for me,
A son of the soil, by right of toil
   Entitled to my fee.   70
No alms I ask, give me my task:
   Here are the arm, the leg,

The strength, the sinews of a Man,
   To work, and not to beg.

Still one of Adam's heirs,
   Though doom'd by chance of birth
To dress so mean, and to eat the lean,
   Instead of the fat of the earth;
To make such humble meals
   As honest labour can,   80
A bone and a crust, with a grace to God,
   And little thanks to man!

A spade! a rake! a hoe!
   A pickaxe, or a bill!
A hook to reap, or a scythe to mow,
   A flail, or what ye will—
Whatever the tool to ply,
   Here is a willing drudge,
With muscle and limb, and woe to him
   Who does their pay begrudge!   90

Who every weekly score
   Docks labour's little mite,
Bestows on the poor at the temple door,
   But robb'd them over night.
The very shilling he hoped to save,
   As health and morals fail,
Shall visit me in the New Bastile,
   The Spital, or the Gaol!

Suggestions by Steam

When Woman is in rags, and poor,
   And sorrow, cold, and hunger teaze her,
If Man would only listen more
   To that small voice that crieth—"Ease her!"

Without the guidance of a friend,
   Though legal sharks and screws attack her,
If Man would only more attend
   To that small voice that crieth—"Back her!"

So oft it would not be his fate
   To witness some despairing dropper   10
In Thames's tide, and run too late
   To that small voice that crieth—"Stop her!"

Stanzas

Farewell, Life! My senses swim;
And the world is growing dim;
Thronging shadows cloud the light,
Like the advent of the night,—
Colder, colder, colder still
Upward steals a vapour chill—
Strong the earthy odour grows—
I smell the Mould above the Rose!

Welcome, Life! the Spirit strives!
Strength returns, and hope revives;   10
Cloudy fears and shapes forlorn
Fly like shadows at the morn,—
O'er the earth there comes a bloom—
Sunny light for sullen gloom,
Warm perfume for vapour cold—
I smell the Rose above the Mould!

Abbreviations

Notes

Sources of Illustrations

Index of Titles and First Lines

General Index

_____

Abbreviations

Bohn	*The Pictorial Handbook of London,* Bohn's Illustrated Library (London, 1954)
Boswell's Johnson	*Boswell's Life of Johnson,* ed. R. W. Chapman (London, 1957)
CA	*Comic Annual* (1830-1839, 1842), 11 vols.
Clubbe, *VF*	John Clubbe, *Victorian Forerunner: The Later Career of Thomas Hood* (Durham, N.C., 1968)
DNB	*The Dictionary of National Biography,* ed. Sir Leslie Stephen, Sir Sidney Lee et al. (London, 1921-1922), 21 vols.
FMN	*Forget Me Not*
FO	*Friendship's Offering*
HM	*Hood's Monthly Magazine and Comic Miscellany* (1844-1845)
HO	Thomas Hood, *Hood's Own: or, Laughter from Year to Year* (London, 1839)
Jerrold, *TH*	Walter Jerrold, *Thomas Hood: His Life and Times* (New York, 1909)
LG	*Literary Gazette*
LM	*London Magazine*
LS	*Literary Souvenir*
Memorials	*Memorials of Thomas Hood,* ed. by his Daughter [Frances Freeling Broderip], with a preface and notes by his Son [Tom Hood] (London, 1860), 2 vols.
Morgan	Peter F. Morgan, "Thomas Hood's Literary Reading, as Shown in His Works," unpub. diss. (University of London, 1959)
NMM	*New Monthly Magazine*
O & A	[Thomas Hood and John Hamilton Reynolds,] *Odes and Addresses to Great People* (London, 1825; 3rd ed., 1826)
OED	*The Oxford English Dictionary* (Oxford, 1933), 12 vols.
Oxford Ed.	*The Complete Poetical Works of Thomas Hood,* ed., with notes, by Walter Jerrold (London, 1906). Oxford Edition
Partridge	Eric Partridge, *A Dictionary of Slang and Unconventional English,* vol. I, 6th ed. (London, 1967)
Percy	Thomas Percy, *Reliques of English Poetry,* with Memoir and Critical Dissertation by the Rev.

	George Gilfillan; text ed. by Charles Cowden Clarke (London, n.d.), 3 vols.
The Plea	Thomas Hood, *The Plea of the Midsummer Fairies, Hero and Leander, Lycus the Centaur, and other Poems* (London, 1827)
Poems (1846)	Thomas Hood, *Poems* (London, 1846), 2 vols.
Reid	J. C. Reid, *Thomas Hood* (London, 1963)
Timbs	John Timbs, *Curiosities of London* (London, 1855)
TLS	*Times Literary Supplement*
Tylney Hall	Thomas Hood, *Tylney Hall* (London, 1834), 3 vols.
W & O (1)	Thomas Hood, *Whims and Oddities* (London, 1826; 2nd ed., 1829)
W & O (2)	Thomas Hood, *Whims and Oddities, Second Series* (London, 1827; 2nd ed., 1829)
Whimsicalities	Thomas Hood, *Whimsicalities, A Periodical Gathering* (London, 1844), 2 vols.
Works	*The Works of Thomas Hood,* ed., with notes, by Tom Hood and Frances Freeling Broderip (London, 1869-1873), 10 vols.
Young	*Early Victorian England: 1830-1865,* ed. G. M. Young (London, 1934), 2 vols.
Whitley, "Keats and Hood"	Alvin Whitley, "Keats and Hood," *Keats-Shelley Journal,* V (Winter 1956), 33-47

Notes

In the notes to the poems, variant readings, including a few emendations, are given in a paragraph at the end of the notes to each poem. The head-note to each poem gives the date and place of first publication to the best of my knowledge. I mention that a poem was reprinted in *Poems* (1846) only if the poem was not republished in volume form during Hood's lifetime or if I have used a variant reading from this edition.

Introduction

1. Empson, *Seven Types of Ambiguity*, 3rd ed. (Norfolk, Conn., 1953), p. 110; *19th Century British Minor Poets*, ed., with an introduction, by W. H. Auden (New York, 1966), p. 17.
2. *The Victorian Temper* (New York, 1964), p. 10.
3. *Works*, VI, 412.
4. *Ibid.*, p. 386.
5. *Memorials*, II, 13–14; Thackeray, "On a Joke I once heard from the late Thomas Hood," *Roundabout Papers* (New York, 1885), pp. 71–72.
6. See Cornelius M. Cuyler, "Thomas Hood: An Illustration of the Transition from the Romantic to the Victorian Era," unpub. diss. (Johns Hopkins University, 1943), p. 267.
7. *The Poetical Works of Thomas Hood* (London, 1873), p. xxxi.
8. *Memorials*, I, 5.
9. *Ibid.*, p. 3.
10. *A Second Gallery of Literary Portraits* (New York, 1850), pp. 106, 104–105.
11. *Sonnets of this Century* (London, 1887), p. lv.
12. *The Listener*, 29 Aug. 1963, p. 320.
13. Whitley, "Keats and Hood," pp. 39, 43.
14. In his "Literary Reminiscences" of 1838 (*Works*, I, 452).
15. Reid, p. 241; Brander, *Thomas Hood* (London, 1963), p. 16.
16. *Works*, X, 32.
17. *Pen and Pencil* (New York, 1858), pp. 132, 134.
18. *Seven Types of Ambiguity*, p. 109.
19. See *The Letters of Charles Lamb*, ed. E. V. Lucas (London, 1935), III, 3–4, 7–8.
20. *Miscellaneous Prose*, ed. E. V. Lucas (London, 1912), I, 335.
21. "Hood's Poems," *Edinburgh Review*, LXXXVIII, no. clxviii (April 1846), 382, 383. The *Wellesley Index* attributes the article as "probably" by Leigh Hunt.
22. See "Miss Kilmansegg and Her Precious Leg," l. 1881 and note, p. 377.
23. For an account of Hood's dramatic career see Alvin Whitley, "Thomas Hood as a Dramatist," *University of Texas Studies in English*, XXX (1951), 184–201.
24. *Robert Browning* (London, 1952), p. 3.

25. See the brilliant exposition of this theme in Hood in John Heath-Stubbs, *The Darkling Plain* (London, 1950), pp. 49–61.
26. See, for example, H. F. Chorley's appreciative evaluation in the *London and Westminster Review*, XXIX, no. i (April 1838), 138–144.
27. *Letters,* ed. Lucas, III, 419–420.
28. *Letters of Thomas Hood from the Dilke Papers in the British Museum,* ed. Leslie A. Marchand (New Brunswick, 1945), pp. 15–17, 19–20, 22–23.
29. *Works,* VI, 413.
30. *HM,* III, no. vi (June 1845), 609–610. The writer is probably F. O. Ward.
31. *Athenaeum,* 17 Oct. 1840, p. 829. A modern diagnosis of Hood's health sees him suffering from an increasingly severe case of "pulmonary edema," with syphilis, perhaps contracted prenatally, as the main disease. In any account of Hood's achievements and failures, his health is a vital factor. It remains, in the end, the factor hardest to assess. For further comment, see Clubbe, *VF,* pp. 32, 229–231.
32. *Works,* IX, 37.
33. Whitley, p. 47.
34. Hood to Watson, 8 Oct. 1844, National Library of Scotland, Edinburgh. Alvin Whitley first established this point ("Keats and Hood," p. 33).
35. *Times,* 26 March 1844, p. 8.
36. *Works,* IX, 238.
37. N.s., XIX (March 1846), 293.
38. *Memorials,* II, 257. This letter to Peel was written in February 1845.
39. *Ibid.,* I, xvii.
40. *Times,* 20 July 1854, p. 10.

I. Romantic Poems

I remember, I remember

First published in the annual *FO,* 1826. Text: *The Plea.* Cf. John Hamilton Reynolds, "Stanzas on Revisiting Shrewsbury," beginning "I remember well the time,—the sweet school-boy time."

2: The house where I was born. Strictly speaking, the poem is not autobiographical. Hood was born in the Poultry, in the heart of London; when he was eight the family moved to Islington, then a suburb separated from London by green fields, and it is likely that he recalls memories of his life there. The idyllic landscapes and the memories of the lost innocence of childhood, which echo Wordsworth and Lamb, should be considered a poetic, rather than an autobiographical, recreation of childhood happiness.

Variants. 13: robin; *FO,* robins. 15: laburnum. Thus *FO. The Plea:* liburnam. 16: The tree; *FO, The tree.* 19: must rush; *FO,* would rush. 27: tops; *FO,* spires. 31: farther; *FO,* further.

A Retrospective Review

First published in the annual *LS*, 1827, signed. Text: *The Plea*. In the *LS* the poem has the motto "Ah that I were once more a careless child," which is l. 14 of Coleridge's "Sonnet to the River Otter." The disillusioned awakening into maturity in this poem, in "I remember, I remember," and in "The Ballad" contrasts dramatically with the savagely ironic memories of childhood education in the "Ode on a Distant Prospect of Clapham Academy." Cf. the opening lines with the clown Feste's concluding song in *Twelfth Night*, V, i, 398–417, beginning "When that I was and a little tiny boy." The title puns on the name of a contemporary journal.

7–8: A hoop was an eternal round / Of pleasure. Cf. Gray, "Ode on a Distant Prospect of Eton College," ll. 28–29: "What idle progeny succeed / To chase the rolling circle's [hoop's] speed . . ." (Morgan).

14–15: Elgin's lord . . . taw. Lord Elgin brought back to England from the Parthenon and the Erechtheum Greek sculptures, including the statue of Theseus, and sold them in 1812 to the British government. They were on public exhibit. Both Theseus and the "taw" are "marbles."

26: dumps. 1. "A roughly-cast leaden counter, used by boys in some games" (*OED*); 2. fits of melancholy or depression.

29: hoop. Hood puns on "whoop" (*LS*: whoop) and on a child's barrel-hoop, and possibly intends a further pun on "hoop" as "one of the iron arches used in croquet" (*OED*). Cf. "Ode on a Distant Prospect of Clapham Academy," l. 79.

30: call. In contemporary commercial usage a "call" was "a demand for the payment of money" (*OED*). Also a "whistle."

65: an Alexandrine child. The "Alexandrine child" or "formal man" (l. 64) might well be taller by one "foot" than the boy. Cf. l. 54 of the "Ode on a Distant Prospect of Clapham Academy": "And push us from our *forms!*"

66: A boy of larger growth. Cf. Dryden, *All for Love*, IV, i, 43: "Men are but children of a larger growth" (Morgan). Fond of the phrase, Hood uses it several times elsewhere.

68: sky-blue. Thin, watery milk with a bluish tint.

70: Turk. Uncouth brat.

72: fag. A boy in an English public school who acts as a servant for another boy in a higher form or class.

76: "kiss the rod." Cf. Prov. 13:24: "He that spareth his rod hateth his child: but he that loveth him chasteneth him betimes."

85: *omne bene*. The "all good." The context suggests that *"omne bene"* may be here either the Latin master's comment on his work or "the prize of merit," presumably the "silver pen" of l. 90.

91: home, sweet home. Popular song that first appeared in the opera *Clari, the Maid of Milan* (Covent Garden, 1823); words by John Howard Payne, music by Sir Henry Bishop.

96: No "satis" to the "jams." *Satis jam:* enough now. Cf. Horace, *Odes*, Book I, 2, l. 1 (*"Jam satis"*) and *Satires*, Book I, 5, l. 12 (*"Ohe! Jam satis est"*: "Ho! That is enough!"). Hood, his son recalls, "had a rare facility for twisting the classics" (*Memorials*, II, 125).

102: To cast a look behind. Cf. Gray's "Ode on a Distant Prospect of Eton College," 1. 38: "Still as they run they look behind" (Morgan).

Variants. 3 (and 99): blithe; *LS*, blythe. 29: hoop; *LS*, whoop. 55: O; *LS*, Oh (the next three stanzas also begin thus).

Fair Ines

First published in the *LM*, Jan. 1823, signed "H." Text: *The Plea*. The present third stanza was not included in the *LM* version.

1: O saw ye not fair Ines. Cf. Burns, "Oh saw ye bonnie Leslie" (Morgan).

Ruth

First published in the annual *FMN*, 1827. Holograph MS: Hood Collection, University of California, Los Angeles. Text: *The Plea*. Only the more important of the many textual variants are noted. This poem, like many others in *The Plea*, draws its immediate inspiration from Keats, in this instance from ll. 65–67 of the "Ode to a Nightingale," and ultimately, through Keats, from the book of Ruth. Hood's "patient maiden" Alvin Whitley finds "not unlike . . . [Wordsworth's] Solitary Reaper" ("Keats and Hood," p. 42).

Variants. 1: breast high amid; MS, breasthigh amidst; *FMN*, breast-high amidst. 4: glowing kiss; *FMN*, burning kiss. 5: cheek; MS, cheeks. 10: blackest; *FMN*, darkest. 12: That; MS, Which. 13–14: tressy forehead dim; *FMN*, forehead darkly dim. 15: amid; *FMN*, among. 16: sweetest looks; MS, grateful looks; *FMN*, her sweet looks.

The Sea of Death: A Fragment

First published in the *LM*, March 1822, signed * * *. Text: *The Plea*. Morgan notes: "Coleridge's poem 'Limbo,' though dated 1817, was not published until 1834, but there are striking resemblances between its subject, language, and form, the heroic couplet, and those of 'The Sea of Death' " (p. 597).

37–39: Time / Slept, as he sleeps upon the silent face / Of a dark dial in a sunless place. Cf. Coleridge, "Limbo," ll. 15–18 (Morgan), and Thomas Moore, "Love and the Sun-dial," ll. 1–2: "Young Love found a Dial once, in a dark shade, / Where man ne'er had wander'd nor sunbeam play'd."

Ode: Autumn

First published in the *LM*, Feb. 1823, signed "H." In this version the first two stanzas are combined. Text: *The Plea*. Of the many verbal parallels that exist between the poems of Hood and those of Keats, I have pointed out in the notes only a few of the more obvious. For an excellent, succinct discussion of Keats's influence upon Hood's poetic development, see Alvin Whitley, "Keats and Hood," 33–47; see also Federico Olivero, "Hood and Keats," *MLN,* XXVIII (Dec. 1913), 233–235. For fuller discussions see the relevant chapters in Morgan and Cornelius M. Cuyler, "Thomas Hood: An Illustration of the Transition from the Romantic to the Victorian Era," unpub. diss. (Johns Hopkins University, 1943). The model for this poem is obviously Keats's "To Autumn," but others of Keats's poems provide verbal echoes. Cf., for example, the first stanza with Keats's "Hyperion," ll. 1–14. Whitley presents a splendid comparative analysis of Hood's Ode and Keats's in his article (pp. 41–42).

3: no lonely bird would sing. Cf. Keats, "La Belle Dame sans Merci," l. 4: "And no birds sing." Cf. also Hood's "Autumn" ("The Autumn skies are flush'd with gold"), l. 5, and "Miss Kilmansegg and Her Precious Leg," ll. 1248–1251.

9: Where are the songs of Summer?—With the sun. *LM:* Where are the songs of day-light? In the sun. Cf. Keats, "To Autumn," l. 23: "Where are the songs of Spring? Ay, where are they?"

17: And tear with horny beak their lustrous eyes. Keats, "Ode to a Nightingale," l. 29: "Where Beauty cannot keep her lustrous eyes."

33–34: And honey bees have stor'd / The sweets of Summer in their luscious cells. Cf. Keats, "To Autumn," ll. 9–11: "And still more, later flowers for the bees . . . For Summer has o'er-brimmed their clammy cells."

36–37: But here the Autumn melancholy dwells, / And sighs her tearful spells. *LM:* Autumn Melancholy. Several critics have pointed out Hood's seeming inconsistency in the sex of "Autumn" (see l. 4, "his hollow ear") but, as Audrey Jennings observes (*TLS,* 26 June 1953, p. 413), the inconsistency disappears if the capitalized "Melancholy" of the *LM* version is considered the antecedent of "her." Jennings further suggests a comparison between Hood's "Melancholy" and Dürer's *Melencolia.*

39–40: Alone, alone, / Upon a mossy stone. Cf. Wordsworth, "She Dwelt among the Untrodden Ways," l. 5: "A violet by a mossy stone."

42: With the last leaves for a love-rosary. Cf. Keats, "Ode on Melancholy," l. 5: "Make not your rosary of yew-berries."

62: To frame her cloudy prison for the soul. Keats, "Ode on Melancholy," ll. 29–30: "His soul shall taste the sadness of her might, / And be among her cloudy trophies hung."

Variants. 2: Stand shadowless like Silence, listening; *LM,* Stand shadowless, like Silence listening. 9: Where are the songs of Summer?—With the sun; *LM,* Where are the songs of day-light? In the sun. 21: from her; *LM,* among. 24: all twinkling; *LM,* wind-wanton. 36: Autumn melancholy; *LM,* Autumn Melancholy. 39–40: Alone, alone, / Upon a mossy stone; *LM,* written as one line ("Alone—alone—upon a mossy stone"). The following line omitted in *The Plea:* "Until her drowsy feet forgotten be." 43: Whilst all the wither'd world looks drearily; *LM,* Whilst the all-wither'd world spreads drearily. 48: O go; *LM,* Aye, go. 51: and a face of care; *LM,* like a constant care. 53: and enough of gloom; *LM,* and eternal gloom. 56: living bloom; *LM,* exquisite bloom. 59: the earth; *LM,* this world.

Autumn ("The Autumn skies are flush'd with gold")

First publication and text: *The Plea.*

Autumn ("The Autumn is old")

First published in *FO,* 1826, signed. Text: *The Plea.*
Variant. 2: sere; *FO,* sear.

Ode to Melancholy

First publication and text: *The Plea.* "Hood's 'Ode to Melancholy,'" writes Alvin Whitley, "is not the fine soul's appreciative awareness of the fated death of beauty but rather a moral lament of 'Neglectful pride,' 'cankering scorn,' and 'honour's dearth' in the world of men and a memento that death knocks at every door, interwoven with distressing episodes of the deaths of mothers and lovers. Religious consolation is provided" ("Keats and Hood," p. 43). Whitley suggests that the poem was modeled on the octosyllabic couplets of "The Eve of St. Mark." Federico Olivero observes "that Keats's sadness [in the "Ode on Melancholy"] arises from excess of happiness, while Hood's feeling has its source in the fact that the aspirations of the soul are weighed down by the base tendencies of matter" (ll. 109–122). In addition, he finds the "rural setting" and the "contemplative attitude of mind" reminiscent of "Il Penseroso" ("Hood and Keats," *MLN,* XXVIII [Dec. 1913], 233). Several writers have pointed out the indebtedness of ll. 1–34 to Keats's "Ode to a Nightingale."

35: my mother. Although Hood's mother died in 1821, it is unlikely the poem is autobiographical.

47–52: Ay, let us think of Him . . . raven plume. "Him" is Charon. Cf. the canceled (and then unpublished) first stanza of Keats, "Ode on Melancholy," which, Léonie Villard conjectures, Hood has access to through Reynolds (*The Influence of Keats on Tennyson and Rossetti* [Paris, 1914], p. 20). Of Hood's imitations of Keats, George H. Ford writes: "they seem so obvious that one is tempted to wonder whether Hood imagined, in view of the neglect of Keats, that he could borrow openly without many readers becoming aware of it" (*Keats and the Victorians* [New Haven, 1944], p. 10).

64–66: the best, the worst . . . in one common ruin hurl'd. Cf. Pope, *Essay on Man, Epistle I,* ll. 88–89: "A hero perish, or a sparrow fall, / Atoms or systems into ruin hurl'd."

87: Dis. The Roman name of the Greek Pluto.

106: the lad. Endymion.

115–116: Like the sweet blossoms of the May, / Whose fragrance ends in must. Mustiness. Hood cannot resist a pun on "musk" (May / must).

121–122: There's not a string attun'd to mirth, / But has its chord in Melancholy. Cf. Keats, "Ode on Melancholy," ll. 25–26: "Ay, in the very temple of Delight / Veil'd Melancholy has her sovran shrine."

Song ("There is dew for the flow'ret")

First publication and text: *Memorials,* II (published in the section entitled "Literary Remains"). Tom Hood dates the poem 1825 and provides the following note: "The first two verses of this poem were written by my father, the last two were added by Barry Cornwall, at my mother's request, with a view to its being published with music" (*Works,* V, 104). The two stanzas by "Barry Cornwall" (Bryan Waller Procter) are as follows:

> There is care that will not leave us,
>   And pain that will not flee;
> But on our hearth, unalter'd,
>   Sits Love—'tween you and me.

> *Our* love, it ne'er was reckoned,
>   Yet good it is and true—
> It's *half* the world to me, dear,
>   It's *all* the world to you.

Ballad ("It was not in the winter")

First publication and text: *LS,* 1827, signed. Republished in *Poems* (1846), II, with the two final stanzas omitted; and in *Memorials,* II, with many changes in orthography and punctuation. Cf. Herrick, "To the Virgins to Make Much of Time."
Variant. 13: thy. Thus *Memorials; LS,* my.

Still glides the gentle streamlet on

First publication and text: *Tylney Hall,* II. Republished in *Poems* (1846), II, with the title "To_____." The Oxford Ed. gives the poem the title "The Streamlet." Cf. J. H. Reynolds, "Song" ("Go, where the water glideth gently ever"). Traditionally, the poem was for Jane Hood.
Variant. 4: do not; *Poems* (1846), never.

The Forsaken

Holograph MS: Hood Collection, University of California, Los Angeles. First publication and text: *The Plea.* Republished in *Works,* IV, 443–444, with the following note by Tom Hood: " 'The Forsaken,' however, which is noted in the commonplace book [of Thomas Hood] as 'for head of Madeline,' I imagine, from its date, must have appeared in some annual about this time [1824]."
9: My Mother. Although Hood's much-loved mother died in 1821, it is unlikely the poem is autobiographical.
Variants. 7: steal; MS, win. 11: loves; MS, love. 14: gray; MS, grey. 17: The useless lock; MS, That useless tress.

Queen Mab

First publication and text: *Works*, VI, 302–303. Tom Hood supplies the following note: "It was probably during this year [1834] that the little poem of 'Queen Mab' was written." Cf. Mercutio's long speech in *Romeo and Juliet*, I, iv, and Drayton's *Nymphidia*.

Lear

First publication and text: *Poems* (1846), II. Republished in *Works*, VIII, 254, with a note by Tom Hood indicating that the poem "was probably written earlier" than 1842.

False Poets and True

First publication and text: *Poems* (1846), II. Republished in the Oxford Ed. with the subtitle "To Wordsworth."

5–6: tho' they die / Obscur'd. Hood refers—and again in l. 13—to the recent deaths of Keats and Shelley; the poem has many echoes of Shelley's *Adonais*, which Hood read soon after its first publication.

13: lark and nightingale. Shelley ("To a Skylark") and Keats ("Ode to a Nightingale"). Cf. also Wordsworth, "To a Sky-lark" ("Ethereal minstrel!").

Sonnet Written in Keats's Endymion

First publication and text: *LM*, May 1823, signed "T." In this sonnet, deemed by Alvin Whitley ("Keats and Hood," p. 43) "Hood's finest Keatsian poem," Edward S. LeComte suggests that Hood was the first to call Keats Endymion (*Endymion in England* [New York, 1944], pp. 146–147).

Sonnet ("It is not death, that sometime in a sigh")

First published in the *LM*, June 1823, signed "T." Text: *The Plea*. The *LM* version is entitled "Death." Jerrold (*TH*, p. 200) compares the thought of this sonnet to George Eliot's "O may I join the choir invisible"; Whitley ("Keats and Hood," p. 41) suggests a comparison between the movement of this sonnet and Keats's "When I have fears that I may cease to be."

Variants. 1: sometime; *LM*, some time. 3: That sometime these bright stars, that now reply; *LM*, That some time the live stars, which now reply. 14: resurrection; *LM*, resurrections.

Sonnet: Silence

First published in the *LM*, Feb. 1823, signed "T." Text: *The Plea*. Jerrold (*TH*, p. 200) suggests a parallel between the opening lines of this poem and Byron, *Childe Harold's Pilgrimage*, IV, cxxviii, beginning, "There is a pleasure in the pathless woods." Hood's "deep deep sea" echoes Byron's "deep Sea," as his "wide desert" echoes Byron's "Desert" of the previous stanza.

Variant. 4: desert; *LM,* desart.

The Death-Bed

First publication and text: *Englishman's Magazine,* Aug. 1831. Republished in *Poems* (1846), II. In *Memorials,* I, 5, Tom Hood observed: "The lines entitled 'The Death-Bed' . . . were written at the time of her death" (Hood's sister Anne's in 1821). J. M. Cohen, however, states that Anne "lived on into old age" but offers no conclusive evidence ("Thomas Hood: The Language of Poetry," *TLS,* 19 Sept. 1952, p. 605). In *Works,* V, 102, Tom assigns the poem to the year 1825 and states that it was "not written before this time—nor yet can I think very much after . . . I remember very well that my father had no copy of this, and had lost sight of it until when, after his return to England [in 1840], he found it as a newspaper cutting in a scrap-book of Miss Lamb's—the sister of his old friend Elia . . . I cannot refrain from quoting entire the elegant Latin translation of these lines which appeared in the 'Times' shortly after my father's death [reprinted in *Works,* V, 102]. I have since learned they are from the pen of the Rev. H. Kynaston, Master of St. Paul's School." Tom notes further: "This poem, besides being lost sight of as mentioned above, has undergone much that is strange. The editor of a collection of English poetry [Francis Palgrave in early editions of *The Golden Treasury*] calmly dropt out the two middle verses as 'ingenious'; and Mrs. Stowe inserted it in 'Dred' with so much American assimilativeness that it might have passed for her own, and was indeed set to music as one of the 'Songs from Dred, by Mrs. Beecher Stowe.' "

The Ballad

First publication and text: *Juvenile Forget Me Not,* 1832. The poem, signed, recalls the earlier "I remember, I remember" and "A Retrospective Review." The accompanying engraving by William Chevalier, also entitled *The Ballad,* is based on a painting by Robert Farrier.

3–4: strips of song . . . hung along . . . old walls. In Hood's youth the long dead wall of Hyde Park (which later became open railing) was hung with ballads.

10: Newland's bills. I.e., Bank of England notes, after Abraham Newland, chief cashier of the Bank of England from 1782 to 1807.

19: In dismal sort. Feeling dismal.

20: "Chevy Chase." The "Ancient Ballad of Chevy Chase" celebrates a famous Border skirmish over hunting rights.

34: Babies in the Wood. In the ballad the babes, left in a wood, die during the night and Robin Redbreast covers them with leaves.

48: "an old song." Cf. *Twelfth Night,* II, iv, 3: "That old and antique song we heard last night."

II. Comic Poems

To a Critick

First publication and text: *LM*, Feb. 1822, signed "Anthony Rushtowne." The sonnet appeared in "The Lion's Head," the *LM*'s answers-to-correspondents column, which Hood directed. He introduced it thus: "The remonstrance of Juvenis is indeed pathetic; but in spite of the Sonnet which he has quoted in his behalf, we must adhere, though with regret, to our refusal; but if, as we suspect, he is Old Anthony himself, we shall be happy to hear from him again." In this poem, "The Fall of the Deer," and "The Carelesse Nurse Mayd," Hood imitates Thomas Chatterton's Rowley poems.

The Fall of the Deer

First published in the *LM*, Nov. 1822, in "The Lion's Head," untitled and unsigned. It was set in Gothic type and introduced with these words: "The following is taken, as Nimrod [C. J. Apperley] assures us, from a real 'Old Poem,' upon hunting, and indeed it has the appearance of having never been young." Text: *W & O* (1). I have noted only the more important of the many textual changes. The poem bears distant kinship to Wordsworth's "Hart-Leap Well" and perhaps also recalls William Cowper, *The Task*, III, 108–111.

7–8: the wild Stag how he stretches / The naturall Buck-skin of his Breeches. Cf. *As You Like It*, II, ii, 33–38: "a poor sequest'red stag . . . did stretch his leathern coat / Almost to bursting."

36: Under the Jawes of Dogges and Death. Cf. *King John*, V, ii, 113: "Even in the jaws of danger and of death."

Variants. 2: the Bark; *LM*, ye Bark. 3: The House Wife; *LM*, Ye Housewife. 6: Deer Dogges; *LM*, Deer-Dogs. 10: Bailiffes; *LM*, Bayliffs. 17: Silver Dish; *LM*, silver Dishe. 18: wish; *LM*, can wishe. 23: Faileth; *LM*, Failes. 24: From runninge slow he standeth faste; *LM*, He runs not slow but standeth faste. 29: Dogge; *LM*, Dog. 35: Craven; *LM*, Coward.

She is far from the land

First publication and text: *W & O* (1). The poem, which occurs in the middle of a prose sketch of this title, is a remote parody of Thomas Moore's song "She Is Far from the Land."

19: Sallee-men. Moorish pirate ships.

Ode on a Distant Prospect of Clapham Academy

First publication and text: *NMM*, April 1824, signed. Republished unchanged in *Poems* (1846), I. Hood attached to the title the note "No connexion with any other ode," and thus expected his readers to recall Thomas Gray's "Ode on a Distant Prospect of Eton College," which his poem frequently and closely echoes. Hood had received part of his education at Nicholas Wanostrocht's Academy for Young Gentlemen at Camberwell, and this academy he describes, with the locality changed, in the "Ode." Jerrold, *TH*, writes: "Seeing that Hood, when living at Camberwell, pointed the house out to his son, and that his son gives the master's name, it may safely be assumed that when the poet wrote his 'Ode' he purposely changed the locality to Clapham because the Alfred House Academy was then still flourishing" (p. 16). Furthermore, Clapham, a London suburb, was an Evangelical center and home of the "Clapham sect." Given Hood's life-long distaste for Evangelical religiosity, his choice of locale can hardly be accidental. Cf. Tom Hood's comments in *Memorials*, I, 6n, and *Works*, X, 23–24n, and Hood's own recollections of his education in the "Literary Reminiscences" of 1838 (*Works*, I, 451–453). Cf. also Lamb, "The Old Familiar Faces."

2: That classic house, those classic grounds. Gray's "Ode" begins, "Ye distant spires, ye antique towers." On the two poems see Donald J. Gray, "The Uses of Victorian Laughter," *Victorian Studies*, X, no. 2 (Dec. 1966), 169–170.

5: little captives. Cf. Gray, "Ode," l. 52: "little victims."

25: Mrs. S*** . . . (Like Pallas in the parlour). Hood recalls in the "Literary Reminiscences" his experiences at a preparatory school prior to his going to Wanostrocht's finishing school. "Accordingly, my memory presents but a very dim image of a pedagogical powdered head, amidst a more vivid group of females of a composite charter—part dry-nurse, part housemaid, and part governess,—with a matronly figure in the back ground, very like Mrs. S., allegorically representing, as Milton says, 'our universal mother.' But there is no glimpse of Minerva" (*Works*, I, 450). The "Mrs. S." referred to in the "Literary Reminiscences" is probably the famous tragic actress Sarah Kemble Siddons. It seems likely that Hood had the "Ode" before him when he wrote his "Literary Reminiscences."

28: The Little Crichtons. In the "Literary Reminiscences" Hood ironized: "And now, it may be reasonably asked, where I did learn anything if not at these establishments, which promise Universal Knowledge—extras included—and yet unaccountably produce so very few Admirable Crichtons" (*Works*, I, 452–453). The original Admirable Crichton was James Crichton (1560–1585?), who is reputed—at the age of seventeen—to have disputed on scientific questions in Paris in twelve languages.

30: bohea. Though considered a superior kind of black tea at the beginning of the eighteenth century, by the time Hood wrote it had become, being the last crop of the season, the least esteemed.

36: Love and Cottage-bread. Cf. note to l. 101 of "Miss Kilmansegg and Her Precious Leg," p. 364–365.

37–42: Randall . . . Carew. Presumably fictitious persons. In the "Literary Reminiscences" Hood remarks: "In spite of hundreds of associates, it has never happened to me, amongst the very many distinguished names connected with science or literature, to recognize *one* as belonging to a school-fellow" (*Works*, I, 453n).

44: "the Greys." The Royal Scots Greys (2nd Dragoons), raised in 1678.

47: the *wane* of life. Hood puns on "wain," much the more common spelling.

50: Owhyee. The Hawaiian Islands.

52: All, all are gone—the olden breed! Cf. the refrain of Lamb's "The Old Familiar Faces": "All, all are gone, the old familiar faces."

54: "And push us from our *forms!*" Cf. "A Retrospective Review," l. 64: "How can this formal man be styled . . ." Hood also puns on "forms" in the sense of "shape of the different parts of a body."

59: crony arms. British school slang for arms of a close friend.

65: Mac-Adamized. I.e., rendered level or easy.

79: at hoop. Playing croquet.

80: *fives*. A kind of handball.

81: taw. Large, fancy marble.

82: curvets. Leaps.

83: Cob. Both a short thickset horse and a fellow pupil.

95–96: Far happier is thy head that wears / That hat without a crown! Cf. *II Henry IV*, III, i, 30–31: "Then, happy low, lie down! / Uneasy lies the head that wears a crown."

105: *dumps*. See note to l. 26 of "A Retrospective Review," p. 333.

106: The Elgin marbles. Cf. "A Retrospective Review," ll. 14–15.

113: We look behind. Cf. Gray's "Ode," l. 38: "Still as they run they look behind."

117: sky-blue. Thin, watery milk with a bluish tint.

Faithless Sally Brown. An Old Ballad

First published in "The Lion's Head," *LM*, Feb. 1822, unsigned. Text: *W & O* (I). In the *LM* the poem was prefaced as follows: "We cannot sufficiently express our gratitude to Common Sense, jun., of Leeds, for the patience and skill with which he has attempted to couch the Eyes of Lion's Head. Will Common Sense, jun. frankly tell us, (in a *frank* if he pleases,) what we are to think of the following ballad?—" In *W & O* (1) it was prefaced thus:

> I have never been vainer of any verses than of my part in the following Ballad. Dr. [Isaac] Watts, amongst evangelical nurses [muses?], has an enviable renown—and Campbell's Ballads enjoy a snug genteel popularity. "Sally Brown" has been favoured, perhaps, with as wide a patronage as the Moral Songs [by Watts], though its circle may not have been of so select a class as the friends of [Campbell's] "Hohenlinden." But I do not desire to see it amongst what are called Elegant Extracts. The lamented [John] Emery,—drest as Tom Tug, sang it at his last mortal Benefit at Covent Garden;—and, ever since, it has been a great favourite with the watermen of Thames, who time their oars to it, as the wherrymen of Venice time theirs to the lines of Tasso. With the watermen, it went naturally to Vauxhall:—and over land, to Sadler's Wells. The Guards—not the mail coach, but the Life Guards,—picked it out from

a fluttering hundred of others—all going to one air—against the dead wall at Knightsbridge. Cheap Printers of Shoe Lane, and Cow-cross, (all pirates!) disputed about the Copyright, and published their own editions,—and, in the mean time, the Authors, to have made bread of their song, (it was poor old Homer's hard ancient case!) must have sung it about the streets. Such is the lot of Literature! the profits of "Sally Brown" were divided by the Ballad Mongers:—it has cost, but has never brought me, a half-penny.

In this preface Hood speaks of "my part in the following Ballad" and of "the Authors," thus implying that the poem is not his alone. His collaborator, if indeed he had one, was John Hamilton Reynolds. Although Reynolds' sister Charlotte claimed that each poet contributed alternate stanzas (*Letters of John Keats,* ed. M. Buxton Forman, 4th ed. [London, 1952], pp. xxxix–xl), in Reynolds' copy of the *LM,* now in the Keats House, Hampstead, the poem is marked "T. Hood." It seems unlikely that Reynolds' share went beyond a few verbal suggestions, for the poem has a unity which argues a single author. On the question of authorship see Reid, p. 73, and P. F. Morgan, "John Hamilton Reynolds and Thomas Hood," *Keats-Shelley Journal,* XI (Winter 1962), 88. Jerrold in the Oxford Ed. points out that about 1829 the ballad was set to "Wapping Time" by Jonathan Blewitt, as no. 2 of *The Ballad Singer.*

6: a press-gang crew. Name given to a body of men who formerly carried out the impressment of those liable to forced service in the army or navy. At this time impressment was used with much harshness and scandal to recruit men for the navy.

18: elf. I.e., "a poor devil."

28: Eye-water. 1. Natural tears; 2. gin (slang). W. H. Hudson, writing in 1915, deplored this "dreadful cockney pun."

30: old Benbow. Admiral John Benbow (1653–1702), British naval hero and subject of a popular song.

42: 'The virgin and the scales.' Both constellations (Virgo and Libra) are seen together and both are signs of the zodiac. Cf. *Paradise Lost,* X, 676: "By *Leo* and the *Virgin* and the *Scales.*"

51: Ben. I.e., sweetheart.

60: to pipe his eye. A colloquial usage for "to weep." In the *LM* this line has the following footnote: "Catullus has imitated this: Ad dominam solam usque pipi-abat. *Printer's Devil.*" Cf. Catullus, *Poems,* III, 1. 10: "it [Lesbia's sparrow] would keep on peeping to its mistress only."

Variant. 35: "The Tender-ship," cried Sally Brown; *LM,* The Tender, cried poor Sally Brown.

Faithless Nelly Gray. A Pathetic Ballad

First publication and text: *W & O* (1). This ballad, the Oxford Ed. points out, was set to music by Jonathan Blewitt, and published about 1829 as no. 4 of *The Ballad Singer.*

8: The Forty-second Foot. Or the Black Watch, now officially the Royal Highlanders.

11: wooden members. Hood scoffs at "wooden" members of Parliament.

15: his devours. I.e., his respects (French *devoirs*).

36: Badajos. Fortified city in Estremadura, southwest Spain. Wellington besieged and took the city from the French in 1812.

56: the Line. Also the regular, usually front-line troops in the British army.

62: nail. 1. Partridge cites J. H. Vaux, *Flash Dict.* (1812), "A person of an over-reaching, imposing disposition"—i.e., a "shrewdy," a crook—"is called a nail, a dead nail, a nailing rascal." 2. "A measure of weight for wool, beef, [cheese] etc. usually equal to eight pounds" (*OED*). Hood puns on both meanings.

68: With a *stake* in his inside. According to old custom, suicides were usually interred at crossroads on public highways, with a stake driven through the heart.

Mary's Ghost. A Pathetic Ballad

First publication and text: *W & O* (2). Like most of Hood's ballads, "Mary's Ghost" echoes and parodies past ballads, particularly "Sweet William's Ghost," "James Harris (The Daemon Lover)," and David Mallet's "Margaret's Ghost," an eighteenth-century refurbishing of "Fair Margaret and Sweet William." Cf. also John Lowe's popular "Mary's Dream." The ballad was set to music by Jonathan Blewitt and published as no. 1 of *The Ballad Singer*. Hood states in the preface to *W & O* (2) that "my hope persuades me that my illustrations cannot have degenerated, so ably as I have been seconded by Mr. Edward Willis." The accompanying woodcut to "Mary's Ghost," *Gin a Body meet a Body* (the title is from Burns's "Coming through the Rye") is not, as most of the others in the volume are, initialed "W" or "EW." It is presumably Hood's.

1–4: 'Twas in the middle of the night, / To sleep young William tried, / When Mary's ghost came stealing in, / And stood at his bed-side. Cf. "Margaret's Ghost," ll. 1–4: " 'Twas at the silent solemn hour, / When night and morning meet; / In glided Margaret's grimly ghost, / And stood at William's feet" (Percy, III, 273).

11: my long home. The grave. Eccles. 12:5.

13: The body-snatchers. Hood refers to the activities of the "Resurrection Men" or "Resurrectionists," though the poem antedates by several years the notorious William Burke and William Hare of Edinburgh, who in 1829 were convicted of rifling graves to sell the bodies for dissection by doctors and students at the School of Medicine. Cf. "Miss Kilmansegg and Her Precious Leg," l. 862 and note, p. 371.

18: chary. Cherished.

19: Mary-bone. Burial grounds attached to St. Mary-le-Bone (St. Mary-at-the-Bourne) at the end of High Street.

22: Dr. Vyse. Not definitely identified. Perhaps Vyse is an English spelling based on the pronunciation of the German name Weiss. (Hood's inability to read German at this time increases the likelihood of this possibility.) A John Weiss, M.D., practiced as an instrument-maker in London during the 1820's. He was the author of several works, including *An Account of inventions and improvements in Surgical Instruments, made by J. Weiss . . .*, which reached a second edition in 1831. Weiss was also an acquaintance of Sir Astley Cooper and probably of many other leading medical men, since they were his customers.

24: Guy's. Guy's Hospital in London.

27: Doctor Bell. Probably Sir Charles Bell (1774–1842), discoverer of the distinct functions of the sensory and motor nerves.

31: Bedford Row. In Holborn, about half a mile east-northeast of St. Paul's Cathedral.

32. the city. The most ancient part of London, the area around St. Paul's Cathedral.

34: Doctor Carpue. Joseph Constantine Carpue (1764–1846), surgeon to the National Vaccine Institution, lecturer at the Duke of York's hospital until 1832.

36: Pickford's van. Of Messrs. Pickford and Co. (the "Mr. P." of l. 37), the largest moving company in London. Their vans were a common London sight.

41: The cock it crows. The signal for ghosts to vanish. Cf. *Hamlet,* I, ii, 217–219: "But even then the morning cock crew loud, / And at the sound it [the Ghost of Hamlet's father] shrunk in haste away / And vanish'd from our sight."

44: Sir Astley. Sir Astley Cooper (1768–1841), famous surgeon and lecturer in anatomy at Guy's Hospital.

Tim Turpin. A Pathetic Ballad

First publication and text: *W & O* (2).

1: gravel blind. Cf. *The Merchant of Venice,* II, ii, 37–38; the clown Launcelot speaks of "my true-begotten father who, being more than sand-blind, high-gravel blind, knows me not"—i.e., something more than sand-blind and less than stone-blind. Cf. also Scott, *The Heart of Midlothian,* chap. 31.

5: like a Christmas pedagogue. Some kind of blindman's buff seems indicated. Perhaps Hood puns on St. Paul's saying that the Law, until "the faith which should afterward be revealed" came, was a pedagogue guiding men to Christ (Gal. 3:23).

15: like Pyramus. Who exchanged vows with Thisbe through a chink in the wall (a "wall-eye," l. 16) that separated the houses of their parents.

87: Horsham-drop. The trap-door of the gallows at Horsham, West Sussex, about forty miles from London.

Death's Ramble

First published in the *LG,* 9 June 1827, signed "T. H." Text: *W & O* (2). Tom Hood supplies the following note on the poem: "Mr. [William] Jerdan . . . tells me that it was suggested by an argument relative to the authorship of the 'Devil's Walk,' mentioned accidentally in connection with Holbein's [wood engravings of] 'The Dance of Death.' The poem was subsequently published separately, with coloured illustrations, by [Charles Joseph] Hullmandel" (*Works,* V, 157). In 1799 Coleridge and Southey coauthored a humorous satire, "The Devil's Thoughts" (which Southey expanded in 1827), describing the Devil promenading and delighting in the sight of human vices; their poem was imitated by Shelley in his "Devil's Walk" (1812) and by Byron in his "Devil's Drive" (1813). It is the Coleridge-Southey poem that prompted the "argument relative to the authorship," Southey having to defend his and Coleridge's joint authorship against the rival claim of Richard Porson.

15: the mutes. An old legal term for prisoners who, when arraigned for treason or felony, refused to plead or gave irrelevant answers.

43–44: "fee" / Was a prelude to "faw" and "fum." The nursery rhyme runs: "Fee, fi, fo, fum, / I smell the blood of an Englishman; / Be he alive or be he dead, / I'll grind his bones to make my bread." Cf. *King Lear,* III, iv, 188–189: "His [Childe Rowland's] word was still 'Fie, foh, and fum, / I smell the blood of a British man.' "

Variants. 36: summon'd; *LG, summon'd.* 43: that. Omitted in *LG* and *W & O* (2), 1st ed.

John Day. A Pathetic Ballad

First publication and text: *CA,* 1832. Republished in *HO.*

7: a Christmas box. A box in which contributions of money were collected at Christmas.

19: outsides. Outside passengers on a coach.

35–36: Coventry . . . to Stroud. Over sixty miles apart.

39: The course of love was never smooth. Cf. *A Midsummer Night's Dream,* I, i, 132: "The course of true love never did run smooth."

54: his being's link. A "link" was until the advent of gas illumination a torch for lighting people along the streets.

Variants. 11: thro'; *HO,* through. 15: though; *HO,* tho'. 20: hers. Thus *HO. CA:* her's.

Sally Simpkin's Lament; or, John Jones's Kit-Cat-Astrophe

First publication and text: *CA,* 1834. Republished in *HO.* The *OED* defines "simkin" (or "simpkin") as "a fool" and "kit-cat" as "a particular size of portrait, less than half-length, but including the hands" (see ll. 3–4). The motto that Hood cites from "Bryan and Pereene, A West-Indian Ballad" is not in the version given in Percy (I, 264–266) but is probably

Hood's comic variation of the following lines in the ballad: "When, ah! a shark bit through his waste: / His heart's blood died the main!"

A Waterloo Ballad

First publication and text: *CA,* 1834. Republished in *HO.* Cf. Thomas Campbell, "The Wounded Hussar."

8: Ninety-Second dear. The 92nd (Gordon Highlanders) Regiment of Foot (1798–1861). It served with distinction in the Peninsula Campaigns of 1809–1814 and at Waterloo.

19: March of Intellect. Cf. Southey, *Sir Thomas More: or, Colloquies on the Progress and Prospects of Society,* 2nd ed. (London, 1831), II, 268–269: "The march of intellect is proceeding at quick time" (Colloquy 14: "The Library").

39: the Gazette. The *London Gazette,* an official journal, which listed those "wounded, dead, and missing" (l. 40).

44: French bricks. Loaves of French bread *(briques de pain).*

49: Its billet every bullet has. "Every bullet has its billet," i.e., its destination assigned. See John Wesley, *Journal,* 6 June 1765 (attributed to King William III) and Scott, *Count Robert of Paris,* chap. 25.

52: "crooked billet." "Billet" in the sense of "lodging" has the alternate spelling of "bullet."

56: *steel'd his breast.* Cuirassiers wore steel breastplates.

60: Quarter-day. One of the four days regarded as beginning a new quarter of the year—the day troops were paid.

68: *Coldstream.* The Coldstream Guards, one of the five regiments of Foot Guards raised by General Monk in 1659–60.

74: royal Guelph. Political party in medieval Italy which supported the Pope; the English kings were descendants of the Guelphs.

75: Butcher. *HO:* butcher. Possibly a reference to General G. L. von Blücher (1742–1819), the Prussian general whose unexpected arrival at the Battle of Waterloo caught Napoleon off guard and helped make it an overwhelming victory for Wellington and his allies.

79: My shillingsworth of 'list. The new recruit was given a shilling, his "bounty" (l. 77), to enlist in the army.

88: a *tester.* 1. A tester bed has a head canopy; 2. a sixpence.

96: th' Illuminations. The lighting up of a town with colored lights, artistically arranged, in token of festivity or celebration. Cf. Byron, *Don Juan,* VII, 44.

The Carelesse Nurse Mayd

First publication and text: *CA,* 1830. Republished in *HO.* In this poem Hood imitates Thomas Chatterton's Rowley poems.

Variant. 8: Ane other; *HO,* Another.

Domestic Asides; or, Truth in Parentheses

First publication and text: *CA*, 1831. Republished in *HO*.
12: Brussels. Brussels carpet.
16: dabby. Moist.

Domestic Poems

First publication and text: *CA*, 1837. The poems were prefaced thus:

It has often been remarked—and never more likely than after hearing
"John Anderson, my Jo," sung by Broadhurst, at a public dinner—that
there is a species of Poetry, indigenous to Scotland, which might em-
phatically be called Domestic. The Land of Cakes is, indeed, peculiarly
rich in songs and ballads of household interest, which, like their stock
Tragedy of Douglas, may be said to be Home-made. The Caledonian
Muse does not merely take a walk round the premises, speculating on
the domestic comforts, or discomforts, the household affections, or dis-
affections, within; but she is invited and goes *ben,* far ben; makes her-
self quite at home; and is "treated as one of the family." She sits down,
like a gossip as she is, at the ingle side; takes a peep into the muckle pat;
pries into the cradle; and does not hesitate to spier into the dubious
parentage of "young wee Donald." She gauges the meal-tub; and informs
herself of the stock of siller in hand. There are no secrets with her. The
gude wife and gude man unfold to her their most private affairs. They
describe to her how they sleep, with a pint stoup at their bed feet; and
confide to her all their particular gratifications and grievances. Johnny
complains of a weary pound of tow,—that his wife does not drink hooly
and fairly,—and hints that he should not be sorry to see the termagant
dished up in her winding-sheet:—Jeanie tells of his extravagance, in
not wanting to take his old cloak about him; and asks counsel on the
state of his grey breeks. The Daughter, if she be at home, gets the Muse
in a corner, lets her into the names and number of her lovers; describes
the modes and freedoms of their wooings; and repeats all their love-
nonsense verbatim. In short, a Familiar of the Inquisition could not be
more familiar with all the recesses of their private life: only what the
Muse knows she publishes; and, in the shape of ballads and songs, spreads
her home news, scandal and all, throughout the parishen.
  The English, on the contrary, have few Poems of this nature. The
Muse does not sing like a cricket from our hearths; and with an abun-
dance of home-made wines, we have scarcely a home-made song. This
is a gap in our literature, a vacant shelf in our Family Library, that ought
to be filled up. I cannot suppose that we are nationally deficient in the
fireside feelings and homily affections which inspire a domestic ditty;—
but take it for granted, that the vein exists, though it has not been
worked. In the hope of drawing the attention of our Bards to the subject,

I venture to offer a few specimens of Domestic Poems, "such as"—to use the words of Doctor Watts—"I wish some happy and condescending Genius would undertake and perform much better."

The preface is introduced by two mottos. "It's hame, hame, hame" occurs in Allan Cunningham's song "Hame, Hame, Hame," and "Be it ever so humble, there's no place like home," in the song "Home, Sweet Home," originally a part of John Howard Payne's opera *Clari, the Maid of Milan* (1823).

I. Hymeneal Retrospections ("O Kate! my dear Partner")

8: like gooseberries boil'd for a fool. "Gooseberry-fool" is "a dish made of gooseberries stewed or scalded and pounded with cream" (*OED*). "Gooseberry" was a colloquial term for "fool."
11–12: Time . . . driving his plough. Cf. Shakespeare, Sonnet 22, and Burns, "To a Mountain Daisy," stanza ix.

II. Hymeneal Retrospections ("The sun was slumbering in the West")

20: Southend. Popular bathing resort, at the mouth of the Thames, forty-five miles from London.
24: *nus*. Latin: mind, understanding.

III. A Parental Ode to My Son, Aged 3 Years and 5 Months

Republished in *Blackwood's Magazine*, XLI, no. cclvi (Feb. 1837), with the following comment: "We are weary of modern poetry. It wants force. The truth of nature might be as well looked for on the opera stage . . . But we give a specimen of another style, the true mixture of the romantic and the real which touches every heart at once." Hood's wife was named "Jane" (l. 14) and his son Tom (born 19 January 1835) would have been just under two years of age at the time of the poem's publication, but the "Ode" is probably no more autobiographical than that. Cf. Wordsworth's "To H. C. Six Years Old" and "Ode: Intimations of Immortality from Recollections of Early Childhood," ll. 85ff., both addressed to Hartley Coleridge.
24: From ev'ry blossom in the world that blows. Cf. Wordsworth, "Ode: Intimations of Immortality from Recollections of Early Childhood," l. 202: "the meanest flower that blows."

Stanzas, Composed in a Shower-Bath

Holograph MS: Hood Collection, Yale University. First publication and text: *CA*, 1838. Though the MS shows only punctuation variations from the published version, on the same sheet there is a crossed-out version which shows that the poem was originally conceived as "Sonnet:—The Shower Bath." It has interest in revealing the kind of changes Hood made in his poetry.

Naked—as stood old Adam, *ere the Fall,*
To pluck the stalk so fatal to his blood,
So stand I here, alas! before the Flood!
On my own head a punishment to call—
Yet thought of gasping like a drowning pup
Will chill & paralyze the nervous pow'r,—
One moment I invoke the tumbling show'r
The next I hope the weather may hold up.
My eyes are closely seal'd; my teeth are set;
"Expect some heavy rain about this time"
But where's the stoicism so sublime
That will not shrink to ring for wringing wet?—
Of going their whole hogs some folks talk big,
Let them just try to go the whole cold pig!

The tail-piece *Operation for the Cataract* is given in the *CA*'s list of plates as designed by J. Scott, but, as Hood mentions it in the manuscript, presumably it is his. The lines he cites as motto occur not in *Remorse* but in *Osorio:* "Drip! drip! drip! drip!—in such a place as this / It has nothing else to do but drip! drip! drip!" (IV, i, 1–2). A cold bath—a hot bath would have been considered effeminate—was still uncommon at this time except in a few aristocratic families. Shower baths—taken in sentry-box like cabinets—were still more uncommon.

17: Of going hogs. To go the whole hog.

18: *the whole cold pig.* "Cold pig" (or "cold pie") is "the application of cold water to wake a person" (*OED*).

Variant. 5: How like; MS (crossed out), Such was.

The Bachelor's Dream

Holograph MS: Hood Collection, Yale University. First publication and text: *CA,* 1839.

Variants. 4: is sitting; MS (crossed out), reposing. 26: What work he; MS (crossed out), that mischief.

No!

First published in the *NMM,* Nov. 1842. Text: *Whimsicalities,* I.

8: the Crescents. A row of houses built in the inner form of the crescent moon.

18: No Park—no Ring. The Ring in Hyde Park was the fashionable haunt for horseback-riding.

24: November. In *NMM* written as part of preceding line.

To Minerva. From the Greek

First publication and text: *Memorials,* II. The poem dates from about the year 1844.

3: Thyrsis. One of the traditional names for a shepherd-poet.

7: Pallas . . . thine Owl. Pallas Athene (Minerva) had the owl as symbol.

III. Verse Narratives

Bianca's Dream. A Venetian Story

First publication and text: *W & O* (2). The poem was apparently written in 1820. According to Hannah Lawrance, Hood read a story in verse, entitled "Juliet," at the opening meeting in Oct. 1820 of a literary society to which they both belonged. "This, under the name of 'Bianca's Dream'— but slightly altered—subsequently appeared in the second series of 'Whims and Oddities'; but, as originally given, it was followed by a capital appendix of 'Learned Notes, after the manner of the Learned Martinus Scriblerus'" ("Recollections of Thomas Hood," *British Quarterly Review*, XLVI [Oct. 1867], 328). The poem's parody of romantic love, its Venetian setting, and its *ottava rima* verse form recall Byron's *Beppo*.

7–8: Each eye of hers had Love's Eupyrion in it, / That he could light his link at in a minute. Eupyrion was "the name given by the inventor [Hertner] to a contrivance for obtaining a light instantaneously" (*OED*); here used in a figurative sense. A link was a kind of torch.

12: Flambeaux. Torches.

16: Flints. Flint, Ray, Nicholson & Co., 12 Grafton St., Soho, fashionable haberdashers.

29: padusoy. Usually paduasoy, a corded silk cloth, or a garment made from it, used extensively in the eighteenth century.

30: beaver. A man's silk hat, originally made of this fur.

56: put the *crater* out. 1. Extinguished the "volcano"; 2. put the "creature" out-of-doors.

75: Thisbe. She stabbed herself when she discovered that her lover Pyramus, thinking her slain by a lion, had killed himself; the blood of the lovers stained purplish-red the white fruit of the mulberry tree. See Ovid's *Metamorphoses*, IV, 55–169.

77: Sappho. For the legend of her love for Phaon and her leap from the Leucadian cliff, see Ovid's "Epistle of Sappho to Phaon," *Heroides*, XV, which Hood probably knew in Pope's rendering.

80: those old *suitors* lived beyond their last. Hood probably puns on the proverb *Ne sutor ultra crepidam* (Let the cobbler stick to his last). "Sutor" is also Scots for "cobbler."

82: his corks. A piece of cork, used to support a swimmer in the water.

90: 'tis horrible to die. Cf. *Measure for Measure*, III, i, 118–128: "to die . . . 'tis too horrible."

94: spunging-house. A place where debtors were held until they either paid their debts or were put in prison for nonpayment.

95: personals. Persons.

102–103: an immortal light. / Like that old fire. Perhaps Greek-fire, or wild-fire, readily ignited and difficult to extinguish.

109: zephyr light. Soft, mild light.

118: Deh Vieni. *Deh vieni alla finestra* (Look down from out your window, I now implore you), canzonetta which Mozart's Don Giovanni, wearing Leporello's cloak, sings to the waiting-woman of Donna Elvira (*Don Giovanni*, II, iii).

120: a Bridge of Sighs. Venice's famous *Ponte dei Sospiri* leads from the Doge's Palace to a notorious prison. It is so named from the sighs of the doomed prisoners on their way to execution. Cf. Hood's "The Bridge of Sighs" and Byron, *Childe Harold's Pilgrimage*, IV, 1.

127: Sagittarius. A southern constellation outlining a centaur shooting an arrow.

128: Aquarius. A central constellation outlining a man pouring water from a container in his right hand.

129: listing. Listening.

164: the seventh stage. Jaques divides life into "seven ages" in *As You Like It*, II, vii, 141–166: "Last scene of all . . . Is second childishness and mere oblivion, / Sans teeth, sans eyes, sans taste, sans every thing" (163–166).

168: A compound (like our Psalms) of tête and braidy. A "tête" is "a woman's head of hair, or a wig, dressed high and elaborately ornamented, the fashion of the second half of the 18th c." (*OED*). A "braidy" is a braid or braids, probably in this sense: "In 19th c. sometimes applied to the flat bands of [false] hair, worn at one time by ladies over the side of the face" (*OED*). Professor Wesley Kort, Department of Religion, Duke University, suggests that "tête" and "braidy" refer respectively to the heady or *instructive* and the decorative or *ornamental* nature of poetry, and that Hood's use of the words would be in keeping with the traditional interpretation of the Psalms. In the *Apologie for Poetrie* (1583), for instance, Sidney speaks of poetry as both teaching and delighting and gives as an example the Psalms of David. In 1740 Isaac Watts and Charles Wesley published metrical versions of the Psalms that were used mostly in nonconformist churches. Hood was a religious nonconformist: thus his use of the expression "like our Psalms."

169: Saturn. Loosely used by Hood to represent "Time" (l. 177). The planet Saturn, on account of its remoteness and slowness of action, was supposed to have a baleful effect upon human affairs.

174: pensioners called In and Out. Paid hirelings in and out of favor with their patrons, "first and second rater" (l. 175).

180: "winsome marrow." Cf. William Hamilton (1704–1754), "The Braes of Yarrow": "Busk ye, busk ye, my bonny bonny bride, / Busk ye, busk ye, my winsome marrow."

184: Glassite. Member of the religious sect founded by the Rev. John Glas, a minister of the Established Church of Scotland who was deposed in 1728. But Hood uses "Glassite" and "Quaker" (l. 184) to complete a pun begun with "spectacles and palsy" (l. 183).

208: Gloster. Richard, duke of Gloucester, successfully woos for political motives Lady Anne, whose father and husband he has murdered (see *Richard III*, I, ii).

227: English telegraphs. One of the many signaling apparatuses in use before the invention of the electric telegraph in 1838. Hood probably alludes to a device, invented in 1792, "consisting of an upright post with movable arms, the signals being made by various positions of the arms according to a pre-arranged code" (*OED*).

233: "Be thou my park, and I will be thy dear." Cf. Shakespeare, *Venus and Adonis,* l. 231: "I'll be a park, and thou shalt be my deer."

249: sparks. Gallant blades.

264: Insipid things—like sandwiches of veal. "Insipid" because a calf intended for veal is bled to exhaustion.

Variants. 72: his girth; *W & O* (2), 1st and 2nd eds., her girth. 91: our. *W & O* (2): out. *W & O* (2), 1st ed.: our. 159: heart. *W & O* (2): heat. *W & O* (2), 1st ed.: heart.

The Last Man

First publication and text: *W & O* (1). Hood's verse narrative stands comparison well with other romantic treatments of the same theme: Byron's poem "Darkness" (1816), Thomas Campbell's poem "The Last Man" (1823), Thomas Lovell Beddoes' fragmentary play *The Last Man* (1823–1825), and Mary Shelley's novel *The Last Man* (1826). Cf. also Jean de la Bruyère: "Je suppose qu'il n'y ait que deux hommes sur la terre, qui la possèdent seuls, et qui la partagent toute entre eux deux: je suis persuadé qu'il leur naîtra bientôt quelque sujet de rupture, quant ce ne seroit pour les limites" (I postulate that there are only two men on earth, that they enjoy sole possession of it, and that they divide the whole between themselves: I am convinced that some bone of contention will soon arise between them, even if only about the boundaries.) (*Les Caractères ou les moeurs de ce siècle,* V, 47). John Wilson comments perceptively on the poem and the accompanying woodcut *The Last Man* in his review essay, "Hood's *Whims and Oddities*," in *Blackwood's Magazine,* XXI, no. cxxi (Jan. 1827), 54–57. For more recent critical estimates see A. J. Sambrook, "A Romantic Theme: The Last Man," *Forum for Modern Language Studies,* II (Jan. 1966), 25–33, and Arthur McA. Miller, "The Last Man: A Study of the Eschatological Theme in English Poetry and Fiction from 1806 through 1839," unpub. diss. (Duke University, 1966). Morgan points out striking similarities between Hood's poem and Jean Paul Richter's "Farewell to the Reader" (pp. 135–137) and notes that Hood would have known of Richter through De Quincey's appreciative article in the *LM* (Dec. 1821). Both De Quincey and Thomas Griffiths Wainewright, two of Hood's older colleagues on the *LM,* remarked on the affinities between the two writers. Morgan also makes out a cogent case for Hood's indebtedness to Mary Shelley's *The Last Man,* published in February 1826—Hood's poem was not published until later in the year (pp. 478–481). Alfred Ainger sees affinities with Coleridge's "Rime of the Ancient Mariner" (*Poems of Thomas Hood* [London, 1897], I, xxxi).

15: orts. Leftover fragments of food, i.e., "snaps" (l. 18).

17: Newgate-bird. Jailbird (after the London prison destroyed in 1902).

109: the beggar man made a mumping face. Cf. Lamb, "The Two Races of Men" in *Elia* (Morgan): the "mumping visnomy" of "your bastard borrower."

152: corals. Teething toy for babies, made of coral.

164: blinded him in his bags. Blindfolded him in his loose clothes (or trousers).

221–222: there is not another man alive, / In the world, to pull my legs. Before the invention of the long drop in executions, friends of the criminal were allowed to pull his legs in order to shorten his sufferings. (The *OED* gives 1888 as the date of the earliest recorded use of this phrase in the sense of deceiving or humbugging.)

Variant. 13: blithe; *W & O* (1), 1st ed., blythe.

Jack Hall

First publication and text: *W & O* (2). The title is a pun on "jackal."

9: Death Fetches. A "fetch" is an "apparition" or "double" of a living person. Hood means "resurrectionists." See note to l. 21.

17: Sacharissa. Lady Dorothy Sidney was celebrated as "Sacharissa" in poems by Edmund Waller (1606–1687). According to John Aubrey, Waller loved the lady passionately, but the poems themselves are decorous.

21: the Faculty. Colloquial term designating the members of the medical profession, some of whom "bid rogues" to resurrect corpses (l. 22). Hood's poem anticipates by several years the case of the notorious "Resurrectionists" Burke and Hare. See note to l. 13 of "Mary's Ghost," p. 344.

35: brother Mute. In Ben Jonson's *The Silent Woman* (1609) Mute is Morose's well-trained servant; bound to complete silence, he rarely breaks his vow.

37: the ferry. Of Charon, who in Greek mythology ferried dead souls across the river Styx to Hades.

54: Pancras' ground. The cemetery attached to St. Pancras-in-the-Fields.

56: the bony knacker. I.e., the devil; but "knacker" perhaps also used in this sense: "one whose trade it is to buy worn out, diseased, or useless horses, and slaughter them for their hides and hoofs, and for making dog's-meat, etc.; a horse-slaughterer" (*OED*).

76: mull. Snuff-box.

117: the Cheshire Cheese. This "famous tap" (l. 118) in Wine Office Court, off Fleet Street, was rebuilt shortly after the Restoration and is still in existence.

123: Deady. Gin (from the name of the distiller, D. Deady).

126: mum. 1. Silence; 2. a kind of beer originally brewed in Brunswick.

141: area rails. Railings which shut off an enclosed, sunken court from the pavement.

258: *bitten.* Swindled. The *OED* gives an obsolete slang usage of "bite" as an "imposition, a deception; what is now called a 'sell'; passing from the notion of playful imposition or hoax, to that of swindle or fraud."

Variant. 27: ghoul; *W & O* (2), goul.

The Demon-Ship

First published in the *LG*, 30 June 1827, signed "T. H." Text: *W & O* (2). The textual changes—almost exclusively punctuation and spelling—are minor. The poem was prefaced in *W & O* (2) as follows:

Stories of storm-ships and haunted vessels, of spectre-shallops, and super-natural Dutch doggers, are common to many countries, and are well attested both in poetry and prose. The adventures of Solway sailors, with Mahound, in his bottomless barges, and the careerings of the phantom-ship up and down the Hudson, have hundreds of asserters be-sides Messrs. [Allan] Cunningham and [Geoffrey] Crayon; and to doubt their authenticity may seem like an imitation of the desperate sailing of the haunted vessels themselves against wind and tide. I cannot help fancying, however, that Richard Faulder was but one of those tavern-dreamers recorded [in *The English Traveller*] by old Heywood, who con-ceived

> "The room wherein they quaff'd to be a pinnace."

And as for the Flying Dutchman, my notion is very different from the popular conception of that apparition, as I have ventured to show by the opposite design. The spectre-ship, bound to Dead Man's Isle, is al-most as awful a craft as the skeleton-bark of the Ancient Mariner; but they are both fictions, and have not the advantage of being realities, like the dreary vessel with its dreary crew in the following story, which records an adventure that befel even unto myself.

Hood's poem parodies and shows occasional verbal indebtedness to Allan Cunningham's "The Legend of Richard Faulder, Mariner," published in *Sir Marmaduke Maxwell* (1822), though he characteristically transforms Cunningham's legendary "Voyage in the Spectre Shallop" into his own more realistic key, which undercuts the supernatural by having the hero rescued not by a specter-ship but by an actual collier. Hood's knowledge of "the careerings of the phantom-ship up and down the Hudson" may have derived, P. F. Morgan suggests, from Part IV of Geoffrey Crayon's (i.e., Washington Irving's) *Tales of a Traveller* (1824). The line from Thomas Heywood's *The English Traveller* Hood would have read in Lamb's *Specimens of English Dramatic Poets*. Morgan suggests a parallel between the opening lines and those of John Clare's "Description of a Thunder-storm" in *The Village Minstrel* (1822).

1: off the Wash. The estuarine inlet of the North Sea on the east coast of England, between Lincolnshire and Norfolk. It is mostly shallow, with low, marshy areas; sandbanks make navigation dangerous.

4: Erebus. The place of nether darkness through which the dead passed before entering Hades.

22: scooping sea. Clare, "Description of a Thunder-storm," l. 24: "scooping rock." "Of a rock, the sea: That forms hollows or depressions" (*OED*). Hood borrowed Clare's apparent neologism—his is the first use of the word the *OED* records—and adopted it for his own purposes.

36: And was that ship a *real* ship. Cf. Coleridge, "The Rime of the Ancient Mariner," ll. 175ff., where the Mariner first realizes that the ship he sees is a skeleton ship.

51: lemures. In Roman mythology the night-walking spirits of the dead.

62: Mahound. The devil (Scots). "Mahoun" in Cunningham's ballad.

67: Loud laugh'd that SABLE MARINER. Cf. Cunningham, "The Legend of Richard Faulder," V: "Loud laugh'd all my mariners." Hood's "SABLE MARINER" (or "GRIMLY ONE," l. 52) resembles Cunningham's "hoary OLD ONE."

Variant. 62: gain'd; *LG,* won.

The Sea-Spell

First publication and text: *W & O* (1). The motto *"Cauld, cauld,* he lies beneath the deep" probably refers to, though does not cite, the *"Old Scotch Ballad"* of "Sir Patrick Spens," where most versions mention the sea "fifty fadom deep, / And there lies guid Sir Patrick Spens."

1: It was a jolly mariner. Cf. Coleridge, "The Rime of the Ancient Mariner," l. 1: "It is an ancient Mariner."

10: a baby's caul. The inner membrane inclosing the foetus before birth or a portion of it enveloping a child's head at birth: superstitiously regarded as a good omen and supposed to be a preservative against drowning.

17–18: His ample trowsers, like Saint Paul, / Bore forty stripes save one. Cf. 2 Cor. 11:24: "Of the Jews five times received I [St. Paul] forty *stripes* save one."

45: per saltum: "Per-salt" the *OED* defines as "a salt formed by a combination of an acid with the peroxide of a metal." "Saltus" is Latin for a "leap." "Per saltum" might then, by extension, mean "through a salty leap."

48: own'd a pique. 1. Peak; 2. ill-feeling; 3. "in *piquet,* the winning of thirty points on cards and play, before one's opponent begins to count" (*OED*).

53: by purchase. Also any device, such as a rope, pulley, windlass, or the like, by means of which power may be brought to bear with advantage.

60: like Gog and Magog snoring. Two huge wooden figures, fourteen and a half feet high, in the Guildhall, King Street, Cheapside. One of Hood's *Comic Melodies* was "Gog and Magog: A Guildhall Duet," with music by Jonathan Blewitt.

62: the grampus. The whale.

120: surge. 1. Billow; 2. woolen fabric.

Variant. 111: The windward sheet is taut and stiff. Thus *W & O* (1), 1st ed.; I have changed "taught" to "taut." 2nd ed.: The sheet's to windward taught and stiff.

The Dream of Eugene Aram, the Murderer

First published in *The Gem* (1829), a literary annual which Hood edited that year. Text: *The Dream of Eugene Aram, The Murderer* (1831), a separate publication in volume form, with eight illustrations by William Harvey. The chief differences between the *Gem* text, where the poem is entitled simply "The Dream of Eugene Aram," and the 1831 publication are reduction in capitalization and some regularization of punctuation; for consistency's sake, a few of the 1829 readings have been silently adopted here. In the 1831 volume the poem bore the following dedication:

To J. H. Reynolds, Esq.

Dear Reynolds,

Induced to this reprint by a series of Illustrations from the pencil of an Artist whose genius you highly estimate;—remembering some partiality you have expressed for the Poem itself;—and, above all, that you stand nearest to me in a stricter form of the brotherhood which the Dream is intended to enforce; I feel that I cannot inscribe it more appropriately or more willingly than to yourself. It will be accepted I know, with the kind feeling which is mutual between you and

Your's ever truly,

Thomas Hood.

The 1831 volume also carried the following preface:

The remarkable name of Eugene Aram, belonging to a man of unusual talents and acquirements, is unhappily associated with a deed of blood as extraordinary in its details as any recorded in our calendar of crime. In the year 1745, being then an Usher, and deeply engaged in the study of Chaldee, Hebrew, Arabic, and the Celtic dialects, for the formation of a Lexicon, he abruptly turned over a still darker page in human knowledge, and the brow that learning might have made illustrious, was stamped ignominious for ever with the brand of Cain. To obtain a trifling property, he concerted with an accomplice, and with his own hand effected, the violent death of one Daniel Clarke, a shoemaker of Knaresborough, in Yorkshire. For fourteen years nearly the secret slept with the victim in the earth of St. Robert's Cave, and the manner of its discovery would appear a striking example of the Divine Justice, even amongst those marvels narrated in that curious old volume, alluded to in The Fortunes of Nigel, under its quaint title of "God's Revenge Against Murther."

The accidental digging up of a skeleton, and the unwary and emphatic declaration of Aram's accomplice, that it could not be that of Clarke, betraying a guilty knowledge of the true bones, he was wrought to a confession of their deposit. The learned homicide was seized and arraigned; and a trial of uncommon interest was wound up by a defence as memorable as the tragedy itself for eloquence and ingenuity;—too ingenious for innocence, and eloquent enough to do credit even to that long premeditation which the interval between the deed and its discovery had afforded. That this dreary period had not passed without paroxyms of remorse, may be inferred from a fact of affecting interest. The late Admiral Burney was a scholar, at the school at Lynn in Norfolk, where Aram was an Usher, subsequent to his crime. The Admiral stated that Aram was beloved by the boys, and that he used to discourse to them of Murder, not occasionally, as I have written elsewhere, but constantly, and in somewhat of the spirit ascribed to him in the Poem.

For the more imaginative part of the version I must refer back to one of those unaccountable visions, which come upon us like frightful monsters thrown up by storms from the great black deeps of slumber. A lifeless body, in love and relationship the nearest and dearest, was imposed upon my back, with an overwhelming sense of obligation—not of filial piety merely, but some awful responsibility equally vague and intense, and involving, as it seemed, inexpiable sin, horrors unutterable, torments intolerable,—to bury my dead, like Abraham, out of my sight. In vain I attempted, again and again, to obey the mysterious mandate— by some dreadful process the burthen was replaced with a more stupendous weight of injunction, and an appalling conviction of the impossibility of its fulfilment. My mental anguish was indescribable;—the mighty agonies of souls tortured on the supernatural racks of sleep are not to be penned—and if in sketching those that belong to blood-guiltiness I have been at all successful, I owe it mainly to the uninvoked inspiration of that terrible dream.

T. H.

With the preface's last paragraph, revealing the deep terror his "visions" caused him, compare Hood's speculative essay, "A Dream" (*Works*, V, 135–142). In the 1831 volume Hood also reprinted (slightly abridged from the *Biographia Britannica*) the text of Aram's defense at his trial (reprinted in *Works*, VI, 439–446). A German translation, *Eugen Aram, oder das Verbrechen als Gegenstand der Kunst* . . . (Bromberg, 1841), by Philip von Franck and H. A. Rühe, reached Hood in 1841 (see *Memorials*, II, 89–93). He wrote on 3 July 1843 to W. J. Broderip: "Charles Lamb once said to me that the most knowing man in the world was one who had done a Murder, & had not been found out:—for example Eugene Aram, during the 14 years that he was unsuspected" (unpublished letter, Folger Shakespeare Library, Washington).

P. F. Morgan notes the poem's strong affinities with Southey's macabre ballad "Jaspar"; and Southey's influence on Hood, as George Saintsbury observes in the *Cambridge History of English Literature*, may have extended to the ballads as well. The narrator's compulsive need to relate his tale of crime and guilt to an unwilling listener makes the poem look backward, as several critics have pointed out, to Coleridge's "Rime of the

Ancient Mariner." Though Aram's story was well-known in the early nine-teenth century, Hood's poem probably inspired Edward Bulwer's three-decker novel, *Eugene Aram* (1832), and may have influenced Oscar Wilde's *Ballad of Reading Jaol* (1898).

6: Like troutlets in a pool. An inaccurate translation of the word "troutlets" called forth one of Hood's exceedingly rare comments on his poetry. Hannah Lawrance writes: "Never was there a closer observer of nature, even in apparently very trifling things. We remember finding him one morning quite delighted, for he had just received from a German friend a translation of his 'Eugene Aram's Dream,' and it was always a delight to him to find any recognition of the merits of *that* poem. The general translation was fairly faithful; 'But look,' he said, 'I wrote—

> "There were some who ran, and some who leaped,
>   Like *troutlets* in a pool."

Now, the translator has substituted 'little fishes,' which is all wrong. Little fishes leap sometimes, but the troutlet leaps *quite out* of the stream, and so is the emblem of boyhood in its utmost joy. How often I have watched these troutlets leaping right out, as though they could not contain them-selves!' " "Recollections of Thomas Hood," *British Quarterly Review,* XLVI (Oct. 1867), 346–347.

17–18: But the Usher sat remote from all, / A melancholy man! Cf. Southey, "Jaspar," ll. 65–66: "He sate him down . . . / A melancholy man!" An usher is a schoolmaster's assistant.

29–30: Much study had made him very lean, / And pale, and leaden-ey'd. Cf. Keats, "Ode to a Nightingale," ll. 26–28: "Where youth grows pale, and spectre-thin . . . And leaden-eyed despairs."

48: "The Death of Abel." English translation (1761) of *Der Tod Abels* (1758) by Salomon Gessner (1730–1788); this idyllic prose pastoral enjoyed extraordinary popularity, though here Hood commits an anachronism: Aram committed his crime in 1745.

101–102: I took the dead man by his hand, / And call'd upon his name. Cf. "The Ancient Ballad of Chevy Chase," ll. 57–58: "He tooke the dede man be the hande, / And sayd, 'Wo ys me for the!' " (Percy, I, 9).

189–190: For I knew my secret then was one / That earth refused to keep. Morgan compares these lines to Lady Macbeth's sleepwalking scene (*Macbeth*, V, i).

204: And my red right hand grows raging hot, / Like Cranmer's at the stake. Thomas Cranmer, Archbishop of Canterbury from 1549 to 1556. Upon the accession of the Catholic Queen Mary, he was tried for treason, convicted of heresy, excommunicated and condemned to death. A few days before his death he recanted, but when asked to repeat the recantation in public at the stake, he refused and placed the hand that had written it into the fire.

216: To the poem's last line Hood attached in *The Gem* the following note, rendered superfluous by the preface of 1831: "The late Admiral Burney went to school at an establishment where the unhappy Eugene Aram was Usher, subsequent to his crime. The Admiral stated, that Aram was generally liked by the boys; and that he used to discourse to them about *murder,* in somewhat of the spirit which is attributed to him in the Poem."

The Desert-Born

First publication and text: *CA,* 1837. The motto "Fly to the desert, fly with me" is the title of a song from Thomas Moore's *Lalla Rookh.* Hood's description of the commanding "oriental queen" (l. 8) owes something to Lady Hester Stanhope (1776–1839), as the poem's nightmarish ride across the Syrian desert recalls her triumphant entry into Damascus and her visit to the ruins of Palmyra. More important, the poem reflects Hood's fascination with the *Arabian Nights,* especially "The Tale of the Ebony Horse," where the king is presented with a horse whose "virtue . . . is that, if one mount him, it will carry him whither he will and fare with its rider through the air and cover the space of a year in a single day" (Sir Richard Burton trans.). Morgan sees a parallel between the "galloping rhythms" of this poem and those of Mrs. Caroline Norton's lachrymose "The Arab's Farewell to his Horse" in her volume *The Undying One* (1830).

56: a mare of milky white. The metamorphosis of the "airy dream" (l. 57) of beautiful maid into the hard reality of milky-white mare recalls several tales of the *Arabian Nights,* especially "The Story of Beder, Prince of Persia": "Quit that form of a woman, and be turned instantly into a mare" (*Works,* V, 398, 402).

61: Meux's giant steeds. Of Henry Meux and Co., 269 Tottenham Court Road, London brewers since 1764.

77: *ridings.* The county of Yorkshire (l. 76) is divided into East, West, and North Ridings (and the City of York).

81: running long. Letting accounts become overdue.

83: in stirrups. I.e., a lord or landowner.

87: "I'm one of those whose infant ears have heard the chimes of Bow!" The celebrated bells of St. Mary-le-Bow Church, Cheapside, usually called Bow Church; the true Cockney or Londoner is one born within "the chimes of Bow."

89: cruel kindness. Cf. *Hamlet,* III, iv, 177: "I must be cruel, only to be kind."

92–93: whatever spot of earth / Cheapside, or Bow, or Stepney, had the honour of your birth. Hood was always proud of his London birth. "The Dragon of Bow Church," he wrote in his "Literary Reminiscences," "or Gresham's Grasshopper, is as good a terrestrial sign to be born under as the dunghill cock on a village steeple. Next to being a citizen of the world, it must be the best thing to be born a citizen of the world's greatest city" (*Works,* I, 449).

109: Like old Redgauntlet, with a shoe imprinted on my forehead. Edward Hugh Redgauntlet, known as "Herries of Birrenswork" in Scott's novel *Redgauntlet* (1824). The Redgauntlet family was marked by a hereditary indenture of the forehead resembling a miniature horseshoe.

163: Mazeppa-like. I.e., stripped naked like the Cossack leader (1644–1709).

202: Wild shriek'd the headlong Desert-Born—or else 'twas demon's mirth. A characteristic example of Hood's use of romantic irony. Whether the horse actually "shriek'd," or whether " 'twas demon's mirth," the reader never learns. Such deliberate ambiguity and undercutting of the dramatic illusion reveal the influence upon Hood of German romanticism. For his probing analysis of its possible evil effects upon unsuspecting readers, see *Works*, VIII, 215–217.

213: Time flapp'd along, with leaden wings. Cf. Richard Jago, "Absence": "With leaden foot time creeps along."

Variant. 29: Dervish; *CA*, Dervise.

The Haunted House. A Romance

First publication and text: *HM*, Jan. 1844. Reprinted in *Poems* (1846), I. Holograph MS (printer's copy) of Part I, ll. 1–60, 97–116: Hood collection, Bristol University Library, England. An engraving by John Cousen entitled *The Haunted House*, after a painting by Thomas Creswick, forms the frontispiece to this number of *HM* and suggested (or was specially engraved for) the poem. In September 1843, three months before he published his poem, Hood visited Edinburgh Castle; there he undoubtedly saw the spot where David Rizzio, the favorite of Mary Queen of Scots, was brutally murdered in 1566; he may have blurred it into the poem's "BLOODY HAND" and unnamed "weighty crime." There is no direct evidence to indicate that Hood knew Edgar Allan Poe's poem "The Haunted House," first published in 1839 as part of "The Fall of the House of Usher." In 1845 Poe praised Hood's poem as the finest he had written (*The Complete Works of Edgar Allan Poe*, ed. James A. Harrison [New York, 1902], XII, 236–237). In 1855 appeared *Domus Portentosa; or, The Haunted House*, a literal rendering of Hood's poem into Latin elegaic verse by the Rev. Philip A. Longmore. Morgan suggests parallels with Tennyson's "Mariana."

32: The place is Haunted. Cf. B. W. Procter, "A Haunted Stream," l. 94: "The place *is* haunted" (Morgan).

52: "shocking tameness." Jerrold in the Oxford Ed. noted the echo of William Cowper, "Verses Supposed to be Written by Alexander Selkirk," ll. 15–16: "They [the beasts] are so unacquainted with man, / Their tameness is shocking to me."

71: green as is the mantled pool. Cf. *The Merchant of Venice*, I, i, 89: "cream and mantle like a standing pond."

175: Dolorous moans. Cf. Wordsworth, "Hart-Leap Well," l. 136: "dolorous groan" (Morgan).

Variants. 16: globe; MS (crossed out), sphere. 45: gray; MS, grey. 87: plums; *HM*, plumbs. 109: side; MS (crossed out), hand. 217: can; *HM*, cann.

IV. Miss Kilmansegg and Her Precious Leg

Miss Kilmansegg and Her Precious Leg. A Golden Legend

First published in the *NMM*, Sept., Oct., Nov., 1840, and Feb. 1841, where it appeared under the rubric "Rhymes for the Times, and Reason for the Season." Text: *CA*, 1842. The *CA* text shows few changes from that in the *NMM*, the chief being more careful punctuation. I indicate changes in diction in the *Variants*. Henry Fothergill Chorley recalled in the *Athenaeum* (11 Dec. 1869) a dinner he had had with Hood at Lake House, where the poet lived from 1832 until early in 1835, and remembered telling Hood about a childhood game involving "a golden leg" that he played at bedtime:

> The play ran thus. A Giant's voice was heard at the bottom of the stair-case, crying "Give me my golden leg." To which the answer from the bed was, "Come up a step further and you shall have it." The pleasure was protracted and enhanced by the number of the steps on the stair-case, by the repetition of the Giant's query *crescendo,* and the mingled fright and audacity of those who tempted him. At last the Giant got into the bed-room with "Give me my golden leg" *fortissimo.* The answer was, "Take it." On which there was a catastrophe, and a smash, and a bolster-ing riot, most vigorously enacted by those in and those not in the bed [cf. ll. 2353–2359] . . . That talk, I fancy, may have helped to the creation of the poem which, among tragical grotesque poems, is, and will remain to be a marvel,—if only because after the story was fairly "cast on" Hood was in search of the catastrophe of the legend (p. 780).

Hood implies on several occasions (e.g., ll. 275–277, 298, 333, 477, and 507) that the presumably fictitious Kilmansegg family was closely related to per-sonages high in London financial, political, and religious circles. The motto of the poem is from *Timon of Athens,* IV, iii, 25–26.

Why Hood named the heroine of his most ambitious poem "Miss Kil-mansegg" and what are that name's allusive qualities have long remained mysteries. Even though Hood apparently did not model his poem upon an actual family, it seems clear that he named his heroine after the Kielmans-egg family (also spelled Kielmannsegg, Kielmannsegge), a leading noble family of the kingdom of Hanover, members of which resided in London. A Kielmansegg came to England with the first George (1714–1727) and the family kept up its English ties through the fourth George (1820–1830), prospering, like many other imported German families, under the patron-age of the English kings who from 1714 until the accession of Victoria in 1837 were also kings of Hanover. During the Regency (1811–1820) these families held sway in society and "their loud voices, aggressive manners, rotund figures, and gaudy dress offended many English aristocrats" (Wil-liam Childers, "Byron's *Waltz*: The Germans and their Georges," *Keats-Shelley Journal,* XVIII [1969], 83). Though by 1840 most of these families, including the Kielmanseggs, were no longer heard of in London social circles, many Englishmen of Hood's generation undoubtedly still remembered the names and ways of these parvenu German emigrés who surrounded the Prince Regent. And in 1840 they had a fresh reminder of past Germanic invasions of English society in the person of Albert of Saxe-Coburg-Gotha, who on 10 February of that year married Queen Victoria. It soon became known that the young queen was pregnant: that the birth of the royal princess Victoria on 21 November coincides almost exactly with the birth of Hood's Miss Kilmansegg cannot be accidental. Though Hood wrote favorably of Queen Victoria when she acceded to the throne and was to offer Prince Albert a copy of the German translation of "The Dream of Eugene Aram" in 1841, by choosing the name "Kilmansegg" he nonetheless capitalized on the latent Germanophobia of large segments of the British public. After a century of noticeable Germans who spoke noticeably bad English, anti-German sentiment was rife in England: Victoria's marriage to Albert recalled to many the corruption, the vulgarity, the predominance of foreign ways in English aristocratic society under the "German Georges"—perhaps recalled also the "long line of royal mistresses and brides imported from Germany" (Childers, p. 87)—and awoke fears of a return of German influence. Not only did "Kilmansegg" carry meaningful connotations for the more alert of his readers, but Hood could also use the name, now that the family no longer resided in England, without fear of retaliation or libel suit. Thus, when we consider the confluence of associations with the Hanoverian Kielmanseggs, the relative safety in using their name, the name's onomatopoeic and Dickensian qualities (Kill-man's-egg), lastly, the unhappy memories of his recent self-imposed exile in Germany (1835–1837) and his resultant dislike of Germans, Hood's choice of name for his heroine becomes understandable—and extremely apt.

Byron in *Waltz: An Apostrophic Hymn* (1812), Childers points out, satirized "the Germans' invasion of London society" and ridiculed, with the use of such names as the Countess of Waltzaway and the Princess of Swappenback, "the many strange and funny-sounding names borne by the Germans who had flocked to London under the sponsorship of the Hanoverian monarchs" (p. 83). Hood's satire, less specific in its targets, has a similar purpose. Though he certainly did not intend a strict correlation between Queen Victoria and Miss Kilmansegg or between Prince Albert and the "Foreign Count" (l. 1464 and illustration) whom Miss Kilmansegg marries, he would have been aware that his more discerning readers—and Hood aimed his punning poems at the intelligent—might see a complex web of indirect associations between political reality and poetical fancy. "Miss Kilmansegg" is then, as its creator intended it to be, very much a "Rhyme for the Times."

7: Sir Harris Nicholas. Sir Nicholas Harris Nicolas (1799–1848), author of *A Synopsis of the Peerage of England*, 2 vols. (1825), *History of the Orders of Knighthood of the British Empire*, 4 vols. (1841–1842), and many other works on genealogy.

18: Colchian sheep. Jason found the Golden Fleece in Colchis, an ancient country on the eastern shore of the Black Sea.

19–20: golden pippins—the sterling-kind / Of Hesperus. A celebrated apple of English origin; the Hesperides were in Greek myth the guardians of the golden apples which Hera received upon her marriage to Zeus.

34: Pactolian water. Water full of gold dust; Midas bathed in the river Pactolus in Lydia and as a result lost the curse of the Golden Touch.

39: Smithfield-market. The famous meat and poultry market in London. Hood wrote for the 1830 *CA* an "Ode to the Advocates for the Removal of Smithfield Market."

40: the Golden Bulls, Several medieval documents were known by this designation from having been decorated with golden seals (or *bullae*).

47: a Golden Ass. Apuleius' satirical romance *The Golden Ass* narrates the adventures of a young man, Lucian, who is accidentally transformed into an ass. The ass was called "golden" on account of its excellent qualities.

60: "O bella eta del' oro!" The first chorus from Tasso's *Aminta,* translated by Henry Reynolds as "O happy Age of Gould." Tasso refers of course to the Golden Age of classical antiquity, Hood to the modern age of Mammon-worship.

65: Jacob Ghrimes. Hood seems to have in mind the biblical Jacob rather than the loutish Grimes of William Godwin's *Caleb Williams* (1794) or the scoundrelly young Peter Grimes of George Crabbe's *The Borough,* Letter 22 (1810). Jacob's life is a "parable" of how to get ahead through fraud and deceit: "And the man increased exceedingly, and had much cattle, and maidservants, and menservants, and camels, and asses" (Gen. 30:43). Presumably he is the "Patriarch Kilmansegg" who "lived of yore" and "Who was famed for his great possessions" (ll. 12–13).

69: five per cents. Public securities bearing this rate of interest.

73: Clementi. Muzio Clementi (1752–1832), Italian pianist and composer who lived in England. Clementi, Collard & Collard published Hood's *Comic Melodies* in 1830.

79–80: And Farmers reaped Golden Harvests of wheat / At the Lord knows what per quarter. As they did during the Napoleonic wars, which by cutting off imports raised prices at home. The price of bread was artificially kept high from 1815 to 1846 by the Corn Laws.

91: Babbicome Bay. Babbicombe, a Devonshire resort, two miles north of Torquay.

92: Port Natal. The present-day Durban on Natal Bay, an inlet of the Indian Ocean.

97: like Colchester native. The first oysters of the season, Colchester "natives," are eaten at a banquet given by the mayor of Colchester during the third week of October.

101: the prose of Love in a Cottage. Cf. Keats, *Lamia,* Part II, ll. 1–2: "Love in a hut, with water and a crust, / Is—Love, forgive us!—cinder, ashes, dust"; and the elder George Colman, *The Clandestine Marriage,* I, ii: "Love and a cottage! Eh, Fanny! Ah, give me indifference and a coach and six!"

104: Robins. George Henry Robins (1778–1847), the famous auctioneer. Hood made an amusing woodcut of him, *Fancy Portrait of Mr. Robins* (*Works*, I, 234).

105: "a mess of pottage." An expression proverbially current in allusions to the story of Esau's sale of his birthright (Gen. 25:29–34). Not in the King James version of 1611, but in the Bibles of 1537 and 1539, and in the Geneva Bible of 1560.

106: Fortunatus's kin. Fortunatus was a hero of medieval legend to whom Fortune gave an inexhaustible purse.

114: Bulbul rare. A much-admired songbird, the "nightingale" of the East.

115: garden of Gul. Garden of Roses ("Gul" is Persian for "rose"). Cf. Byron, "The Bride of Abydos," I, 8: ". . . the Gardens of Gúl in her bloom."

118: She [Peggy] hates the smell of roses. Ruskin twice makes the comparison (*Works*, ed. E. T. Cook and Alexander Wedderburn [London, 1903–1912], XIII, 520, and XXVIII, 183) between Mephistopheles' hatred of roses (*Faust*, II, penultimate scene) and Peggy's, but it is unlikely that Hood ever read the second part of *Faust*.

128: mangles. Machines "for rolling and pressing linen and cotton clothing etc. after washing" (*OED*).

133–134: born . . . with a silver spoon / In her mouth, not a wooden ladle. Cf. headnote to "A Lay of Real Life."

136: Plutus. The blind god of wealth in Greek mythology.

142: "in the straw." In childbed.

149: Otto of Roses. Attar (the fragrant essence) of roses.

164: Grecian fable. The legend of Phaeton, a son of Apollo, who took his father's chariot and led the horses of the sun on a disastrous course through the heavens.

175: at Owen Glendower's birth. When "the heavens were all on fire, the earth did tremble," and other marvelous portents occurred, all of which "signs" proclaimed Glendower "extraordinary" (*I Henry IV*, III, i, 13–50).

189: botargoes. A Rabelaisian relish made of the roe of the mullet or tunny.

190: the Birth of the Babe in Rabelais. Of Gargantua, giant son of Grandgousier and Gargamelle, in Rabelais' *Gargantua* (I, iv).

192: the guests at Circe's horrible feasts. Circe turned Odysseus' men into swine (*The Odyssey*, Bk. 10).

197: the Naples Spider. The tarantula; in parts of southern Italy its bite is still considered to bring on religious ecstasy.

199–205: King John . . . "whizzable." *King John*, IV, ii, 182–185: "My lord, they say five moons were seen to-night; / Four fixed, and the fifth did whirl about / The other four in wondrous motion." Cf. Brutus' calm before lightning in *Julius Caesar*, II, i, 44–45: "The exhalations whizzing in the air / Give so much light that I may read by them." "Maroons" (l. 201) were contemporary fireworks that imitated in exploding the report of a cannon. Cf. l. 212.

215: Croesus's issue. Croesus was the last, fabulously rich king of Lydia. His "issue" did not succeed him.

220: Gros de Naples. A heavy silk fabric, originally made in Naples.

223–224: Curaçoa, Maraschino, or pink Noyau. Sweet liqueurs.

231: Heliogabalus. Elagabalus, debauched Roman emperor (218–222 A.D.). But Hood means Heliodorus, who was sent to Jerusalem by the king of Syria with orders to steal the Treasury but was driven from the temple by the apparition of a great horse that battered him with its forefeet (2 Macc. 3:25).

235: They gave her no vulgar Dalby or gin. Dalby's carminative was a preparation used especially for children. Gin is here used as a medicament.

237: Dantzic Water. Gold-water, a cordial to which a small quantity of "leaf of gold" (l. 236) has been added.

244: Earl Spencer. John Charles Spencer, Viscount Althorp and third Earl Spencer (1782–1845), member of various governments, retired from politics in 1834. Well-known as a breeder of cattle.

245: "What's in a name?" Romeo and Juliet, II, ii, 43–44: "What's in a name? That which we call a rose / By any other word would smell as sweet."

248: Doctor Dodd. The Rev. Dr. William Dodd (1729–1777), hanged for forgery in a celebrated case. His conduct is described in J. P. Malcolm, *Anecdotes of the Manners and Customs during the Eighteenth Century* (London, 1810), I, 84–85, as "inconsistent beyond parallel." Active in behalf of "penitent prostitutes" and "the relief of prisoners confined for Small Debts," he was yet "a luxurious spendthrift, and a violator of the penal laws of his country, to support unjustifiable extravagance and splendour of living." Samuel Johnson wrote in his support (see *Boswell's Johnson, passim*.)

271: rich as a Mexican. Presumably very rich; Mexican currency was then held in high esteem and symbolized wealth.

276–277: Uncles—rich as three Golden Balls / From taking pledges of nations. Probably an allusion to the Rothschild family (cf. l. 283), which during the Napoleonic wars raised £100,000,000 for the European governments. The "three Golden Balls" are the traditional sign of pawnbrokers and were first used by Lombard moneylenders in medieval London. At this time Lionel Nathan de Rothschild (1808–1879) was head of the important London house; his son Nathaniel Meyer (1840–1915) was, presumably coincidentally, born at about the same time (8 November) as Miss Kilmansegg.

288: Pozed Ali Baba's brother's wife. The wife of Kasim, Ali Baba's brother, was "pozed" or puzzled why Ali Baba's wife would wish to borrow her scales. She smeared the "bushel" with suet and wax and it came back with a gold coin adhering to the cup ("Ali Baba and the Forty Thieves").

289: Coz-lings. Little coz or cousin. A nonce word, Hood's being the only usage recorded in the *OED*.

292: "Goslings." 1. Young (golden) geese; 2. foolish, inexperienced youths.

298: His lordship the May'r with . . . two Gold Sticks. Hood puns on the English title—*The Devil on Two Sticks*—of Alain René Le Sage's novel *Le diable boiteux* (1707), which was also dramatized under the same English title by Samuel Foote in 1768. Asmodeus, the Devil on Two Sticks of the novel, serves as the Mephistophelian companion to Don Cleofas (cf. also l. 379).

301: M or N. Usually "N or M," here used to designate a repentant sinner ready to mend his ways. N or M is "the answer given to the first question in the Church of England Catechism; and it means that here the person being catechized gives his or her *name* or *names*" (*Brewer's Dictionary of Phrase and Fable*).

306: niddle-nodded. Nodded rapidly.

322–323: the common phrase . . . about a rich complexion. The reverse of the proverb: Cold of complexion, good of condition. By l. 2095 Sir Jacob is dead.

325: dead-leaf satin. Dull-colored, very fine satin.

334: that temple. St. Paul's Cathedral, London.

342: Humboldt's "El Dorado." Alexander, Freiherr von Humboldt (1769–1859), noted explorer of Central and South America, published an account of his voyages in twenty lavish folio volumes (1805–1834). English editions and translations were very expensive. "El Dorado" was the name given to an imaginary fabulous country in the interior of South America, said to abound in gold and precious stones. Humboldt in his work mentions being told of the land while exploring the Upper Orinoco, though Hood may be recalling Voltaire's account in *Candide*.

358: "the dew of her youth." Cf. Ps. 110:3: "thou hast the dew of thy youth."

375: Rundell and Bridge's. 32 Ludgate St., goldsmiths and diamond-jewelers to the Crown.

379: one of the Gold Sticks. See note to l. 298.

380: "the Lass with the golden hair." Cf. Christopher Smart's poem "The Lass with the Golden Locks," where the amorous shepherd abandons "pipe" and "flock" to sing the beauties of his "lass of the golden locks."

383: Danaë. Mother of Perseus, visited by Zeus in the form of a shower of gold.

385: Doctor James. No contemporary identification is certain, but Hood, as so often, seems to have someone definite in mind. On this occasion it may have been Edward Coppleston (1776–1849), whose Tory politics and High Church Anglicanism a liberal nonconformist like Hood would have abhorred. Coppleston was from 1827 until his death Dean of St. Paul's; this position, Hood makes very clear, was that held by "Doctor James" (see ll. 333–335). Several clergymen named "James" were well-known at this time, but Hood in choosing the name may have remembered the famous quack Robert James (1705–1776), whose celebrated "Dr. James's Fever Powder" both Sir Robert Walpole and Oliver Goldsmith swore by. It was still sold in Hood's day and apparently was still in good repute.

396: little Phelim. "The ever good," a common Irish name, often translated as "Felix." Ll. 396–409 portray the conditions of the urban Irish in England at this time.

423: Tickler's ground. Name of a children's game (usually "Tom Tiddler's ground"). "One of the players is Tom Tiddler, his territory being marked by a line drawn on the ground; over this the other players run, crying 'We're on Tom Tiddler's ground, picking up gold and silver.' They are chased by Tom Tiddler, the first, or sometimes the last, caught taking his place" (*OED*). Cf. Dickens' Christmas story of the same name (1861).

430: a bait for the "Nix my Dolly" set. I.e., a temptation for slatterns to steal. "Nix my dolly," a then current cant term meaning "Never mind!" was popularized by W. H. Ainsworth's song in *Rookwood* (1834), III, v: "Nix my dolly, pals, fake away."

438: Highbury. A northern suburb of London.

440: gilded queens on St. Bartlemy's day. St. Bartholomew's Day, 24 August, the day in 1572 when the "gilded queen," Catherine de Medici, ordered a general massacre of French Protestant leaders. "Gilded queens" would be some kind of candy, eaten by English Protestant children.

449: a swing. Indulgence.

450: a dust. An uproar.

450–451: the flaming gilded thing / On the top of the Fish Street column. The copper-gilt urn on top of the Fish Street Monument, London, simulating a ball of fire; the monument was erected to commemorate the Great Fire of 1666.

458: "Impressions before the letters." Proofs taken from an engraved plate before the lettering is inserted.

469: "cramm'd." Then colloquial. Probably also in the sense of "to deceive with lies" (Partridge).

472: L. S. D. Pounds, shillings, pence.

478: Edgeworth's page. Maria Edgeworth (1767–1849), Irish novelist, author of *Castle Rackrent* (1800) and other tales of strong moral flavor.

480: Barbauld and Trimmer. Mrs. Anna Letitia Barbauld (1743–1825), author of moral prose essays and poems, including nature studies entitled *Hymns in Prose*. Mrs. Sarah Trimmer (1741–1810), author of exemplary tales, educational works, and children's books. Cf. Hood's satire "Trimmer's Exercise, for the Use of Children" and the accompanying woodcut (*Works*, II, 257–259).

501: Solon. Sage and lawgiver of Athens whose famous maxim was "Know thyself."

527: Butler, and Enfield, and Entick. Joseph Butler (1692–1762), Bishop of Bristol, author of *Fifteen Sermons* and other religious and moral writings. William Enfield (1741–1797), English divine, author of numerous collections of sermons. John Entick (1703?–1773), miscellaneous writer.

528: "Early Lessons" of every sort. Various religious and educational primers, though Hood specifically refers to Maria Edgeworth's popular *Early Lessons,* 2 vols. (London, 1809), which, by 1855, had reached 4 vols. and an 18th ed.

529: Souvenirs, Keepsakes, and Pledges. Names of popular literary annuals.

530: Old Johnson. Dr. Johnson's *Dictionary* (1755) is meant.

531: one night when he went to the play. At the first performance (1749) of his tragedy *Irene* Johnson "appeared . . . in a scarlet waistcoat, with rich gold lace, and a gold-laced hat" (*Boswell's Johnson,* p. 142).

532: Louis Chambaud (d. 1776), author of *Fables choisies, à l'usage des enfants et des autres personnes qui commençent à apprendre la langue françoise* (1751), *A new dictionary, English and French, and French and English,* 2 vols. (1778), and other books on the French language. Hood also puns: "Sham-beau."

533: Lindley Murray. English grammarian (1745–1826), born in America. His *English Grammar* (1st ed., 1795) enjoyed tremendous popularity and became a standard nineteenth-century text for English and American schoolchildren.

537: Howell and James's. Warehousemen, 9 Regent St., Pall Mall, fashionable showrooms for expensive furniture and decoration.

540: Promessi Sposi. *The Betrothed* is the usual English translation of Alessandro Manzoni's famous novel *I Promessi sposi* (1827).

542: Coutts in the Strand. Important private bank, 59 Strand, founded in the seventeenth century.

544: Golconda. The old name of Hyderabad, proverbially famous for its diamonds.

545: Potosi. A mountain famous for its silver mines, once the richest source of silver in the world, and a city in Bolivia.

553: Cucumber called the Gigantic. Probably the serpent or snake cucumber, which attains the length of six feet.

554–556: Eastern Tales . . . Of the Purse of Oriental make, / And the thousand pieces they put in it. Cf. the *Arabian Nights,* stories of Ghanim (nights 38–45), Ali Ben Bekkar (nights 153–169), and Abou Hassan (nights 349–351).

559: Field of the Cloth of Gold. An open plain in northern France where Henry VIII of England met with Francis I of France in 1520 in a pavilion of golden cloth. Cloth of gold is "a tissue consisting of threads, wires or strips of gold, generally interwoven with silk or wool" (*OED*).

592: Like the Steed in the fable. Cf. Aesop's "A Horse and an Ass," "A Laden Ass and a Horse," and "The Horse and the Ass."

613: Calmuck. Usually "Kalmuck" (Mongolian). Hood probably intends "Tartar."

618: it's catching a Tartar. "To get hold of one who can neither be controlled nor got quit of" (*OED*). A Tartar was, figuratively, a savage, a vixen.

621: his horse is a tit for Tat. *NMM:* Tatt. A "tit" is a small horse or nag. Hood intends a pun on Tattersall's, founded in 1766 by Richard Tattersall, known as "Old Tatt." Located near Hyde Park Corner, Tattersall's was one of the principal markets in England for riding and carriage horses and the headquarters for the turf. "Tat[t]" could sell a "tit" only "to a very low bidder" (l. 622).

632: Ballad of Leonora. Gottfried August Bürger's enormously popular "Leonore," (1774) which Hood probably read in Sir Walter Scott's translation (cf. ll. 1690–1691 and note). One further ominous allusion (cf. Pactolian water, Croesus, etc.): as Leonore rides with her ghostly sweetheart to her death, so Hood's heroine "is chasing Death" (l. 647).

634: Turpin's ride to York. Dick Turpin (1706–1739), the notorious highwayman, made his famous ride to York on his mare Black Bess. Hood knew W. H. Ainsworth's dramatic account in *Rookwood* (1834).

635: clipper. A splendid horse.

636: the Ring. Miss Kilmansegg, after circling the Ring in Hyde Park, clears the gate (since removed) at Hyde Park Corner, gallops down Piccadilly, past Green Park on the right, Dover Street on the left, before finally being thrown by Banker beyond Old Bond Street.

637: Mazeppa. Cossack leader (1644–1709), who was stripped naked and tied to a wild horse, sent bounding over the plains. Hood probably knew Byron's *Mazeppa* (1819).

640: the Oaks. A race for three-year-old fillies, founded in 1779, and run at Epsom on the Friday after the Derby.

641: Jockeys disparages. Thus both *NMM* and *CA*, 1842. "Jockeys disparage" woud be grammatically correct, but Hood may use "Jockeys" here contemptuously to mean any man of the common people (cf. l. 762) who would not use correct grammar; or perhaps he puns on "jockeys"—short for jockey-boots or top boots—which might "disparage" too rapid a "pace."

643: "arrowy Rhine." Cf. Byron, *Childe Harold's Pilgrimage*, III, 46, "majestic Rhine," and III, 71, "arrowy Rhone."

649: blood of Guelph. Political party of medieval Italy which supported the Pope and engaged in much slaughter with the Ghibellines, supporters of the Emperor.

671: that Persian daughter. Parizade, a princess whose adventures are related in the "Story of the Sisters Who Envied Their Younger Sister" in the *Arabian Nights*. In her last adventure she finds a "magical Golden Water," a small quantity of which, put into a basin, would fill it and form a beautiful fountain that would continually play without overflowing.

678: "Dash at the heavy Dover!" Damn the heavy horse (?): from "put this reckoning up to the Dover waggoner," according to Partridge a catchphrase of ca. 1820–1840.

725: a Staffordshire crate. Staffordshire is still the center of English earthenware and porcelain manufacturing; the northern industrial district is called the Potteries.

727: Singleton's "Golden Ointment." A popular eye ointment, possibly the oldest English proprietary remedy. It can still be bought.

728: "As the twig is bent, the tree's inclined." Pope, *Moral Essays, Epistle I,* l. 150.

753: St. George's altar. Of St. George's Cathedral (completed 1848), the largest Roman Catholic church in England of its day and under construction at the time Hood wrote "Miss Kilmansegg."

780: a corking-pin. A very large pin.

812: pure as from Mexican barter. Mexican gold was unalloyed.

818: the Court of Scander-Beg. "Scanderbeg" was a name given by the Turks to George Castriotes (1403?–1468), Albanian national hero and crusader against the Turks. The adjective "scander-begging" means "rascally." Hood implies that "the Court of Scander-Beg" was a "Court of Rascals." Cf. l. 924.

823: County. End of the September installment in the *NMM.*

833: Kitty Clover. Title of a humorous poem by Carrie W. Thompson.

842: the whole Dead Weight. The *OED* cites this obsolete usage: "A name given to an advance by the Bank of England to Government on account of the half-pay and pensions of the retired officers of the Army and Navy."

855: *rumpuses.* Hood used the word as a pun, perhaps implied here, in his "Ode to the Advocates for the Removal of Smithfield Market," ll. 59–60: "But, sirs, for pity's sake! / We don't want oxen at our doors to *rump-us!*"

862: Burked. The word, derived from the name of the notorious criminal William Burke, executed in 1829 for smothering many people in order to sell their bodies for dissection, has two meanings, the first more likely here: 1. "to kill secretly by suffocation or strangulation"; 2. "to smother, 'hush up,' suppress quietly" (*OED*).

862: the very essays of Burke. Here viewed as embodiments of common sense.

863: Wealth over Wit plays the Turk. I.e., runs roughshod.

869: 'Change—the Alley—the Bank. 1. The Royal Exchange, Cornhill, meeting place of merchants; 2. Sweetings Alley, location of the Royal Exchange, where securities were traded; 3. the Bank of England.

871–872: It made as much stir as the fossil shank / Of a Lizard coeval with Adam. Hood refers to one of the recent geological or paleontological discoveries that had sharply divided those defending the Mosaic cosmogony and those leaning toward more liberal interpretations. Such a discovery would indeed cause "much stir."

873: Greenwich and Chelsea elves. London charity hospitals occupied, respectively, by naval and military pensioners. "Elves" often refers to children but is used here in the deprecatory sense of "poor creatures," "poor devils."

881: Stratford-le-Bow. Northern suburb of London, northwest of the Regent's Canal.

887–888: a run . . . the "go" and the "Kick." Terms in rugby.

899: Belles of Wapping. Filthy street of tenements adjoining the Tower of London. A "wapping-dell" is a whore.

900: St. Giles's Beaux. Stylish roughnecks. The neighborhood of St. Giles-in-the-Fields was, before the making of New Oxford Street, the haunt of thieves, prostitutes, and pickpockets.

908–912: Bardus . . . looking down at his kerseymere. I.e., a foppish "bard" admiring his trousers made of cassimere, a fine, twilled woollen cloth. Hood perhaps recalls Pope's devastating portrait of "Sporus" (Lord Hervey) in the *Epistle to Dr. Arbuthnot,* ll. 305–333.

921: Fiddle-headed. Empty-headed.

932: the Cherokee talks of his cab and cob. I.e., the nouveau riche Indian talks of his carriage and horse. In 1835 a small number of Cherokees signed a treaty—generally characterized as disgraceful and fraudulent— with the United States stipulating that in return for receiving the equivalent of $5,000,000 the entire tribe would emigrate to lands west of the Mississippi. Six hundred tribal aristocrats received large sums of money from the U.S. Government and emigrated in 1837 with their negro slaves and droves of fat cattle. By 1840 one parvenu had apparently arrived in London.

934–936: Cards like that hieroglyphical call / To a geographical Fancy Ball / On the recent Post-Office covers. Among the numerous works of William Mulready (1786–1863) "was the first penny postage envelope issued by Rowland Hill in 1840. It was adorned with a design emblematical of Britannia sending winged messengers to all quarters of the globe" (*DNB*). John Leech, the illustrator of "Miss Kilmansegg," made it the subject of a celebrated caricature in *Punch.*

938: Latakoo. Probably New Guinea or the Islands of Melanesia, from "lakatoi," the dug-out canoes used by some sea-faring tribes of New Guinea.

939: Prince Le[e] Boo. Of the Pelew Islands. He died of smallpox on a visit to England in 1784. "That unfortunate Sandwich scion" (l. 940) was, however, King Liholiho (Kamehameha II) of the Sandwich Islands, who with his queen visited London in May 1824. Both caught measles and died there in July. Hood has amalgamated the two monarchs.

947: Mathew. Theobald Mathew (1790–1856), Catholic priest, signed the pledge of total abstinence on 10 April 1838. Several hundred thousand in England and Ireland followed his example and became teetotalers, at least temporarily.

948: antiphlogistic. Allaying excitement.

960: Schwalbach pigs. Rhineland spa—which Hood would have seen— near Frankfurt-am-Main, famous (in Hood's eyes) for its underfed hogs. Hood drew humorous woodcuts of lean and hungry German swine for the

CA, 1836, opposite p. 15, and for his novel-travelogue satirizing German life, *Up the Rhine* (London, 1840), opposite pp. 134 and 283.

967: the cap. Nightcap.

991: inward man. Cf. Eph. 3:16: "inner man."

993: "gutted." Then colloquial. "To gut" has the meaning of "to rob."

998: smalls. Knee breeches.

1011: a Congress of Nations. Hood's amalgam of the "Battle of the Nations" (1813) at Leipzig and the various congresses of post-Napoleonic Europe.

1017: Shacabac. The famished but intelligent beggar in the *Arabian Nights* who is tempted by several illusory feasts and finally rewarded with a sumptuous real one.

1018: Tom, and Jerry, and Springheel'd Jack. Corinthian Tom and Jerry Hawthorn: two chief characters in Pierce Egan's *Life in London* (1821). Spring-heel'd Jack: "The marquis of Waterford, in the early parts of the nineteenth century, used to amuse himself by springing on travellers unawares; and from time to time others have followed his silly example" (E. Cobham Brewer, *The Reader's Handbook* [London, 1923]). His exploits formed the subject of popular adventure stories.

1023: the stiffest of covers. Also in this sense: "a confederate who screens the operations of a thief or pickpocket" (*OED*).

1041: Wang-Fong and Il Bondocani. *Whang Fong; or, The Clown of China* (1812), pantomime by Charles Dibdin the Younger; *Il Bondocani; or, The Caliph Robber* (1802), comic opera by Thomas John Dibdin.

1042: dump. See note to l. 26 of "A Retrospective Review," p. 333.

1046: the Spectre in "Don Giovanni." The Ghost of the Commandante in Mozart's opera (1787) appears at the end to drag the Don down to hell.

1054: Crescent. Also in the sense of "shape."

1057: stomacher. "An ornamental covering for the chest (often covered with jewels) worn by women under the lacing of the bodice" (*OED*).

1077: checks. In chess, a threat to the king; on a "blazon" (l. 1078), "a pattern of cross lines forming small squares" (*OED*).

1099: to leg-bail Embarrassment's serf. To escape from a bailiff's custody (?).

1100: a Leg. Or black-leg: a turf swindler.

1103: "Plain Gold Rings." An echo of Thomas Moore's song "Rich and Rare Were the Gems She Wore," the second line of which is, "And a bright gold ring on her hand she bore." Hood illustrated Moore's song mock-heroically in a woodcut, *W & O* (1), opposite p. 13, showing a squaw with adornments of fish-bones and dog's teeth, her head surmounted by a huge marrow-bone.

1108: nid-nodded. Nodded repeatedly.

1114: the Muse of History. Clio, who presumably "talk'd" prosaically.

1117: Trojan fraction. Precious stones and metals are weighed by the pound troy, divided into 12 ounces and 5760 grams (less than the pound avoirdupois).

1128: Cuddies. Simpletons.

1133–1134: "Rich and Rare / Were the gems she wore." See note to l. 1103.

1144: Tom Tug. A fool. Name of the honest young waterman who wins as wife Wilhelmina, the gardener's daughter, in the elder Charles Dibdin's *The Waterman* (1774). Cf. headnote to "Faithless Sally Brown," p. 342.

1150: Minuet de la Cour. A slow, stately dance, introduced in France in the seventeenth century.

1156: *Figuranté*. Ballet dancer.

1166: Rosina's pastoral bevy. Hood refers in this stanza to rustic dances in which country children "dance for bread" (l. 1165), i.e., coins.

1172: poussette. "To dance round and round with hands joined, as a couple in a country dance" (*OED*).

1176: hopper. "A brewer's vat in which the infusion of hops is prepared to be added to the wort" (*OED*), but a multiple pun: 1. dancer (a hop-pestere—the "leg" of l. 1170—is a female dancer); 2. a person engaged in picking "hops" (l. 1178).

1177: those limbs forlorn. Probably either Irish or from the London slums or both (thus the public indignation reflected in ll. 1179–1180).

1182: "Money Musk." A country dance tune.

1187: Giant of Castle Otranto. In Horace Walpole's gothic novel *The Castle of Otranto* (1764).

1196: the Great Enchanter's charm. George Henry Robins (1778–1847), the famous auctioneer.

1198–1199: An arm like the Goldbeater's Golden Arm / That wields a Golden Hammer. Presumably a good auctioneer's arm is like that of a goldsmith of Goldsmiths' Hall, London; gold is pounded persistently and with great force. Cf. Dickens, *Pickwick Papers:* "with twenty gold-beater force" (chap. 24).

1204: ICE and . . . PINES. Ice cream and pineapples, the latter very expensive out of season.

1206: The TEMPLE OF TASTE from GUNTER'S DESIGNS. In William Gunter's *Gunter's Confectioner's Oracle, containing receipts for deserts . . . with an appendix, containing the best receipts for pastry-cooks . . . being a companion to Dr. Kitchener's Cook's Oracle* (London, 1830). Gunter's, Berkeley Square, was a fashionable shop for ices.

1211: conners. Inspectors.

1224: cheering. End of October installment in the *NMM*.

1228–1231: The Square . . . was quiet. Cf. Keats, "La Belle Dame sans Merci," ll. 3–4: "The sedge has wither'd from the lake, / And no birds sing."

1271: if Ignorance be indeed a bliss. Cf. Gray ("the Poet" of l. 1270), "Ode on a Distant Prospect of Eton College," ll. 99–100: "where ignorance is bliss, / 'Tis folly to be wise."

1286: Nettlebed. Village in Oxon, northwest of Henley.

1287: Stratford the Stony. Stony Stratford, once a market town, now part of Wolverton, on the river Ouse.

1295: *sleepers.* Ties supporting a railroad track.

1301: Crook-Back'd Tyrant Care. Hood personifies Horace's *Cura (Odes,* Book 2, 16, l. 22, and Book 3, 1, l. 40) with characteristics of Shakespeare's Richard III.

1315: Morbid. Perhaps Hood recalls the unbalanced "Morose" of Jonson's *The Silent Woman* (1609).

1326–1327: dormouse pie, / (An ancient classical dish by the by). Sleep-inducing, as would be "sauce of poppy" (l. 1328). Cf. Petronius, *Satyricon,* 31. Hood probably read the *Satyricon* in William Burnaby's famous translation (1694).

1347: couchant (a bitter cup!). I.e., lying down; "cup" used here in the scriptural sense of a painful experience to be endured.

1399ff.: Eden's happy land. Cf. *Paradise Lost,* end of Bk. 12. Hood embroiders on Milton's description (and Genesis).

1441: Tibbie Fowler. Anonymous Scottish song, arranged in one version by Joseph Haydn.

1447: sparks. Young men of elegant or foppish character.

1464: A Foreign Count. Modeled in part, as is Count Smorltork in Dickens's *Pickwick Papers,* upon Prince Pückler-Muskau, whose attempts to snare a British heiress in 1826–27 proved unsuccessful.

1466: fore-cabin. Inferior accommodations for second-class passengers.

1476: stock. A thrusting sword.

1476: a frock, well trimm'd with braid. See note to l. 2158.

1477: frogs. Either an ornamental fastening to the front of a military coat or an attachment to the waist-belt in which a sword may be carried.

1485: "Retail Order." "Retail" in the sense of "petty," "trivial."

1488: Proverbs of France. Plays in which a proverb is the foundation of the plot.

1522: crooked tester. Bent sixpence.

1526: Cis. Cisley or Ciss, a dairy maid.

1533: as red as haws and hips. Fruit of the hawthorn and wild rose.

1535: Roger's blue ribbons. Bought at James Rogers & Co., 3 Upper Marylebone St., a fashionable haberdasher.

1549: the Golden Horn. An arm of the Bosporus forming the main harbor of Istanbul, so called because of the rich cargoes unloaded there.

1550–1551: the Barge . . . Like Cleopatra's Galley. In Shakespeare's *Antony and Cleopatra,* II, ii, 196–202.

1556: Golden dragons, and Golden cocks. See note to ll. 92–93 of "The Desert-Born," p. 360.

1572: St. James's sonorous steeple. The fashionable St. James in Piccadilly.

1596: had Gog been Groom. Gog was one of two huge wooden figures, fourteen and a half feet high, in the Guildhall, King Street, Cheapside.

1625: the head of the Young Pretender. Charles Edward Stuart (1720–1788), upon whose head a reward of £30,000 was set in 1745.

1631: Anson. Admiral George Anson (1697–1762) captured the Manila (not Mexican) galleon on 20 June 1743.

1643: bow'd like a Guelph. Servilely. The Guelphs were supporters of the Pope.

1652–1653: Beaux / Quite fine enough for Ideals. Hood puns on "beau ideal," the suitors ("Beaux") being perfect types or models ("Ideals").

1658: Jim the Crow. James or Jemmy: a burglar's crowbar. "Crow" is thieves' slang for a person who keeps watch while another steals.

1659: Jack i' the Green. "A man or boy inclosed in a wooden or wicker pyramidal framework covered with leaves, in the May-day sports of chimneysweepers, etc." (OED).

1679: schipper. Skipper.

1690–1691: Such were the future man and wife! / Whose bale or bliss to the end of life. Cf. Scott's translation of Gottfried August Bürger's "Leonore" (entitled "William and Helen"): "His will, that turn'd thy bliss to bale, / Can change thy bale to bliss" (ll. 51–52).

1713: Those wedding-bells. Probably an echo of Thomas Moore's song "Those Evening Bells." Hood wrote a parody, similarly entitled, of Moore's song (Works, II, 331).

1731: nick. Moment.

1735: Good Queen Bess. Queen Elizabeth I (1533–1603).

1736: hippocampus. One of the seahorses of Neptune.

1738: toast and the Chinese leaf. Queen Elizabeth was abstemious over food and drink.

1739: grampus. Whale meat.

1763: tits. Horses.

1769: butchers in blue. Butchers wore dark blue aprons (butcher's blue is a shade of dark blue).

1770: Whitechapel. Whitechapel Market. See note to l. 423 of the "Ode to Rae Wilson, Esquire," p. 388.

1775: Yellow Boys. Sovereigns, or other gold coins.

1776: cattle. Mob.

1780: rattle. Coach.

1784: Old Brentford. Part of the town of Brentford, Middlesex, now of Greater London.

1786–1787: That hill, named after one of her kin, / The Hill of the Golden Farmer. "Near Bagshot [in West Surrey] there is a public-house called the Jolly Farmer, a corruption of the GOLDEN FARMER, a nickname obtained by one of the former possessors on account of his wealth, and his custom of paying his rent always in guineas." Jacob Larwood and John Camden Hotten, The History of Signboards (London, 1900), p. 352. The Weekly Journal of 29 March 1718 mentions "the Gibbet where the Golden Farmer [was] hanged in chains." Cf. ll. 1918 and 1964.

1789: the trust. The trustees of Miss Kilmansegg's estate.

1795: breaking. End of November installment in the *NMM*.

1803–1804: To some a full-grown orb reveal'd, / As big and as round as Norval's shield. That of the valiant warrior Young Norval in John Home's romantic tragedy *Douglas,* based on a Scottish ballad and first acted in 1756. Hood's lines echo Norval's description: "The moon which rose last night, round as my shield" (Act II). See also Hood's woodcut, *Home's Douglas* (*Works,* II, 300).

1805: burner Bude-lighted. A new gas burner capable of producing a very bright light.

1818: In Juliet's . . . eyes. Cf. *Romeo and Juliet,* II, ii, 15–22.

1823: Savory's. A. B. Savory & Sons, 14 Cornhill and 5 Finsbury Place South, famed London dealers in expensive goldware and silverware.

1829–1830: Wilderness Row into Paradise Place, / And Garlick Hill to Mount Pleasant. All actual places in and outside London.

1838: Oh, happy, happy, thrice happy state. Cf. Keats, "Ode on a Grecian Urn," stanza 3.

1846: double X ale. Cf. Byron, *Don Juan,* XVI, 67: "A mighty mug of . . . double ale."

1852–1853: There's double beauty whenever a Swan / Swims on a Lake, with her double thereon. Cf. Wordsworth, "Yarrow Unvisited," ll. 43–44: "The swan on still St. Mary's Lake / Float double, swan and shadow!"

1881: Dennises. John Dennis (1657–1734), English critic, took "offense" in his "Remarks on the Rape of the Lock" at Pope's puns, "by which the Author frequently shocks not only the Dictates of *Good Sense,* and the Rules of *true Pleasantry,* but those of *Grammar* and *common English.*" *The Critical Works of John Dennis,* ed. Edward Niles Hooker (Baltimore, 1943) II, 341, 347. Hood in the next line, "A double meaning shews double sense," defends his use of the pun. Cf. also the preface to the *CA,* 1834, where, refuting "certain reviewers," he asserts: "I shall persist in using the double barrel as long as meanings will rise in coveys" (*Works,* VI, 296–297). For another defense see *Works,* V, 171. Though modern taste may regard that "species of wit," as Boswell asserts Johnson did, with "great contempt," Hood could have cited in support of the pun Coleridge's remarks in his *Lectures and Notes on Shakspere* and Lamb's in the essay "Distant Correspondents" and in one of the "Popular Fallacies" ("That the worst puns are the best").

1900: the "Young May Moon." Title of a romantic song by Thomas Moore.

1937: "O rus! O rus!" "O, the country! O, the country!" Horace, *Satires,* Book II, 6, l. 60. The town-country antithesis that Hood develops at length in this section (ll. 1897–1982) recalls Horace, his favorite Latin poet. Cf. Hood's ode "Town and Country" (originally entitled "An Ode in Imitation of Horace") in *Works,* V, 302–305.

1953: Leipsic's flocks. The vast plain surrounding Leipzig favors the breeding of large flocks of sheep. Hood probably saw these flocks in his march across Germany in 1836.

1954: Vauxhall tune. Popular air. Vauxhall, once a fashionable pleasure garden on the outskirts of London, was at this time attracting less elegant clientele.

1978: ring fences. Those which completely encircle estates or large pieces of ground.

1995: "moon and honey for two." Perhaps words from a comic song inspired by one of the numerous imitations of John Tobin's popular play *The Honey Moon* (1804).

2028: "Barber of Seville." Rossini's opera (1816), based on the comedy of Beaumarchais. The hero and heroine, Count Almavira and Rosina, several times exchange notes expressing their love and warning each other of dangers to it.

2038: Home-made pop. Probably ginger-beer.

2052–2054: There's a Golden Bird that claps its wings, / . . . and sings / With a Persian exaltation. A tale of the *Arabian Nights* seems indicated. In the "Story of the Sisters Who Envied Their Younger Sister" (see note to l. 671), Parizade undergoes three adventures, searching for a Talking Bird, the Singing Tree, and the Yellow Water. The Bird not only talked and reasoned like a human being, but called all the singing birds in his neighborhood to come and join in his song. Hood may also have in mind the pantomime by Charles Dibdin the Younger, *The Talking Bird; or, Harlequin and Perizade* (1805). Cf. Marvell, "The Garden," ll. 52–54: "My soul . . . / There, like a bird, it sits and sings, / Then whets and combs its silver wings"—which may have inspired the famous lines in the second stanza of Yeats's "Sailing to Byzantium."

2065: "gilded lilies." Cf. *King John,* IV, ii, 11: "To gild refined gold, to paint the lily."

2103: Like the fabled pearls that the pigs neglect. Cf. Matt. 7:6: "cast ye [not] your pearls before swine."

2124–2125: *strange* gentlemen . . . in the Fancy Line. Probably low-bred enthusiasts of the prize-ring. "Fancy man" was nineteenth-century slang for a man who lived upon the earnings of a prostitute.

2130: Cara Sposa. Dear wife.

2132: mill. Boxing arena.

2134: Miller. Boxer.

2134: Mendoza. Daniel Mendoza (1764–1836), a notable pugilist of his day.

2148: Giant Despair. In Bunyan's *The Pilgrim's Progress* (1678) he imprisons Christian and Hopeful in Doubting Castle.

2156: Hocks. Hochheimer; by extension other white wines.

2158: Stultz's frocks. Stultz, 10 Clifford St. and Bond St., fashionable tailor. Frocks, here articles of men's clothing, were various kinds of tunics, long coats, and mantles; possibly a coat with long skirts used as a military uniform is meant (as in l. 1476).

2159: Manton and Nock's. John Manton & Son, 6 Dover St., Piccadilly, patent gun maker to the royal family. Samuel Nock, 43 Regent Circle, Piccadilly, gun and pistol maker.

2160: Barrels and locks. Of guns.

2161: blue rocks. Rock doves or rock pigeons.

2162: jocks. Jockeys.

2163: Buskins and socks. Shoes worn, respectively, by actors in Greek (and Roman) tragedy and comedy.

2165: fighting-cocks. A dying sport in 1840, pursued by the low-bred and shady.

2174: in flash. In underworld slang.

2175: badger. Banking account.

2178: Vice's Walpurgis revel. Cf. *Faust*, I, "Walpurgis Night."

2179: muffles. Boxing gloves.

2179: bulldogs. Dogs used in bull-baiting (a sport outlawed in England in 1835).

2205–2207: That instead of playing musical airs, / Like Colin's foot in going up-stairs— / As the wife in the Scottish ballad declares. A reference to the song "Are Ye Sure the News is True?" which says, apropos of a character named Colin, "His very foot has music in't / As he comes up the stair."

2317: Like the Thane who smote the sleeping. The "worthy thane" Macbeth slew the sleeping Duncan (*Macbeth*, II, iii).

2332: the Mayor in his gilded carriage. Dick Whittington, thrice Lord Mayor of London.

2366: the "Golden Bowl was broken." Death. Eccles. 12:6–7: "Or ever . . . the golden bowl be broken . . . Then shall the dust return to the earth as it was."

2372: Felo de Se. In England suicide, legally termed *felo-de-se*, is a crime that entails penalties against the deceased's estate.

Variants. 145: chamelion; *NMM*, chameleon. 159: Shewing; *NMM*, Showing. 446: shews; *NMM*, shows. 621: Tat; *NMM*, Tatt. 624: handsome; *NMM*, well-bred. 649: gratis; *NMM*, fearless. 1041: Bondocani; *NMM*, Bondicani. 1308: God himself; *NMM*, nature herself. 1353: mayhap; *NMM*, may hap. 1765: bridle; *NMM*, *bridal*. 1783: fated. Thus *NMM*. *CA*, 1842: faded.

V. Poems of Social Protest

Ode to H. Bodkin, Esq.

First publication and text: *O & A*, a volume coauthored with John Hamilton Reynolds. For the various attributions of the poems in this volume see Whitley, "Keats and Hood," p. 36, and P. F. Morgan, "John Hamilton Reynolds and Thomas Hood," *Keats-Shelley Journal*, XI (Winter 1962), 86–87. One authority cited by Morgan labels the Bodkin ode

"Joint," but on the authority of Walter Jerrold (Oxford Ed.) and M. Buxton Forman (ed., *The Letters of John Keats*, London, 1952) it is here ascribed to Hood. Stylistically the poem seems certainly Hood's, though Reynolds may have had a hand in it (see J. M. Cohen, "Thomas Hood: The Language of Poetry," *TLS*, 19 Sept., 1952, pp. 605–606).

The "Ode to Bodkin" protests the Vagrancy Act of 1824, which divided vagrants into "idle and disorderly persons, rogues and vagabonds, incorrigible rogues and other vagrants." William Henry Bodkin (1791–1874) was appointed honorary secretary to the Society for the Suppression of Mendicity in 1821. According to the *DNB*, "he wished to encourage the systematic giving of relief, but at the same time to extirpate the gross abuses to which the poor laws had become liable in his time." He published in 1821 "Brief Observations on the Bill now pending in Parliament to amend the Laws relative to the Relief of the Poor in England." In the *LM* (June 1822) appeared Lamb's essay "A Complaint of the Decay of Beggars in the Metropolis," inspired by the activities of the special committee appointed by the House of Commons to investigate the vagrancy laws. The poem's motto is from *Much Ado About Nothing*, III, iii, 24–25.

9–10: Oh, when I take my walks abroad, / How many Poor I *miss*. Hood parodies the first two lines of Isaac Watts's poem "Praise for Mercies Spiritual and Temporal": "Whene'er I take my walks abroad, / How many poor I see!" (*Divine Songs for Children*, IV). The poems of "Dr. Watts" (1674–1748)—educator and author of many well-known hymns as well as the *Divine Songs*—were required memorization work for children in the nineteenth century; Lewis Carroll brilliantly parodies some of them in *Through the Looking-Glass*.

16: The eye that never sleeps. Of Argos (or Argus), the monster with a hundred eyes whom Hera sent to watch her rival Io.

17: Belisarius. The greatest of Justinian's generals (505?–565). Accused of conspiring against Justinian's life, he was deprived of all his property. According to legend but not history, his eyes were put out and he lived as a beggar in Constantinople. "Belisarius begging for an *obolum*" is semi-proverbial and also in Lamb's essay.

18: Benbow. Admiral John Benbow (1653–1702) lost his right leg on 24 May 1701 fighting the French off Jamaica. He was the hero of a very popular melody.

21: Street-Handels. I.e., street-musicians. Seemingly Hood's own neologism based on "street-pitchers" or "ballad singers." Handel often raised money for charity, especially for the Foundling Hospital.

23: *scraper*. 1. A foot-scraper; 2. a derogatory term for a fiddler.

25: Sweeper. Crossing-sweeper. A well-known London sight, crossing-sweepers kept the streets free of mud, horse dung, and refuse—and obtained coins from passers-by in appreciation of their humor.

26: the Carstairs with his chalk. Street-drawing was then a popular means of begging. The "Carstairs" may also be the man " 'working a board' on which have been painted various exciting scenes in some terrible drama, the details of which the *street-pitcher* is bawling out" ([John C. Hotten], *The Slang Dictionary* [London, 1870]). "Carstairs" is Hood's neologism, after Joseph Carstairs, author of *The Fashionable Penman* (1823) and other books on penmanship.

27–28: the Cripple . . . cannot sell his walk. I.e., the circuit or "beat" of a beggar.

30: The Camels hide their humps. I.e., great, awkward hulking fellows hide their fits of ill humor or vexation. Hood may be referring, as does Lamb in "A Complaint," to Samuel Horsey, a man of huge frame, "half a Hercules," who, according to E. V. Lucas, "is stated to have been known as the King of the Beggars, and a very prominent figure in London" (*Elia and the Last Essays of Elia,* ed. E. V. Lucas [London, 1912], II, 393). The sequence of character types described in Hood's poem closely follows that in Lamb's essay.

31: Witherington. Roger Withrington ("Wetharryngton" in Percy), the gallant squire in "The Ancient Ballad of Chevy Chase"; his legs having been cut off, he continued to fight "upon his stumps."

39–40: St. Paul, / Hung round with holy flags. For Lord Mayor's Day, 9 November, when pensioners, dressed in uniform and armed, form part of the traditional parade. The houses along the route are decorated with flags.

46–47: when the Beggar Crew / Bring their petitions. The "Beggar's Petition" was a stock poem for infant recitation at this time. It begins thus: "Pity the sorrows of a poor old man / Whose trembling limbs have borne him to your door."

52: "With a bare *Bodkin*" end. *Hamlet,* III, i, 76.

Variants. 18: No Benbow lacketh legs; 1st ed., No Benbow, lacking legs. 43: guard; 1st ed., nurse. 49: Doubtless; 1st ed., Of course.

Ode to Mr. Malthus

Holograph MS of the first version of the poem: Bristol Central Library, England. The second version of the poem was first published in the *CA,* 1832. Reprinted in *HO.* Text: *CA,* 1832.

Thomas R. Malthus (1766–1834) argued in *An Essay on the Principles of Population* (1798; 2nd rev. ed., 1803) that "population would soon increase beyond the means of subsistence and that checks on this increase are necessary." Hood disagreed with Malthus, chiefly on humanitarian grounds, and frequently mocked his doctrines in his poetry and letters.

In a letter to J. H. Reynolds Hood suggested—in vain—"Malthus" as a fit subject for the 1825 *O & A* (Jerrold, *TH,* pp. 163–164), but not until early 1826 did Hood write the first substantial but incomplete draft of his "Ode to Mr. Malthus.—Author of an Essay on the Principles of Population.—" On this first version of the poem Hood marked "Lent to Colburn 16th. Feby./26," but Henry Colburn chose not to publish it in the *NMM.* Either he did not return it to Hood or the poet lost track of it, for the version published in the *CA,* 1832, is very different. The four lines of the earlier version given here show that the influence of Mary Shelley's novel *The Last Man* (1826) did not confine itself to Hood's poem of that title:

> Alas, this is a vision
> Of mine & Mrs. Shelley's. Population
> Is growing ten times faster than provision
> And the Last Man will perish of starvation.

11: the two-back pair. Probably the back room on the second floor.

14: Ponty Pool. Pontypool, market town in Monmouthshire, Wales, nine miles north of Newport.

23: Harrow's steeple. The lead spire of St. Mary's Church on Harrow Hill, then outside London, and visible from a great distance.

25: the King. HO: the Queen. Respectively: King William IV (reigned 1830–1837) and Queen Victoria (reigned 1837–1901).

47: the Serpentine. A long, canal-like body of water dividing Hyde Park from Kensington Gardens. Nearby was the receiving house of the Royal "Humane Society" (l. 45), which kept up a police and medical staff to aid people in danger of drowning. "By their design" the "two banks of the Serpentine" were thus "Saving Banks."

65: Mr. Irving's chapel. The Regent Square Church in London, built by the Scottish clergyman Edward Irving (1792–1834), who had by this time lost his enormous popularity.

68: I'd make the Lord Mayor's a perpetual station. The Lord Mayor of the City of London was (and is) elected annually.

75: Great Swing. "Captain Swing" played in the early 1830's the part which "Captain Ludd" had played twenty years earlier and terrorized the countryside, breaking agricultural machinery and firing hayricks and mills. "Swing" denotes the swinging stick of the flail.

78: the Foundling. The Foundling Hospital, Guildford Street, at this time an asylum for poor illegitimate children whose mothers were known.

81: the little Blue-coats. Charity school scholars wearing the almoner's blue coat, the costume from which the name Blue Coat School is derived. Christ's Hospital is the most noted of these schools.

82: by bit or sup. By too little food and drink. "Easter Monday, / That wine and bun-day" (ll. 79–80), would be a special occasion on which the children proceed to the Mansion House, the official residence of the Lord Mayor, and return with him and the City authorities to Christchurch to hear the sermon. Not until the next day, Tuesday, do the children again go to the Mansion House and pass before the Lord Mayor, each boy receiving a glass of wine, two buns, and a shilling.

83: Some meddling Marplot. The well-meaning but blundering "busy-body" of Susannah Centlivre's comedy *The Busie Body* (1709).

89–90: that great day / In June or May. The anniversary meeting of the charity children took place about the beginning of June, at morning service in St. Paul's Cathedral, and was attended by the City authorities in state.

Bohn's *Handbook* waxes rhapsodic: "This is perhaps the finest spectacle which can be witnessed in this metropolis—the assemblage of between *seven and eight thousand* boys and girls, clothed and educated by voluntary subscriptions. The effect of the mass of treble produced by this multitude of youthful voices is beyond description, and must be witnessed by all who desire to hear the harmony produced by unison singing" (p. 629). Though some found the spectacle a "gratifying sight" (l. 98), it left Hood "sad" (l. 99).

105: Some humane Martin in the charity *Gal*-way. Richard Martin (1754–1834), called Humanity Martin, sponsored and supported many humanitarian acts. Hood here puns on Martin's Galway ancestry. For the *O & A* of 1825 he had written "Ode to Richard Martin, Esq., M. P. for Galway."

110: Islington—Wapping—or Pall Mall way. Sites of charity schools.

111: goose's egg. Which was of gold. Hood means the rich. Cf. "Miss Kilmansegg and Her Precious Leg," ll. 16–17.

114: cajeput. A pungent medicinal oil obtained from the cajuput tree.

118: you and I are crying "Orange Boven!" "Three cheers for Orange!": the cry of Orangemen, members of a political society formed in 1795 for the defense of Protestantism and the maintenance of Protestant ascendancy in Ireland. The movement, as Hood implies, caused much "turning pale" (l. 116) in English ruling circles.

122: the Cholera Morbus. The cholera, so called in earlier ages; cholera epidemics still raged at this time.

Variants. 25: the King; *HO,* the Queen. 26: he; *HO,* she. 46: the thanks; *HO,* thanks.

Answer to Pauper

MS (rough draft): Dilke Papers, British Museum (Add. 43899 f. 193 v). First publication and text: *Athenaeum,* 18 Feb. 1832. The poem answers another, "Reply to a Pastoral Poet," signed "Pauper," which appeared in the *Athenaeum* of 28 Jan. and which Hood's son, on the word of C. W. Dilke, attributed to B. W. Procter (*Works,* X, 547).

12: Pay for window-light. The window tax (not repealed until 1851) was levied on all windows or openings for light beyond a total of eight.

20: breaking stones. Highway labor assigned to the parish poor.

24: eighteen-pence a week. The usual weekly wage.

28: you are farm'd. The workhouse poor were often "farm'd" to contractors, who had every inducement to put economy before compassion.

A Lay of Real Life

First publication and text: *CA,* 1835. Reprinted in *HO.* The poem's semi-proverbial motto is from Goldsmith, *Citizen of the World,* CXIX (*Collected Works of Oliver Goldsmith,* ed. Arthur Friedman [Oxford, 1966], II, 465).

17: a Turk. Here a bad-tempered, cruel woman.

23: my post. 1. place in life; 2. whipping post(?).

47: the pump. Meaning punishment by subjection to a stream of water from a pump.

Ode to Rae Wilson, Esquire

First publication and text: *Athenaeum,* 12 Aug. 1837. Reprinted in *Poems* (1846), I. The following letter "To the Editor of the *Athenaeum*" (Charles Wentworth Dilke) prefaced the poem.

> My dear Sir,—The following Ode was written anticipating the tone of some strictures on my writings, by the gentleman to whom it is addressed. I have not seen his book; but I know by hearsay that some of my verses are characterized as "profaneness and ribaldry"—citing, in proof, the description of a certain sow, from whose jaw a cabbage sprout—
>
> > Protruded, as the dove so staunch
> > For peace supports an olive branch.
>
> If the printed works of my Censor had not prepared me for any mis-application of *types,* I should have been surprised by this misapprehension of one of the commonest emblems. In some cases the dove unquestionably stands for the Divine Spirit; but the same bird is also a lay representative of the peace of this world, and, as such, has figured time out of mind in allegorical pictures. The sense in which it was used by me is plain from the context; at least, it would be plain to any one but a fisher for faults, pre-disposed to carp at some things, to dab at others, and to flounder in all. But I am possibly in error. It is the female swine, perhaps, that is profaned in the eyes of the Oriental tourist [Wilson]. Men find strange ways of marking their intolerance; and the spirit is certainly strong enough, in Mr. W.'s works, to set up a creature as sacred, in sheer opposition to the Mussulman, with whom she is a beast of abomination. It would only be going the whole sow.
>
> > I am, dear Sir, yours very truly,
> >
> > Thos. Hood

William Rae Wilson (1772–1849) was a moneyed Scot, known for his piety and for his narrow Protestant views. A wide-ranging traveler, he recounted his experiences in half a dozen books, now resting in total and deserved oblivion. In them he often attacked Hood as one of the most irreligious men of his time. The two lines he characterized as "profaneness and ribaldry" (in *Notes Abroad and Rhapsodies at Home,* "by a Veteran Traveller," 2 vols. [London, 1837], I, 295, and II, 67) are from Hood's poem, "The Blue Boar," ll. 110–111, published in the *CA,* 1837 (*Works,* VI, 340–349). The poem satirized Evangelical distaste for the proposed Hebrew Emancipation Act, the "Blue Boar" of the title being an Evangelical "bore," supporter of Sunday "blue laws" and other repressive measures. The poem's humor would have escaped Wilson, and the context of the controversial lines clearly supports Hood's claim that they are not irreverent. For an account of the Hood-Wilson fray see Alfred Ainger's "Memoir" prefacing his *Poems of Thomas Hood* (London, 1897), I, liii–lvii; and also Clubbe, *VF,* pp. 66–73 *passim.* The poem's first motto is from Coleridge's "Kubla Khan," ll. 51–54; the *"Old Ballad"* Hood quotes from for the second is none other than his own "Mary's Ghost," ll. 15–16.

1: A wanderer . . . from my native land. Hood had moved in June 1837, from Coblenz on the Rhine to Ostend on the Belgian coast, the "foreign sand" of l. 4.

5–6: Beyond the broadest Scotch . . . Beyond the loudest Saint. Wilson himself, a "Saint" who spoke "Scotch." "Saint" was Hood's (and the age's) contemptuous slang term for a "pious" (in Hood's view "hypocritical") Evangelical.

8: A friendly missive. Probably from Dilke.

20: Ushers of Beelzebub's Black Rod. Ushers of the devil. The Gentleman Ushers of the Black Rod (the black rod is their symbol of office) are the chief Gentleman Ushers of the Lord Chamberlain's department of the Royal Household.

34: Exeter Hall. On the Strand; Evangelical groups held frequent meetings there.

42: "Within the limits of becoming mirth." *Love's Labour's Lost,* II, i, 67.

46: To frame a Sabbath Bill. Sir Andrew Agnew four times sponsored a "Lord's Day Observance Bill" designed "to prevent all manner of work on the Lord's day." Only the death of King William in 1837 prevented this bill, which had gone before Parliament four times before it secured a majority, from becoming law. Hood chided Agnew for his religious intolerance in his 1834 "Ode to Sir Andrew Agnew, Bart." (*Works,* VI, 298–303) and caricatured him "with his bill" in a humorous woodcut (*Works,* IV, 205). Cf. also Dickens's article on Sabbatarianism "Sunday under Three Heads" (1836).

46: or forge a Bull. A reference to the virulent anti-Catholicism of some Evangelical groups and their practice of "Bull-baiting."

57: Billingsgate's slang-whanging tartars. Billingsgate is the chief fish market of London; "to slangwhang" is standard English according to the *OED* and means to assail with violent language or vituperation.

58: great Ernest. Ernest Augustus (1771–1851), fifth son of George III. A strong supporter of the Protestant religion and markedly anti-Catholic, he opposed Catholic emancipation and the Reform Bill of 1832. In 1837 he became King Ernest I of Hanover.

58–59: play . . . Fox and Goose with Fox's Martyrs. Fox and geese, a game on a board with pegs, draughtsmen, or the like; John Foxe (1516–1587), martyrologist, author of *Actes and Monuments* (1563), popularly known as the "Book of Martyrs."

62: sham Abr'am saints. I.e., hypocritical Evangelicals. "Abraham-men were beggars who feigned madness, hence sham-Abraham for those guilty of hypocritical pretences" (Oxford Ed.).

66: a Spiritual Pry. *Paul Pry*, title and name of the principal character of John Poole's (1786?–1872) best-known comedy (1825). Pry was an idle, meddling fellow, perpetually interfering in other people's affairs. In 1826 Hood published "Hints to Paul Pry" (*Works*, X, 577–580).

74: Otaheitan cooks. Of Otaheite, former name of Tahiti.

80: the old Hill of Howth. Five hundred and sixty feet high, on the north side of the entrance to Dublin Bay.

82: victuals in his mouth. "Victuals" possibly used in the now obsolete Scots usage of "corn"; i.e., mealy-mouthed.

84–86: Socrates or Plato . . . / Once taught a jay to supplicate the Gods, / And made a Polly-theist of a Parrot. Both Xenophon's *Recollections of Socrates* and Plato's *Apology* list one of the charges against Socrates at his trial as not paying respect to the gods whom the state respected, but the introduction of a trained "jay to supplicate the Gods" must be assigned to Hood's fanciful invention. But he may, as is likely, simply be punning: a "jay" is also a "simpleton," as a "parrot" (or "popinjay") is a contemptuous term for one who mechanically imitates the speech or actions of others.

88–89: a Mantis,— / An insect, of what clime I can't determine. The name "mantis," meaning a "diviner," was first used by the ancient Greeks. Though the insect is common to southern Europe and North America, the professor of cant of l. 87 (pun on "Kant"), Hood implies, is common to all climes.

93: *nous*. Greek: mind, reason; the highest intellect.

94: thro' the lobby. I.e., of "the House" of Commons (l. 96).

98: The Scottish member's legislative rigs. Sir Andrew Agnew's Sabbatarian bills; see note to l. 46. A "rig" is a trick or scheme.

99: That spiritual Pinder. Hood puns on "pinder," an officer of a manor, whose duty is to impound stray beasts, and on John Wolcot (1738–1819), "Peter Pindar," comic moralist in verse.

118–119: some fellow . . . / Fresh from St. Andrew's College. I.e., an Evangelical bigot. See note to l. 46.

122–124: schemes . . . / That frown upon St. Giles's sins, but blink / The peccadilloes of all Piccadilly. I.e., Agnew's Sabbatarian bill once again. The neighborhood around St. Giles-in-the-Fields was as disreputable as Piccadilly was fashionable. Hood believed, as did Dickens, that Agnew's "Lord's Day Observance Bill" would indirectly favor the rich: all repressive measures limiting Sunday amusement would chiefly affect the poor as Sunday was their only free day.

138: dole. In the now obsolete sense of "guile" or "deceit."

148: your last Journey-Work. Wilson's *Notes Abroad and Rhapsodies at Home* (see headnote).

151: A very Guy, deserving fire and faggots. Guy Fawkes (1570–1606), whose plot to blow up the Houses of Parliament with gunpowder on 5 November 1605 was foiled. He was executed 31 January 1606 on the scaffold, not, as Hood implies, with "fire and faggots."

154: Mawworms less than merry maggots. "Mawworms," hypocritical pretenders to sanctity, after the character Mawworm in Isaac Bickerstaffe's play *The Hypocrite* (1769); "merry maggots," old English country dance tunes, usually coupled with someone's name.

157–158: I have "sat at good men's feasts," / And I have been "where bells have knoll'd to church." Cf. *As You Like It,* II, vii, 114–115. Hood reverses the order of the lines.

159–162: Dear bells . . . breezy dells. Cf. William Cowper, *The Task,* VI, 6–9: "How soft the music of those village bells / Falling at intervals upon the ear / In cadence sweet! now dying all away, / Now pealing loud again."

179: yon servitor of God and Mammon. Cf. Matt. 6:24: "Ye cannot serve God and mammon."

181: trading gammon. I.e., business acumen. In backgammon, a gammon is a victory in which the winner gets rid of all his men before his opponent gets rid of any.

182: A black-leg saint. A crooked, dishonest Evangelical.

192: Ponder's End. Village in Middlesex, twelve miles north of Liverpool St. Station, London.

200: sure-*ly.* "With the second syllable stressed and lengthened . . . a mere intensive, *dial.* or *vulgar colloq." (OED).*

203–204: Church is "a little heav'n below, / I have been there and still would go." Cf. Watts, *Divine Songs for Children,* XXVIII, ll. 5–6 (Hood reverses Watts's lines).

209: in formâ pauperis. The Latin "plea of poverty."

215: a "world ayont." "A World Beyond" is the title of a poem by Nathaniel Ingersoll Bowditch (1773–1838).

225: Cuddie Headrigg's mother. The old Covenanter Mause in Scott's *Old Mortality.*

228: you have been to Palestine. Wilson recounted his experiences in *Travels in Egypt and the Holy Land* (1823), which ran through several editions. See headnote.

234: human heats. Fits of anger or passion.

251: to carve the carvers. Of the images (in Catholic lands). Wilson frequently expressed his disgust over these images, the carving of which, he believed, violated the second commandment.

251: Scotch collops. A savory dish made of sliced veal, bacon, forced meat, and other ingredients.

254: like male Mrs. Trollopes. Mrs. Frances Trollope (1780–1863), author of travel books and novels, is today best remembered for her satiric *Domestic Manners of the Americans* (1832), but Hood has in mind here her markedly anti-Catholic *Belgium and Western Germany* (1834).

261: Hurlothrumbo. Or "The Supernatural," a free-wheeling burlesque (1729–30) that enjoyed an extraordinary run, by the actor and dramatic writer Samuel Johnson (1691–1773).

267: griffinish excess of zeal. Characteristic of a "griffin," a newcomer or greenhorn.

269: Dolls I can see in Virgin-like array. Madonna-worship aroused some of Wilson's most bitter bursts of indignation. Morgan cites his *Travels in Norway* . . . (1826), p. 523, and *Records of a Route through France and Italy* . . . (1835), pp. 41, 62.

271: Like crazy Quixotte at the puppet's play. Don Quixote, watching a puppet play, sees a puppet knight errant and his damsel about to be overtaken by a Moorish army and, in his delusion believing them real, destroys them all (Part II, chap. 26).

272: "offence be rank." Cf. *Hamlet,* III, iv, 36: "my offence is rank."

291–292: as I went / From Liège . . . to Ghent. In June 1837.

307: "PRIEZ POUR LES MALHEUREUX." Pray for the wretched.

325: He felt "the eyes of Europe" on his tail. "Eyes" are spots near the end of a peacock's tail-feathers.

345: Partlet. Hood's tale (ll. 320–346) echoes Chaucer's story (or a retelling of it) of the proud Chaunticleer and the prudent Pertelot in the "Nun's Priest's Tale."

355: "Lucifers." Friction matches.

365: a lignum-vitae bowl. A hard, heavy ball, used in bowling and the games of bowls; it would roll very slowly.

398: *Voluntaries.* 1. Those who advocate that the Church should be maintained by voluntary gifts and be independent of State support; 2. organ solos.

399: The *willing* advent of the rich and poor. As a "voluntary" may be, in still another sense, a "willing sacrifice," so Hood seems to pun on *"willing"* in the sense of "voluntary."

419: Sunday pippins and old Trots. Well-dressed, rosy-cheeked girls and decrepit old women.

423: Whitechapel's ancient shambles. The chief London market, ancient and dilapidated, "for the sale of butchers' meat and for the sale of the Jews' killed butchers' meat . . . Many slaughter-houses . . . are at the backs of the houses, to which there is no access but through the front shop. The animals, however infuriated, have to be forced, usually by the tail-twisting process, into these huddled-up slaughter-houses" (Bohn, p. 612).

431: dee-dash-dee'd some other flocks. I.e., damned-drove-damned Evangelical congregations.

432: blocks. Blockheads—referring to the sheep.

455: *nolens volens.* Willy-nilly.

459: *con*ciliated. A "con" is a blow. Cf. l. 417 and note to l. 423.

471: asinine new milk. Ass's milk, lighter and easier to digest than cow's milk, was a tonic prescribed for weak constitutions.

483: chalk and water. "In 17–18th c. [chalk] . . . is often mentioned as eaten by young women suffering from chlorosis" (*OED*) .

486: Mister Simon Gubbins. I.e., Mister Pure Fool.

496: the milk of human kindness. *Macbeth,* I, v, 18.

Variants. 212: Sun. Thus *Poems* (1846); *Athenaeum,* gun. 381: Choir. Thus *Poems* (1846); *Athenaeum,* choice.

A Plain Direction

First publication and text: *CA*, 1839. The motto "Do you never deviate?" is probably a satiric jab at the virulent Tory weekly *John Bull,* whose political opinions Hood would have found anathema; it may recall Dryden, "Mac Flecknoe," l. 20: "But Sh—— [Shadwell] never deviates into sense."

17: I've read about a famous town. London. Ll. 17–23 allude ironically to the legend and nursery tale of Dick Whittington. A poor country orphan lad, Dick heard that the streets of London were "paved with gold" (l. 21) and sought his fortune there. He eventually married his former master's daughter, was knighted, and was thrice elected Lord Mayor of London.

36: L. S. D. Pounds, shillings, pence.

45: cheaper than the Ward of Cheap. I.e., very cheap. Cheapside was a poor district near St. Paul's, in the heart of the City of London.

93: George [Henry] Robins. The famous auctioneer (1778–1847).

A Drop of Gin!

First publication and text: *Punch,* 18 Nov. 1843. The poem complemented two illustrations, *The Water Drop* and *The Gin Drop,* by *Punch's* comic artist Kenny Meadows and a humorous temperance article by "Q" (Douglas Jerrold), "Father Mathew's Polly-Put-the-Kettle-on-Icon" (pp. 220–223). Though the conditions that inspired Hogarth's *Gin Lane* had been somewhat alleviated, cheap gin was still at this time, as the author of *Real Life in London* (1821) wrote, "that favourite and heart-warming cordial of the lower orders of society."

2: What magnified Monsters circle therein. In Meadows' illustration *The Gin Drop.*

18: Barebones. Praisegod Barbon or Barebones (1596?–1679), an Anabaptist leather-seller of Fleet Street. The Barebones Parliament, summoned by Cromwell in 1653, was named after him.

18: Prynne. William Prynne (1600–1669), vituperative Puritan pamphleteer. He embodied the Puritan railing against the stage.

50: Mynn. Alfred Mynn (1807–1861), famous cricketer, then at the height of his career.

52: Giant Despair. In Bunyan's *The Pilgrim's Progress.*

61: spiders of Chancery. Clever lawyers of the Court of Chancery.

64: "louping over a linn." 1. Leaping into a pond; 2. looping a rope over a linden or lime tree (?).

75: the Palace of Gin. Jerrold, *TH,* surmises that Hood was the first to use the expression "gin palace" (p. 365), but the *OED* gives earlier uses of 1834 and 1835.

The Song of the Shirt

First publication and text: *Punch,* 16 Dec. 1843. Reprinted in *Poems* (1846), I. The holograph MS of the original copy text of stanza 8, showing minor punctuation changes (presumably editorial) from the published version, is in the Hood Collection, University of California, Los Angeles. The frontispiece to *Memorials,* I, shows a "Fac-simile of a sheet of the original M.S. of the 'Song of the Shirt,' containing a verse hitherto unpublished" (see p. 304). This MS, now in the Bristol University Library, consists of drafts of lines of stanza 10, a few omitted lines, and the following stanza, first published in the Oxford Ed.:

> Seam, & gusset, & band,
> Band & gusset & seam,
>   Work, work, work,
> Like the Engine that works by Steam!
> A mere machine of iron & wood
> That toils for Mammon's sake—
> Without a brain [crossed out: And has not a head] to think
>   [written above "think": ponder], & craze
>   or a [crossed out: An] heart to feel—& break!

M. H. Spielmann conjectured, plausibly to my mind, that the omission of this stanza (easily the poem's weakest) "was simply a matter of make-up" of the page (*The History of "Punch"* [New York, 1895], p. 334). The Oxford Ed. inserts the stanza in brackets between the penultimate (tenth) and last (eleventh) stanza of the poem, but the MS indicates it should come between stanzas 9 and 10.

Mark Lemon, editor of *Punch,* recalled that Hood, not thinking highly of the poem, had told him that he had already sent it off to three journals and that all three had rejected it. He accompanied the manuscript with a note that left it between Lemon's "discretion and the waste-paper basket." Overriding the protests of his colleagues, who thought *Punch* should remain exclusively a comic magazine, Lemon published the poem, giving it a page to itself.

"The Song of the Shirt," the best-known, most popular of Hood's poems, expresses the poet's indignation at the miserable working conditions under which London seamstresses eked out a pitiful existence (for earlier instances of his concern see "Miss Kilmansegg," ll. 123–125 and *Works,* VIII, 370). The poem's immediate inspiration lay in the *Times*'s "Police Report" of 26 Oct. 1843, which recorded the case of "a wretched-looking woman named Biddell." She had contracted to sew trousers together for a slopseller named Henry Moses at 7*d.* the pair. Her wages not sufficing to feed herself and her two children, she pawned several pieces of the material entrusted to her. Unable to redeem the pawn, she had been hauled into court. Moses's foreman maintained that, if "honest and industrious," she could earn a "good living"—which he considered about "7*s.* a week." The account of this case and another of the same day, a stinging leader and a factual article entitled "The White Slaves of London" in the *Times* (27 Oct.), a letter from an outraged reader and Moses's own justification (31 Oct.), an article, "Famine and Fashion," and a poem, "Moses and Co.," in *Punch* (4 Nov.)—all of these Hood probably saw, and all, in varying degrees, influenced the composition of "The Song of the Shirt." See also

Friedrich Engels, *The Condition of the Working Class in England* [in 1844], ed. W. O. Henderson and W. H. Chaloner (London and New York, 1958), pp. 237–240; Spielmann, *History of "Punch,"* pp. 331–336; the full account in Alvin Whitley, "Thomas Hood and 'The Times,' " *TLS,* 17 May 1957, p. 309; and Clubbe, *VF,* pp. 149–155.

27–28: It is not linen you're wearing out, / But human creatures' lives. Cf. Scott, *The Antiquary,* chap. 11: "It's no fish ye're buying, it's men's lives."

43–46: A bed of straw . . . a broken chair. Details from a letter published in the *Times* (31 Oct.).

64: twit. Hood's most famous (or infamous) pun.

The Pauper's Christmas Carol

First publication and text: *Punch,* 16 Dec. 1843.

3: CHARITY's perennial treat. On Christmas day workhouse inmates were treated to a special dinner, the "famous cheer" of l. 6, in which they were regaled with very limited amounts of roast beef, plum pudding, and beer.

The Lady's Dream

First publication and text: *HM,* Feb. 1844. Reprinted in *Poems* (1846), I. As frontispiece Hood designed *The Modern Belinda,* engraved by S. Williams. Lap-dog on her arm and surrounded by skeletal sylphs, Hood's Belinda is meant to recall Pope's in *The Rape of the Lock.*

78: even the sparrow falls / Not unmark'd of God. Cf. Matt. 10:29 and *Hamlet,* V, ii, 230–231: "There's a special providence in the fall of a sparrow."

The Workhouse Clock. An Allegory

First publication and text: *HM,* April 1844. Reprinted in *Poems* (1846), I. The new Poor Law of 1834, which provided for the establishment of union workhouses, divided the poor into two categories: those who were lodged and given work within the workhouse (the "indoor" poor), and those who were given outdoor relief to help maintain themselves in their homes (the "outdoor" poor). The latter (the "Labouring Classes" of l. 6 of Hood's poem) had become many times more numerous than the "indoor" poor. Hood's masses, emerging from the East End slums and streaming through the London streets, seem to converge upon the Marylebone workhouse, largest in London and the only one in the area of the streets mentioned in the poem. The *Times* in an article "Christmas-Day in the Workhouses" (26 Dec. 1842) reported that "the out-door poor of Marylebone this year amount to 5,781, being an increase over last of 1,500, and over the prior Christmas of no less a number than 3,500, or 106 per cent" (p. 6).

8: the Workhouse Clock. Every morning "the Overseer of the Poor" (l. 7) set the workhouse clock to indicate the official beginning of the workday.

60: Whitechapel's meat. London's chief meat market. See note to l. 423 of the "Ode to Rae Wilson, Esquire," p. 388.

61: Cornhill. Street in the City of London, formerly the site of the Corn Exchange.

62: the Poultry. District in the City of London (Hood was born there) named after its association with the poultry market formerly within its precincts.

63: the Street of Bread. Bread St., Cheapside.

65: the street of Milk. Milk St., Cheapside.

66–67: Ludgate Mart . . . Mechanic-Art. Both within the City of London. Ludgate Street contained very fashionable shops.

The Bridge of Sighs

First publication and text: *HM*, May 1844. Reprinted in *Poems* (1846), I. "I have all but done a poem on 'the Bridge of Sighs,' " wrote Hood to F. O. Ward in April 1844, "ie Waterloo and its Suicides" (unpublished letter, John Rylands Library, Manchester). A center of London's squalor, Waterloo Bridge had become a favorite haunt of suicides. Alvin Whitley has pointed out that, like "The Song of the Shirt," Hood's "Bridge of Sighs" had its origin in an actual incident: the case of Mary Furley. For her attempted suicide, the death of her youngest child, her condemnation to death, and the outcry her plight aroused, see the *Times* of 26 March, 1, 17, 19, 20, 27, and 29 April, 2 and 15 May 1844. Nor was the *Times*'s outcry without effect: the execution of Mary Furley was postponed, her sentence eventually commuted to transportation for seven years. Dickens showed his ironic awareness of this case in his "Threatening Letter to Thomas Hood, from an Ancient Gentleman. By Favour of Charles Dickens," which preceded "The Bridge of Sighs" in the May *HM*. See also Charles Mackay, *The Thames and Its Tributaries* (London, 1840), I, 34, 35; *Pickwick Papers,* chap. 16; Whitley, "Thomas Hood and 'The Times,'" *TLS,* 17 May 1957, p. 309; and Clubbe, *VF,* pp. 171–174. Baudelaire, an admirer of Hood's artistic and literary talent, translated "The Bridge of Sighs" (see the *Mercure de France,* 1028 [April 1949], 599–607) and entitled no. xlviii of his *Petits poèmes en prose* "Any Where Out of the World" (after ll. 70–71 of Hood's poem). The poem's motto "Drown'd! drown'd!" is from *Hamlet,* IV, vii, 185 (the Queen announces Ophelia's death to Laertes).

Hood's children later published "the following fragmentary verses" of a "Part II" of "The Bridge of Sighs" (*Works,* IX, 208). Whether a fragmentary second part or a discarded version of the first, these verses adhere more closely to the facts of the *Times*'s reports:

> Weary with troubles
> That Death must deliver
> Once more life bubbles
> Away in the river—
> *　　　*　　　*　　　*

> The moon in the river shone
> And the stars some six or seven—
> Poor child of sin, to throw it therein
> Seemed sending it to Heaven.
>
>   *   *   *   *
>
> Cover her, cover her,
> Throw the earth over her—
> Victim of murder inhumanly done;
> With gravel and sod—
> Hide—hide her from God,
> And the light of the sun!

The National Library of Scotland, Edinburgh, holds a holograph manuscript of "The Bridge of Sighs" without the above verses. It is in a letter addressed to a "W. F. Watson Esqre / 52. Princes Street / Edinburgh." Probably written out upon request, the manuscript shows insignificant variants from the published version.

35–39: Where was her home . . . a brother. Morgan cites *Nicholas Nickleby,* chap. 40: "Where does she live? . . . What have you learnt of her history? Has she a father—mother—any brothers—sisters?"

77–79: Dissolute Man! / Lave in it, drink of it, / Then, if you can! Morgan notes an echo from Lucan, *Pharsalia,* VII, 822: "Has trahe, Caesar, aquas, hoc, si potes, utere caelo" (Draw these waters, Caesar, enjoy this country if you can).

The Lay of the Labourer

First publication and text: *HM,* Nov. 1844. The poem appears in the middle of a prose article bearing the same title (*Works,* IX, 225–246) that was addressed to the Home Secretary, Sir James Graham. Hood pleads in the article for fair treatment for unemployed agricultural workers and in the poem for their right to work. Both article and poem reflect, in general, the widespread rural unrest caused by the agricultural depression of 1844, and, in particular, the case of Gifford White, an unemployed farm laborer who had threatened arson if he and his fellow laborers were not given work. He was sentenced to transportation for life for his threat alone. Hood became acutely sensitive to White's plight, even to the extent of having hallucinations that White's ghost was haunting him (*Memorials,* II, 232–233).

11: swarth. Swath.

16: The tinder or the match. If work were available, farmers need not fear "a flaming barn or farm" (l. 17).

26: haggard's blaze. Burning of a stack-yard.

54: To shun the workhouse walls. The *Times* during the Hungry Forties records many instances of the poor willing to undertake desperate measures—even suicide—to avoid the humiliation of having to go to the workhouse.

97: the New Bastile. One of the new workhouses established by the new Poor Law of 1834, called in popular slang "bastil[l]es."

98: the Spital. Here a hospital for the poor and for those having leprosy, cholera, and other such diseases.

Suggestions by Steam

First publication and text: *HM*, Jan. 1845, signed "T. H." Steam power in vessels was just beginning to come into common use at this time.

4: "Ease her!" An order given on a small steamer to reduce speed.

6: sharks and screws. Swindlers and extortionists.

8: "Back her!" Reverse the action of the engine.

10: dropper. One who drops "in Thames's tide," i.e., commits suicide.

12: "Stop her!" The three orders ("Ease her!" "Back her!" "Stop her!") generally follow one another.

Stanzas ("Farewell, Life! My senses swim")

Holograph MS: Bristol University Library. First publication and text: *HM*, Feb. 1845, signed "H." The poem was Hood's last creative effort.

Sources of Illustrations

Sources are given by poem. Unless otherwise indicated, illustrations were designed by Hood. The title-page vignette is from the *CA,* 1834.

The Ballad: *Juvenile Forget Me Not,* 1832, William Chevalier
She is far from the land: *W & O* (1)
Mary's Ghost: *W & O* (2)
Tim Turpin: *W & O* (2), Edward Willis
Death's Ramble: *W & O* (2), Edward Willis
John Day: *CA,* 1832; the first by J. Hewitt, Jr.
Sally Simpkin's Lament: *CA,* 1834
A Waterloo Ballad: *CA,* 1834
The Carelesse Nurse Mayd: *CA,* 1830, Samuel M. Slader
Domestic Asides: *CA,* 1831
Domestic Poems: *CA,* 1837
Stanzas, Composed in a Shower-Bath: *CA,* 1838
The Bachelor's Dream: *CA,* 1839
Bianca's Dream: *W & O* (2)
The Last Man: *W & O* (1)
Jack Hall: *W & O* (2), Edward Willis
The Sea-Spell: *W & O* (1)
The Dream of Eugene Aram: from the 1831 edition of the poem, William Harvey
The Haunted House: *HM,* Jan. 1844, John Cousen
Miss Kilmansegg: *CA,* 1842; all but the last illustration are by John Leech
Ode to Mr. Malthus: *CA,* 1832
A Plain Direction: *CA,* 1839
A Drop of Gin! *Punch,* 18 Nov. 1843, Kenny Meadows
The Song of the Shirt: *Memorials,* I
The Lady's Dream: *HM,* Feb. 1844

Index of Titles and First Lines

Titles of poems are printed in italics, first lines of poems in roman type

General Index